AUSTRALIA

AN ECOTRAVELLER'S GUIDE

AUSTRALIA
AN ECOTRAVELLER'S GUIDE

HANNAH ROBINSON

Interlink Books

An imprint of Interlink Publishing Group, Inc.
Northampton

First published 2003 by

INTERLINK BOOKS

An imprint of Interlink Publishing Group, Inc.
46 Crosby Street, Northampton, Massachusetts 01060
www.interlinkbooks.com

N.B. The reader goes to these wildlands (and takes the book's suggestions and omissions)
at their own risk.

Library of Congress Cataloging-in-Publication Data
Robinson, Hannah.
    Australia : an ecotraveller's guide /
by Hannah Robinson.
    p. cm.
Includes bibliographical references and index.
ISBN 1-56656-479-4 (pbk.)
1. Ecotourism—Australia. 2. Natural areas—
Australia—Guidebooks. 3. National parks and
reserves—Australia—Guidebooks. 4. Australia—
Guidebooks. I. Title.
G155.A75 R63 2002
919.404'7—dc21

2002010975

Printed and bound in Korea

To contact the author: hannahrepresents@yahoo.com

To request our complete 40-page full-color catalog,
please call us toll free at **1-800-238-LINK,** visit
our website at **www.interlinkbooks.com**, or write
to **Interlink Publishing**
46 Crosby Street, Northampton, MA 01060
e-mail: sales@interlinkbooks.com

Contents

To see a World in a Grain of Sand,
And a Heaven in a Wild Flower,
Hold Infinity in the palm of your hand,
And Eternity in an hour.
—William Blake

1
Sydney and Pacific Ranges

Sydney and Pacific Ranges

Don't Miss

❖ Blue Mountains National Park

❖ Lamington National Park (see previous page and below)

❖ Gordon Colony for the gray-headed flying fox flyout

❖ Native Australian marsupials at Scotia Earth Sanctuary

Touch down in Sydney and start your exploration of the only continent where virtually all the earth's key stages of evolution can be seen. You'll find the cyanobacteria reefs that dominated most of earth's lifetime, ancient Queensland lungfish that are our direct relatives, echidnas and platypuses that were among the first mammals, and some of the world's first flowering plants. This book tells you what to look for, where to find it, and how.

Sydney

Most of the best sightings of wildlife and wilderness are far from cities, but Sydney is an exception, since it is so close to the wilderness of the Blue Mountains. Day hikes over this fissured sandstone plateau explore flower-studded heathland and plunging forests. The sandstone bluffs are characteristically old and infertile, a quality found all across Australia and one that most European farmers took about 200 years to appreciate. Yet somehow Australia's ancient rocks squeeze out enough sustenance to evolve uniquely Australian banksia flowers with colored nectar spikes arrayed as big as your hand

and koalas that conserve energy by functioning on the smallest relative brain size of any animal in the world. It is the appreciation of these unique qualities that makes travel within Australia such an exceptional experience.

Even the city itself offers close-up encounters. From gray-headed flying foxes flapping their 3-foot wingspans around the high-rises from their roost in the Royal Botanic Gardens to the prehistoric rock-climbing fish *Galaxias brevipinnis* that is facing local extinction from home construction around Manley Dam, there is plenty to glimpse of the modern and prehistoric species that make Australia so fascinating.

Sydney Harbour

A visit to Sydney is not complete without ferry rides or a cruise around Port Jackson, Sydney Harbour. Overlooking the harbor on the northern shores are Sydney Harbour National Park and the renowned Taronga Park Zoo at Mossman (02-9978-4786), which can be reached by ferry, 15 minutes from Sydney's Circular Quay. The zoo includes Australian native habitats, nocturnal houses, and a treetop koala walkway as well as international collections. The Sydney Harbour Bridge connects North Sydney with the central city and you can get an awesome view by taking the 3-hour Harbor Bridge Climb 134m/439ft up (02-9252-0077) or by climbing the south pylon. On the south side, the local Sydney Fish Market, Sydney Aquarium (02-9262-2300), and Powerhouse Museum (02-9217-0111) are located around the newly redeveloped Darling Harbour area, which you can reach by taking the monorail along Pitt and Market Streets. The aquarium houses three oceanariums that extend into the bay itself, plus excellent Great Barrier Reef and coral habitats. Go during the week when it is less crowded.

It is a close walk from centrally located Circular Quay and harbor ferries to the Sydney

Sydney Harbour Surprises

This convoluted waterway is fed by the Parramatta River and is packed with 600 species of fish and 2,000 marine invertebrate species. A survey performed in 2000 revealed the Sydney Harbor has far more species than previously found. Leafy and weedy seadragons (*Phyllopteryx taeniolatus*), huge sea spiders, and a newly discovered species of pipefish are some of the unexpected finds. These seadragons are pipefish, related to seahorses, with leaf-flaps that look like the kelp in which they hide. Transparent, undulating pectoral fins waft them around the algae, but they cannot catch the seaweed with their tails as seahorses do. Males nurse a pouch of eggs, protecting the offspring from predators. Seadragons are not found in the Great Barrier Reef but are found along southeastern, southern, and western Australian coasts. The Sydney Aquarium offers a way of getting a close-up view of some of the harbor's fish life in one of its open oceanariums.

Another survey of Sydney Harbour in 2001 showed that the many marina structures provide ideal reef-like environments that are boosting diversity despite the oil and chemical spills associated with high boat traffic.

Flying Foxes Downtown

There are several places where you can see flying foxes close-up in Sydney. Ku-ring-gai Chase Alive Bat Walks allow you to watch the evening fly-out, say hello to a hand-reared flying fox, and learn about insect-eating micro-bats and pollinating macro-bats (02-9457-9853).

The Gordon Colony evening fly-out varies from very small in winter to mobbed from October to March. This peaks 20 minutes after sundown. Take the Northshore Line train to Gordon. Walk for ten minutes to the sign-posted Rosedale Road bridge by the roost. Or watch a sub-colony of the same group in their evening fly-out from the Royal Botanic Gardens.

Opera House or a stroll around the Royal Botanic Gardens. A few blocks south is the Central Railway Station, which is the other main transportation hub for getting around the city and many associated national parks. Harbor-side walking tracks are excellent: Farm Cove Walk along the northern side of the Royal Botanic Gardens leads to Sydney Cove Walk and to Circular Quay via the Opera House. Hermitage Walking Track is 1.6km/1mile from Nielson Park around Rose Bay. The Manly Scenic Walkway, 9.6km/6miles from Manly Cove, can easily be reached from the Manly Ferry, 30 minutes from Circular Quay.

Royal Botanic Gardens

The Royal Botanic Gardens provide good sites to see the Australian white ibis that is common in urban areas, plus black-faced cuckoo-shrikes, superb blue fairywrens, and white-plumed honeyeaters. A noisy colony of gray-headed flying foxes can be easily seen as they roost in tree clusters during the day near the newly planted, much celebrated Wollemi pine. Flying foxes are intelligent creatures that thrive on fruiting trees and eucalypt blossoms. They adjust their body temperature by flapping their 50cm/18in wings for ventilation when too hot. These gray-headed flying foxes switch between a larger camp at Gordon, north of Sydney, where a large fly-out occurs most evenings, to the delight of onlookers.

The Wollemi pine (*Wollemia nobilis*) was discovered in 1994 in Wollemi National Park, north of the Blue Mountains, close enough to Sydney to make it almost a metaphor for the secrets that this continents still holds. The newly named species belongs to an ancient family of the Auracaria pines originating 200 million years ago. This find provides an exciting piece in the puzzle of the evolution of Southern Hemisphere pines, which have flat blades that look quite distinct from the needles

Pea-Brained

Koalas (*Phascolarctus cinereus*) have slashed their energy needs by evolving the smallest relative brain size of any mammal. By comparison, our own brains use one-sixth of our energy budget. A koala's brain is so tiny that it doesn't even fill its skull. This is why they sleep 19 hours a day. Koalas have evolved this uniquely Australian strategy to survive the very low nutrient levels of their ancient ark. Koalas eat eucalypts, which came on the scene about 30 million years ago and have tough, leathery leaves laced with poisonous phenols and protein-suppressing tannins, so koalas rotate between species. One of their favorite foods, manna gum (*Eucalyptus viminalis*), packs its youngest leaves with prussic acid to deter koalas from stripping their new shoots bare. Koalas also eat soil for trace minerals, but this causes a serious fungal disease, which we can catch. Nearly half of all koalas have their own version of the human venereal disease chlamydia. They are protected, though, from some diseases by the cellulose-digesting bacteria in their gut. Young koalas are innoculated with the bacteria by consuming semi-digested material, "pap," from their parents. At night, male koalas can be heard grunting like pigs. You can tell a male koala from a female by his Roman nose and greater size.

of their northern cousins. The tree is one of the many botanical species planted and sign-posted in this excellent park. The Botanic Garden office has a database with the exact location of each species for visitors interested in seeing a specific specimen (guided walks leave the office at 10:30AM). The office also provides identification services for rare wild plants brought in by the public.

These gardens are not old and dusty: the new gold rush for pharmaceuticals is enhancing the move toward making new identifications, particularly of rainforest plants. Step one in the process is to find a newly identified species, and this occurs regularly with researchers here. For example, the nightcap oak (*Eidothea hardeniana*), a relict from the prehistoric Australian rainforest, was found in northern New South Wales in 2001. *Asterolasia buxifolia*, a bush with

Taxol® from Fossil

An important new find, the Wollemi pine, has been planted in the middle of the Royal Botanic Gardens, where it is being carefully researched. One of the rarest species of plant, this pine was found in 1994 in two stands in a wild, deep gorge in Wollemi National Park by David Noble, a national parks officer. A third stand was discovered in another gorge in 2000. The bark of this tree from the hoop pine family looks like bubbling chocolate. The Wollemi pine was previously only known in fossil form 150 million years old. Already, research is generating a lot of excitement, for the pine is proving to be a raft from the dinosaur age that has brought a whole host of animals and plants with it. It is not just a tree but a habitat, and the habitat is intact. As with most other trees, this pine lives in close association with the mycorrhizal fungi that nurture its roots by delivering scarce nutrients. Over 50 fungi have been found associated with this tree, several of which live within the root tissue. One of these internal root strains, *Pestalotiopsis*, is a fungus that stunned researchers when it was found to produce Taxol. Taxol is an anti-cancer agent originally found in the bark of the Northern Hemisphere Pacific yew.

gorgeous yellow flowers originally discovered in the 1830s in the Blue Mountains and thought to have become extinct in the wild, was rediscovered in 2001 in a new location in the Blue Mountains by a Botanic Gardens researcher. When new species are found, they are tested for pharmaceutical possibilities.

Ku-ring-gai Chase National Park

30km/18mi north of Sydney, Ku-ring-gai Chase Park extends across the heathland of the Lambert Peninsula and drops into saltwater fjords and quiet beaches. If you are quiet, you are likely to see swamp wallabies (*Wallabia bicolor*), gorgeously patterned lace monitors, and a host of parrot species. 180 bird species and 800 plant species are found here, but this is hot scrubby bush, not lush meadows, so it may take added care to find what you are looking for. You may hear the imitative calls of the superb lyrebird, although they are hard to see. Aboriginal rock carvings of fish and goannas are found by following some West Head walks. The good America Bay Track can be reached from West End Road, a road that also leads to the Flint and Steel Track, which ends at a small beach for swimming. Two visitor centers offer help and

Eastern spinebill active among non-native fuchsia. They frequently hover as they gather nectar.

maps: Kalkari Visitor Centre on Ku-ring-kai Chase Road 3km/1.8mi east of the Pacific Highway (02-9457-9853) and Bobbin Head Information Centre (02-9457-1049). Bat walks are offered from the Kalkari Visitor Centre. If you do not have a car for the hour's drive from Sydney, take the train to Turramurra, then bus to Bobbin Head or Ku-ring-gai Chase Road (a couple of hours from Sydney). Directly on the other side of the bay from Ku-ring-gai Chase is Woy-Woy, an area of eucalypt forests abounding with Eastern rosella and rainbow and musk lorikeets.

Mount Annan Botanical Garden

Australia's largest and newest botanical garden amasses rare and endangered native plants in several fascinating ways. Beautiful lakes and creeks feed the rainforest habitats and 20km/12mi of walking tracks take you through a Wattle Garden, Banksia Garden, Bottlebrush Garden, and Terrace Garden. The Terrace Garden is perhaps the most interesting of all as it unfolds 2,500 Australian species in family groups terraced over a large hillside according to their evolutionary sequence. The evolution of each group is detailed in one of the garden's brochures. Although the gardens are so new that they may seem ultra-spacious, the plantings are mature enough to present some stunning flower displays. Mount Annan Botanical Garden is a major research site directly linked with the Royal Botanic Gardens, and an enjoyable place to spend a day.

The 400ha/988acre garden is 57km/35mi southwest of Sydney. Take the Southwestern Freeway to the Camden exit NW and turn left immediately onto Mount Annan Drive (02-4648-2477; fax 02-4648-2465).

Royal National Park

The 2001/2 bushfires that surrounded Sydney during "Black Christmas" have caused major destruction to this significant park, which had

Pre-Ferns

When you visit the beautiful billowing architecture of the Sydney Opera House, you'll probably find yourself taking a quick photo from the lower steps. But you may miss one of the most ancient forms of plant architecture emerging from the cracks in the botanic garden wall right behind you. *Psilotum nudum* is a modern species that probably looks and functions the same as its original pre-fern ancestor. It developed with the earliest plants long before leaves and flowers, using spores for reproduction. It is leafless, with six-inch bushy green stems its only source of photosynthesis. It has no roots: match-stick-sized stumps are all that hold it in the ground. Instead of roots, it plugs into the fungi that are associated with this plant species. These mycorrhizal fungi are symbiotic and probably the reason that plants emerged from the ocean in the first place. They offer water, phosphorous, nitrogen, and other micronutrients in exchange for the sugars produced by the plant. Some researchers theorize that plant stems and tree trunks were actually originally fungal structures.

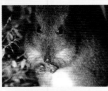

From top: Rufous bettong, long-nosed potoroo, and bridled nailtail wallaby at Earth Sanctuaries. Photos courtesy Earth Sanctuary Ltd.

Earth Sanctuary

Scotia Earth Sanctuary is one of several cutting-edge experiments in for-profit reserves set up by the controversial Dr. John Wamsley. At Scotia you can see numbats, bilbies, mala, bridled nailtail wallabies, woylies, silver boodies, stick-nest rats, plains rats, and hopping mice. These are protected from extinction by removal of all feral animals and encircled by an anti-feral fence. Visitors must book first for any visit, morning or evening tours, or overnight stays. The outcome for the animals has been successful, but finances are still experimental. Scotia is 500km/ 310mi from Adelaide and 1,200km/ 745mi from Sydney between Wentworth and Broken Hill (08-8370-9422; www.esl.com.au).

already been damaged by fires that large native mammals had not yet recovered from. The large park has no natural wilderness corridors for koalas and other bush animals to escape to new food sources.

There are, though, signs of hope. Residents helped capture and release to safety kangaroos and possums, animals that also fled along the beaches. Non-native deer and, paradoxically, small marsupials, including predatory anti-chinuses and dunnarts, plus native rats, had previously recovered after a major fire. Most of these survived by digging or squeezing below ground into holes and crevices. Dirt is so insulating that a mere two inches is deep enough to survive a rapidly moving 2,000-degree Fahrenheit inferno above. Many native plants have evolved to be fire-tolerant and even fire-dependent. But the 2001/2 fires were so unnatural and hot they generated their own cumulonimbus clouds 15,000 feet high, which triggered a lightning storm of their own and cast doubt on natural recovery. Even so, by January 8, 2002, before all the Sydney fires were extinguished, green shoots were already appearing from charred remains in this park.

It appears that the park may recover over time. Full restoration will probably require the reintroduction of some native species using human intervention, a role increasingly played by conservationists as they restore rather than simply protect the wilderness environment.

Blue Mountains National Park

The plunging sandstone forests of the huge Blue Mountains National Park are easily accessible. The journey is just over an hour's train-ride from Sydney. The forests' renown drew Charles Darwin during his Beagle expedition and appealed to an unenthusiastic John Muir during brief visits. If you leave your preconceptions behind, you'll discover more. The appreciation of what this cliff-lined area has to offer has been one of the historic driving forces behind the

*Heath banksia (*Banksia ericifolia*)*

Australian wilderness movement. The area has just been added to the list of World Heritage sites of outstanding natural value. And the site's international standing is likely to grow as a result of this new UNESCO status. In practical terms, though, the Blue Mountains can become unpredictably fog-bound and cold even in midsummer, so hike prepared with layered raingear, food, and water.

The accessible highlights were not affected by the 2001/2 forest fire, which did rage through the associated much wilder Wollemi National Park to the north and lower Grose River Valley away from the Grose River tourist footpaths, causing enormous damage beyond the usual brush fires.

The dissected sandstone plateau rises 1,000m/3,000ft and provides dramatic sweeping views around its cliff edges, laced by several slender waterfalls. "Scrubby trees of the never-failing eucalyptus genus" is how Darwin interpreted the enveloping woodland, but he may have overlooked the darker green rainforest that interrupts the sun-filled eucalypt

Cooperators

Look closely at the behavior of the gray-crowed babblers, white-winged choughs, laughing kookaburras, and noisy miners and see if you can spot any cooperative interactions. One third of Australian birds are cooperative breeders, much higher than any other country, and the highest concentration of cooperative breeding species are found in the Central Rainforest Reserves. Cooperative breeding has various forms and usually involves a community of birds that band together to raise their young, usually more successfully than individual pairs manage it alone. In some types of cooperative breeders, non-breeding helpers assist in defending territory, raising chicks, and feeding young. Breeding pairs are cared for by these helpers. Helpers may never breed. Genetically this challenged Darwinian-based evolutionary theory as it was originally thought that no genes were passed down to confer the non-breeding helper traits. But even theories evolve. It is now accepted that because helpers at the nest are relatives, some of their genes and traits are passed down through their parents and breeding siblings. The result is that the flock becomes more cooperative over time.

Nectaries

Old-Man banksia (*Banksia serrata*) seedcases (above) evolved to protect the seeds even during forest fires. The case chars and then opens, releasing the seeds to fertile ground. It is a major nectar plant. Heath Banksia (*Banksia ericifolia*) (page 9) is a dense tree-shaped shrub with handsome 20 cm/8 inch tall orange flower spikes that emerge from the foliage like bright candles. This is found on sandy coastal areas and sandstone of the Blue Mountains. It flowers late fall and winter, filling the nectar gap between flowering seasons.

The unusual shape of the 7-spiked mountain devil *Lambertia formosa* (below right, in bud) is found in its close relative, the 5- or 7-pronged chittick (*Lambertia inermis*), which is widespread in faraway coastal Western Australia. These flowers are all members of the large, bizarre-shaped Proteaceae family, which supplies heavy nectar loads to honeyeaters, gliders, and possums. The family's center of origin is in Western Australia.

woodland and dramatically increases species diversity. And the eucalypts themselves support a host of critical species, from dozens of species of Australian termites to the little red flying fox (*Pteropus scapulatus*), which may be seen roosting upside down in Blue Mountain gums during the day before feeding on eucalypt nectar at night. In the open dry forests, look for the red chrysanthemum-like 15cm/6in flowers of waratah (*Telpea speciosissima*), which is common locally.

Scattered hanging swamps on the sandstone ledges are lined with clay and act like sponges to provide water for many endangered species. They also drip-feed gullies of rainforests below the cliffs. The swamps are critical habitats that are the first to bounce back after bush fires and also provide excellent food sources. *Drosera binata* and *Drosera spatulata* are swamp sundews that trap insects for scarce nitrogen and phosphorous. Look for the red and green mired insect that walks over the sundew's glue-dropped, protein-digesting leaves using its unusually long legs to steal the sundew's catch.

The cavernous rainforests below the swamps are refuge areas for fire-sensitive birds and animals during bush fires. Here you may also find the superb lyrebirds displaying their exquisite black, chestnut, and silver feathers during winter months. These otherwise dull brown birds are commonly found scratching the ground for grubs around the accessible Leura Forest and along the Dardanelles Pass. Synthesizer-like, this bird mimics and splices

the songs together from all the other species that you are likely to see here, including the creaks of red-crested gangang cockatoos, disyllabic screeches of crimson rosellas, "currawong" cry of aptly-named currawongs, and taunts of laughing kookaburras. Some of these other species cluster at feeders around the Echo Point visitor center near the Three Sisters. The superb lyrebird can sing two songs simultaneously by using its two bronchae to make separate sounds. It delights in building up a full repertoire of songs. A flute tune learned by a captive lyrebird was passed on to generation after generation of listening wild lyrebirds 50 years after its release.

During the spring the nectar gatherers flock to the heathland flowers on the sandstone bluffs and fill them with song. Listen for eastern spinebills, red wattlebirds, and New Holland honeyeaters, and watch them cluster around the bizarre shapes of the Proteaceae family including grevilleas, banksias, and hakeas. The only place you will find related similar-looking Protea flowers is in South Africa, which was once linked to Australia when the two were part of the supercontinent called Gondwana.

Many visitors to the Blue Mountains visit the Three Sisters, a dramatic highlight at the edge of one section of the plateau. The legend of the Three Sisters is about an overprotective father who turned his daughters to stone to protect them in his absence. He intended to restore them when he returned from his journey, but he was killed on his way home, and the sisters remained imprisoned forever.

To reach the Blue Mountains, take the train to one of the stations in the National Park. The most accessible walks are in two clusters: from Blackheath Station to the northeastern-facing side of the Grose Valley and Govetts Leap waterfall and the dramatic fissured canyons around it, or from Katoomba or Luera Station to the southern-facing Katoomba Creek cliffline with Skyway and Scenic Railway and views of the Three Sisters.

Heath and Rainforest

The Popes Glen Track in the Blue Mountains near Blackheath Station follows a creek dominated initially by silvertop ash (*Eucalyptus seiberi*) and Sydney peppermint (*Eucalyptus piperita*). The creek builds into pools and a hanging swamp at Boyds Beach. Use your tracking skills to follow the trails of swamp wallabies (*Wallabia bicolor*). Along the wind-sheared cliff edges toward Pulpit Rock are sparse heathland flowers dripping with nectar, including banksia, mountain devil (*Lambertia formosa*), and clouds of five-pointed fringe myrtle flowers (*Calytrix tetragona*). The Myrtle family to which this flower belongs is the one from which all eucalypts evolved. The closed Leura Forest is a warm temperate rainforest. The medium-sized predatory marsupial spotted-tail quoll (*Dasyurus maculatus*) is nocturnal and difficult to find, but you may see the parallel stick bowers of the satin bowerbird and the daytime nests or dreys of the ring-tail possum. The rainforest resounds with the characteristic whip-cracks of the male Eastern whistle-bird, followed by the female's response. Look in the spring on the rocks around the rainforest scree for pencil orchid flowers (*Dendrobium teretifolium*), with their striking 3cm/1.5 inch pale flowers striped with purple.

Lyrebirds

Male lyrebirds sing in winter for half the day long, a local dialect that can be heard half a mile away. In fact, you are more likely to hear one than see one. Males imitate up to 16 other bird species, plus sounds of birds flying, machines whirring, and dogs barking. You can tell the difference from other species because they splice different songs together in quick succession. Females defend their own territories from females but not males. Females build huge dome-roofed nests off the ground on boulders or grass clumps. The female forages half the time she incubates the egg, slowing the chick's development to 50 days before hatching, and stays inside the dome 47 days more with the chicks. Australian lyrebirds are found in the southeastern Australian foothills from southern Victoria to southeastern Queensland. The endangered Albert's lyrebird was found in the Queensland rainforest, but now it is almost completely restricted to Lamington National Park. The superb lyrebird is found in the wet forests of southeastern Australia and southwestern Tasmania. It forages in nothofagus and eucalypt forests (especially in mountain ash, *Eucalyptus regnans*) for invertebrates and roosts in the canopy, like fowl.

Blackheath Walks

Blackheath Station is near several Blue Mountains walks radiating from the stunning lookouts around Govetts Leap. "Leap" in this case is the Scottish word meaning waterfall, and refers to Bridal Veil Falls. This small plume spills over the sandstone cliff into Govetts Creek Valley, which opens into the Grose River Valley, visible from 5km/3.1mi away. Tall pale green blue gums (*Eucalyptus deanei*) trace the rich soils along the river banks, and deep green rainforests grow in damper gullies. The oil from these gums creates the blue haze for which these mountains are named. Walks into the valley include the Rodriguez Pass to the Grand Canyon, and most take at least a full day. These are rated hard due to the steep descents and ascents. If you want to avoid this level of challenge, you can get a good immersion in most Blue Mountain habitats by walking along the Popes Glen Track from Blackheath to Pulpit Rock, east of Govetts Leap. Start at the Prince Edward Street parking lot close to Blackheath Station. The track entrance is nearby, starting at Dell Street via Wills Street. At Horseshoe Falls, turn left to Pulpit Rock and enjoy several lookouts across the valley. Add in a western detour to Bridal Veil Falls/Govetts Leap along the Cliff Top Track by turning right when you reach the creek-crossing at Horseshoe Falls. The entire hike takes up to 5 hours one way or 3 hours without the detour, and is rated medium in grade. At dusk, look for vegetarian brush-tailed and ring-tailed possums emerging from their nests along the creek on the return walk. You can also return from Pulpit Rock along Hat Hill Road to Blackheath, which is a quicker, smoother route of 2.3km/1.4mi one way.

Katoomba and Leura Walks

The Three Sisters Lookout can be reached from Katoomba Station by walking 20 minutes down Lurline Street south and continuing along Echo

Point Road to Echo Point Lookout. Or take the bus. From here, you'll see their warmly-colored sandstone pinnacles to your left, weather permitting. If you walk left to Three Sisters Lookout, you can decide whether to take the very steep Giant Stairway 170m/555ft down to the Kedumba and Jamison Valley floor. For those unwilling to climb back up, you can descend on foot and then take the Dardanelles Pass to Federal Pass, which continues to the Scenic Railway, taking 2–3 hours one way from Echo Point. The railway will take you back up the precipitous forest canopy to Prince Henry Cliff Walk and optional Scenic Skyway ride. The cliff walk returns you to Echo Point, across heathland and plunging views. If you turn left at the bottom of the Giant Stairway instead, you'll walk the Dardanelles Pass to Leura Forest, a rainforest trail that passes through superb lyrebird territories. Walk in a loop and return back via the Federal Pass, taking about 3 hours return to the base of the Giant Stairway, plus 45 minutes back up. If you continue to Leura Cascades without looping back, you can climb up the sandstone bluff and return via Leura Station instead of Katoomba Station, but allow a full day.

Possum Flight

Look at night with a flashlight into eucalypt or rainforest almost anywhere in Australia and you are likely to spot one of its many possums or gliders. These fluffy, fun creatures keep the neighborhood in trim. Genetically, Australian gliders appear to have evolved flight three separate times from three possum ancestors, instead of from one leaping possum. And outside Australia, flying squirrels have evolved from entirely separate ancestors to glide on skin flaps in similar ways, an example of convergent evolution. Fluffy gliders (*Petaurus australis*) can sail up to 120m/370ft away, changing course and calling loudly. Possums usually eat eucalypts, flowers, and fruit. Most gliders live off sap, nectar, and pollen, though the greater glider eats eucalyptus leaves exclusively. The Australian possums evolved from the predatory marsupials of the Quoll family, about 30 million years ago. Unlike their American cousins, they are now entirely vegetarian. Common brushtail possum (*Trichosurus vulpecula*) is the commonest possum of the suburbs and are also found in eucalypt forests all over Australia. The common ringtail possum (*Pseudocheirus peregrinus*) (left) builds dreys, or twig-and-leaf day shelters, in holes in tea-trees (*Leptospermum* sp.) and eucalypts.

Blue Bower

The satin bowerbird builds a bower of parallel stick walls on a circular twig mat, painted with saliva and charcoal. Blue objects—from cicada cases, to flowers, to plastic bottle tops—decorate a stage. The male offers the female these objects and, when she accepts, mates with her in the bushes away from the bower.

The male's plumage is black with a purple sheen. Its intense violet eyes with dark pupils are highlighted by the blue *objets d'art* that have been so carefully selected.

The larger, handsome female builds a separate nest. Her plumage is decorated with green spots on a robust silver-gray body the size of a fat pigeon.

A close relative of these birds is the regent bowerbird, a rainforest frugivore with outstanding black and gold plumage. It is common within Lamington and Dorrigo National Parks and around rainforest lodge feeders.

Walking guides for several Blue Mountain excursions are available from the National Park Shop, Blue Mountains Heritage Centre, Blackheath, New South Wales (047-87-8877; fax 047-87-8514).

Pacific Ranges

Dorrigo, Lamington, and Barrington Tops National Parks are part of 16 reserves of World Heritage status collectively named the Central Eastern Rainforest Reserves. They form a chain of parks along several Pacific ranges of mountains immediately parallel to the coast. This area stretches across New South Wales and southern Queensland and includes rainforests of subtropical, dry, warm temperate, and cool temperate types. Ecotravellers interested in birds visit these parks because, with 270 bird species, they are among the most diverse of any areas of Australia. Brisbane, the hub city, is also a wonderful tropical center. Steve Irwin's Australia Zoo is located north of Brisbane near the coast. In Lamington

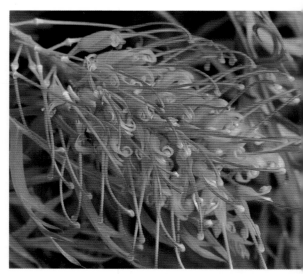

Red silky oak (Grevillea banksii) *is found in Queensland coastal areas as a slender tree or shrub and is planted as an ornamental in gardens. Several unrelated species are named silky oak.*

National Park you can see 200 species of birds during spring. Insect fauna is the second in diversity, ranking after the Queensland Wet Tropics, which no doubt boosts the bird levels. A number of graceful and rare marsupials can be spotted, and platypuses frequent the streams. This is also the land of snails, yet even reptiles include 110 species, of which *Phyllurus* geckoes and *Genocephalus* dragons are largely endemic. The limitations of these sites for ecotravellers is that many of the parks are remnant patches encroached by agricultural land: a real sense of wilderness may be hard to find. As with all Australian wilderness, the animals are elusive because the rainforest birds stay in the canopy and the marsupials are usually nocturnal and shy. But if you sign up for some special-interest weeks at ecotravel lodges, you get close-up encounters firsthand. The faster growth of the tropics is still some way to the north, but the rainforest patches can look similar to the uninitated eye. Due to altitude variations, a large variety of completely different forest habitats may still be seen within a single afternoon. This also creates more "edge" zones, which boost the species diversity and fascination of these forests.

The importance of conservation in this area is underscored by the story of the gastric brooding frogs. These are two frog species that rear their young inside their stomach. In one species, the young secrete a substance that stops the production of gastric juices until they mature. In the other, sticky mucus protects the tadpoles from digestive juices. Both species were discovered in creeks in the Central Rainforest Reserve World Heritage area. But they were last seen in the 1980s and are now missing after a severe drought and increased logging activities, which silted up the streams in which the frogs lived. They are now presumed extinct. There are 43 other species of frogs found in these areas that are now receiving heightened care and research attention.

Leafy sea dragon

Reaching up to 1m/3ft3in, this leafless saprophyte hyacinth orchid (Dipodium punctatum) is common in eucalypt forests in NSW Queensland and Victoria. It removes energy and nutrients from dead and decaying organic matter so it does not need to synthesize much from scratch. It could be said that it functions more like an animal than a plant.

Blueberry (Dianella tasmanica)

Dorrigo National Park

In Bellingen Shire, on the vacation coast between Sydney and Brisbane, lies Dorrigo National Park, 57km/36mi west of Coffs Harbour. Dorrigo is locally popular for its incredibly diverse rainforest vegetation communities— subtropical, warm temperate, and cool temperate—with hiking trails wandering through them all. It is one of four centers of distribution for *Nothofagus moorei*, the Antarctic Beech. The park has a skywalk from which rare birds can often be seen. Take the 400m/1300ft Lyrebird Link Track to the 5.8km/3.5mi subtropical rainforest Wonga Walk. Or near the warm temperate rainforests of Never Never picnic area you can walk to Rosewood Creek Track along this 2-hour walk past rainforest pools. Other options are to take a 4.8km/2.9mi return walk to Casuarina Falls which has a good view of the Great Escarpment, or walk the Blackbutt Track along the escarpment edge.

Look for red-necked pademelons and red-legged pademelons, small kangaroos that live in and around rainforest edges, with the red-legged usually found deeper under the canopy. One hundred and twenty species of birds are found in Dorrigo including canopy birds such as satin and regent bowerbirds, Australian king parrots, and green catbirds; and ground dwellers such as lyrebirds, brush turkeys, Eastern whipbirds, logrunners, noisy pittas, and yellow-throated and white-browed scrubwrens. Take a nightwalk to look for sugar, pygmy, and greater gliders, or brushtail and ringail possums. Reptiles include the land mullet (a tubby skink), carpet and diamond python, lace monitor, and Southern angle-headed dragon. Common subtropical rainforest plants seen around the skywalk include yellow carabeen, booyong, strangler fig, and giant stinging tree. Epiphytic orchids and ferns are common. Common warm temperate rainforest species seen around the Never Never picnic area include coachwood, sassafras, and crabapple. Common moist eucalypt forest species found in the Bellingen Valley include Sydney blue gum, blackbutt, and tallowwood, which is gray-green.

Lamington National Park

Lamington National Park is 176km/110mi south of Brisbane and straddles the lofty escarpment of the 1,100-m/3,630-ft high Borders Range. Its hilly eucalypt bush, cool temperate rainforest, and pristine subtropical rainforest provide one of the best birding sites in Australia. There are 900 species of vascular plants and numerous endemics, with several newly identified species found every few years.

One reason for this park's success in terms of world-wide reputation is that two historic and world-class ecolodges dating back to the 1920s and 1930s offer all that new ecolodges are jumping to mimic: guided walks by experts who live their talk and know the insides of these forests, 160km/96mi of signed walking trails, tree-top structures for canopy walks, "flying-fox" rides, and a full suite of activities that include spotlighting for nocturnal animals. Dedicated ecoexplorers must pay a visit.

Binna Burra Lodge is on the Binna Burra Road via Beechmont and overlooks the sweeping Coomera Valley. The lodge has many

Frogs

During the popular Frog Week at O'Reilly's Guesthouse, the great barred frog (*Mixophyes fasciolatus*) broke the world record in tadpole length at 13cm/5.2in. No wonder: this frog can delay its metamorphosis for a couple of years.

Over 30 frog species are found in the area. The glinting emerald-spotted treefrog (*Litoria peronii*) (below left) is gorgeous. It is common in southeastern Australia, including Lamington, but not in the rainforest. Listen for its low rattle, like a laughing jackhammer. It has a rough patch below its thumb, which in males changes during breeding season to a black patch, like rubber, to better grip the female. Most frogs are best identified by their call, not their color, which can vary enormously. Males of the rare whirring treefrog (*Litoria revelata*) (above) change color completely from day to night. They have orange on the inner fold of their thighs. This species is very small and whirs like a cicada.

100% Australian

Kangaroos range from the rabbit-sized rat kangaroo that represents an intermediate relict caught in evolution from their possum ancestors, to the gigantic Western and Eastern gray kangaroos with head and body length over 2m/6ft6in.

All marsupials have pouches to reduce the metabolic demand on the female during pregnancy. During lean years, if the pouch young dies, it can do this without harming the mother. This is an advantage in an ancient land with low nutrient levels and decadal weather cycles.

The prevailing view about marsupial origins was that they originated in North America. Placental mammals lived side-by-side, but eventually won over, leaving traces of a few opossums in America. Australia was considered to be the marsupial playground because no mammals had arrived to wipe them out.

This theory is now being turned on its head. In 1997 a possible mammal fossil from the Cretaceous was found in Otway Basin, Australia. And a placental fossil, *Tingamarra porteranum*, was found at Murgon in Central Queensland. Mammal fleas have also been found in the Koonawarra fishbeds from the Cretaceous. These finds indicate that all marsupials may well have originated in Australia.

The whiptail or elegant wallaby (Macropus parryi) *has a handsome cheek stripe. It is found in eastern Queensland and northern New South Wales in eucalypt forest, such as Lamington National Park.*

activities for children and adults, including the longest flying-fox ride in the world. This lodge has the edge in offering more activities for younger guests plus a broad set of activities. Walking maps of the extensive, marked trails are available from the National Parks and Wildlife Information Centre on the way to the lodge. Look in the leaf litter for iridescent noisy pittas, on boulders for plump wonga pigeons, and by paths for the parallel-stick bowers of satin bowerbirds.

O'Reilly's Rainforest Guesthouse is at Green Mountain via Canungra. It is at O'Reilly's that David Attenborough, the presenter of many stunning and thought-provoking wildlife films, stays. This recommended guesthouse is designed for naturalists. For the rest, there is a pool and jacuzzi with a plunging view off the mountainside. Significant conservation programs and surveys are sponsored by the O'Reilly family. These are run in conjunction with activity weeks, and guests can participate fully as volunteers. The November Bird Week, which has been running for over 25 years, is the most popular in Australia, and provides the chance to see over 200 species. The *Sorghum leiocladum* is a signal plant growing around eucalypt forests near O'Reilly's that indicates the habitat where you may hear or see the rare Eastern bristlebird.

George is an Albert's lyrebird over 25 years old who may be spotted and heard near Python Rock on one of the extensive forest paths from O'Reilly's. He was still strutting around when I went. An accurate map of walking trails is available at the O'Reilly's guest shop, which also provides an excellent local bird guide sheet. There is a feeding station where Australian king parrots and crimson rosellas delight younger guests and busloads of tourists in from nearby Brisbane, although these crowds rarely stray far into the forest pathways.

Sugar gliders, mountain brushtail possums, red-necked pademelons and exquisitely colored frogs come around the O'Reilly's cabins at night. On a winter's dawn, look along the Border and Pensioner's Tracks in the forest trails for the small trampled stage of Albert's lyrebird, where it fans its silver plumed tail until the feathers drape back over its head. When not displaying, an Albert's lyrebird looks a bit like a drowned pheasant (sorry George.) In fact, even when it is on full show, Albert's does not have the main outer lyres of the superb lyrebird. However, it is a sought-after sight because this endangered species now has a range limited to this National Park and one other area.

Activity Weeks

The two Lamington National Park ecolodges run a series of week-long educational and conservational activities for guests. These are wonderful ways to see rare and hidden species, learn about the rainforest, and meet ecotravellers with similar interests. Expect a full dose of quirky Australian charm.

Binna Burra Lodge

Ecology Week: February
Photography Week:
    February/early March
    & September
Extreme Bushwalkers Week:
    October

O'Reilly's Rainforest Guesthouse

Autumn Birdwatching
    Week: April
Photography Week: May
On-the-Beaten Track Week:
    June
Off-the-Beaten Track, 1 or 2
    weeks: August
Bird Week: November
Frog Week: December

Australian King Parrot

Xanthorrhoea grasstrees, eucalypts, and blady grass growing again after a forest fire.

In the *Nothofagus* forests around Mount Bithonbagel and Mount Wanungara look for the rare rufous scrub-bird in the damp mossy parts with dense undergrowth, especially between Wanungara and Nyamulli Lookouts and the Mount Merino circuit.

The venomless carpet python found in pet shops around the world lives wild around Lamington, in sleek iridescent health. Watch out for harmless, painless leeches around the rainforests that respond to vibration and heat. Just pick them off and watch out that you do not flick them into someone else's eye as you do so. If they make you feel squeamish, consider that many patients undergoing difficult post-surgical care are currently being treated by leeches in the top Western hospitals. Hirudin, a leech saliva compound, is a major part of anti-coagulant medication used in the medications of many heart patients.

On the Lamington National Park Road toward the top of Green Mountain, look around the silvery pine-like casuarina clumps for glossy black cockatoos and into the associated eucalypt woodlands for groups of the elegant pretty-faced wallabies. Koalas are difficult to find, but they are sitting in their favorite eucalypts on some of these hillsides. Aboriginal peoples find koalas by looking for their shadows among the relatively shadow-free dapple of the eucalypt leaves. Eucalypts have evolved to minimize sun impact by turning the leaf blade so the narrowest edge faces the hottest rays, showing up these bulky animals. The rest of us look for koalas by checking for their droppings and sniffing for the strong eucalypt smell that they exude.

2
Lord Howe Island

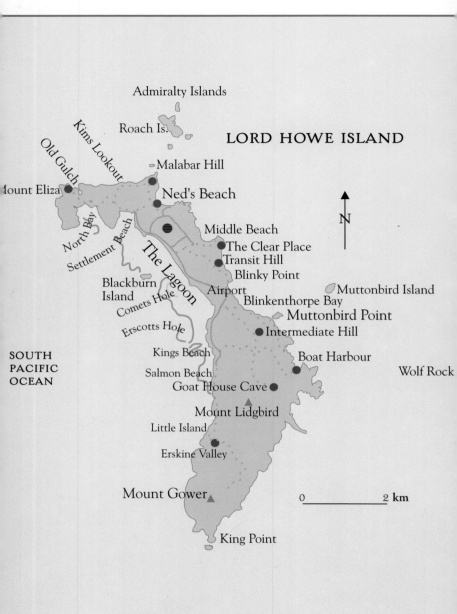

Admiralty Islands

Roach Is.

LORD HOWE ISLAND

Kims Lookout

Old Gulch

Malabar Hill

Mount Eliza

Ned's Beach

North Bay

Settlement Beach

The Lagoon

Middle Beach

The Clear Place

Transit Hill

Blinky Point

Blackburn
Island

Airport

Muttonbird Island

Comets Hole

Blinkenthorpe Bay

Muttonbird Point

Erscotts Hole

Intermediate Hill

SOUTH
PACIFIC
OCEAN

Kings Beach

Boat Harbour

Wolf Rock

Salmon Beach

Goat House Cave

Mount Lidgbird

Little Island

Erskine Valley

Mount Gower

0 ———————— 2 km

King Point

Lord Howe Island

Go to the highly rated Lord Howe Island for the undeveloped, subtropical life of the Tasman Sea and the South Pacific Ocean, two hours by plane from Sydney. This ancient shield volcano has a scattering of houses nestling around a lagoon with coral, algae, and endemic fish species. There are no high-rises or large resorts. You can bicycle from beach to beach for a dip, or walk among the stunning bird life to the dramatic lookouts. Ancient cloud forest ecosystems cling to Lord Howe Island's volcanic summits and native palm groves arc over gullies and slopes. The coral reef is a unique mix of cold-water algae and warm-water corals. Some coral forms look distinct from the separate, warmer Great Barrier Reef, which has a different spawning cycle. Here, corals spawn in January or February during several days around a single full moon.

The 280 resident hosts are relaxed and dedicated to ecotourism. If you ask, your host will provide minute-by-minute updates of seasonal happenings such as turtle and rare bird sightings. Well-established walking tracks and knowledgeable land and reef guides are a major part of the island's offerings. You can easily get around once you have rented your bicycle and snorkeling gear, when you'll see beautiful white terns nesting in spring and summer on the large bare branches of the trees along Lagoon Road and by Ned's Beach. One drawback is that although the roads are relatively flat, many walking trails are steep. If you build up to challenging walks over three days or so, the tougher hikes can be used as preparation for one of the world's best-rated walks. This is the difficult guided Mount Gower day trek that goes almost straight up for 875m/2,870ft to the cloud forest. Here you may come under the inquiring gaze of flightless, endangered Lord Howe Island woodhens as you absorb the fantastic views.

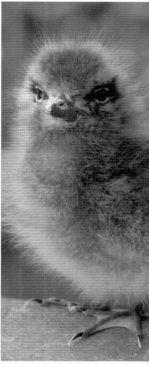

White tern chick (above) on branch, which is all it has as a nest. Blue lagoon (previous page) with Mount Ligbird in distance.

Don't Miss
- Erscott's Hole
- Malabar
- Ned's Beach
- Mount Gower
- Sylph's Hole

Fig Trees

A single *Ficus* tree can create its own forest ecosystem by spreading, using aereal roots that dangle from lofty branches (above). The fig fruits are food for a host of birds and animals. On Lord Howe Island, one *Ficus* extended beyond the length of a football field before being dismantled by a landslide.

EASY WALKS OF UP TO 2 HOURS

Transit Hill is named for the viewing of the transit of Venus, which happened in 1882 and will again in 2004. Start at the Administration Center and walk southeast on the trail through dry forest.

Clear Place is an easy walk for a good panorama on a trail leading southeast from Anderson Road. Kentia palms and huge multi-trunked banyan trees (*Ficus macrophylla columnaris*) shelter muttonbird burrows, so watch your step.

Steven's Reserve is a patch of rainforest and a palm grove in the middle of the island's residential area, accessed from a path off Lagoon Road near the powerhouse. Here you can see one of the island's cash crops, the Kentia palm. These are harvested as seed from wild palms and exported all over the world as house plants, ideally suited to indoor temperatures. In fact, this is an island of palm trees and there are four beautiful species on the island. Palms are an important and beautiful group among the island's 241 native vascular plants, of which 129 plant species are shared with Australia, 102 with New Caledonia, and 75 with New Zealand.

Another short walk, but further away, is found below Mount Lidgbird. The Little Island Track passes a rock outcrop in the lagoon known for picturesque paintings and photographs. Bicycle south along Lagoon Road until it ends at the track. Then walk along the coastline until you are below Mount Lidgbird. Woodhens can be seen on the trail here. You will see the variety of *Pandanus fosteri* that have stilt roots that are much longer and sprout higher up than the Australian mainland variety, perhaps to withstand the Westerlies from the Tasman Sea.

MEDIUM WALKS

Boat Harbour

The trail by Muttonbird Point provides a viewing platform overlooking the colonies of wedge-tailed shearwater, black-winged petrel, masked booby, and common noddy. If you continue to Boat Harbour this will take a day, round trip. There is fresh water at the harbor. You can return over Smoking Tree Ridge by taking a west fork trail at Rocky Run.

Malabar Hill

Malabar Hill (208m/680ft) is about 45 minutes northwest of Ned's Beach up a steep hill track and is highly recommended for its breathtaking plunge-views to the east, and then north until you look directly over cliffs dropping into azure oceans. The red-tailed tropicbirds' aerial circus are also one of the island's attractions. The red-tailed tropicbird is a gorgeous flier, well worth watching for an entire afternoon when they are most active. They perform enormous back-flips and incredible courtship loops over soaring partners.

As you climb, the vegetation changes dramatically from grassland with nesting sooty terns, to stunted hopwood, juniper, and

Evolving Under Our Noses

Pandanus trees, or screw pines, have large stilt roots to colonize river runs and sandy areas without collapsing after floods. The common endemic *Pandanus fosteri* (above) is not the same as the Queensland variety, having much higher stilt roots. This has evolved into a new species after being isolated from its origins. Another screw pine is also on the brink of diversification: there is only one clump of non-endemic *Pandanus pedunculatus* on the island, and if it survives long-term, it may originate another species as well.

Boat Cruises

Glass-bottom boats offer short cruises to North Bay and the lagoon for observation and snorkeling. Take warm clothes as well as swimming gear. Nearby Roach Island, in the Admiralty Islands, is highly recommended for birdwatchers. Landings can be made on very calm days to observe sea birds nesting in summer. Several boat cruises reach the Admiralty Islands for their excellent diving choices. Huge colonies of wedge-tailed shearwaters, gray ternlets, masked boobies, common noddies, and sooty terns squeal and clamor as they fly in and out. Ball's Pyramid is a challenging and other-worldly destination for fishing, birding, and diving. Its 551m/1,800ft spire can be seen from Lord Howe Island. This is the remnant of an eroded coastline or island, the tallest "stack" in the world. Kermadec petrels breed here, the only place in Australia. *Dryococoelus australis* is a huge flightless Phasmid, a prehistoric stick insect, that was recently thought extinct. A search party located several of these in 2001 on Ball's Pyramid, with eggs nearby. This illustrates the importance of isolated islands in protecting the world's genetic bank of obscure species.

bullybush. The endemic epiphyte bush orchid (*Dendrobium macropus howeanum*) bursts with pale yellow flowers in August and September. Look for a large patch of endemic foot-high *Plectorrhiza erecta* orchid flowers in December to the left of a rocky clearing by the track. These are epiphytic orchids with wiry stems that tangle together, woven with white roots. The small flowers are creamy orange with purple dots. Climbing *Jasminum simplicifolium* scents the air sweetly in summer. Tree species change as altitude and humidity increase to include blackbutt, greybark, and hopwood. The hill is full of the rustle of ex-shipboard black rats whose tails can be seen as the animals carefully hide their heads like young children playing peek-a-boo. And you may spot the only endemic reptiles of the island here. These are the rainbow-glowing endemic skink (*Leiolpisma lichenigera*) and gecko (*Phyllodactylus guentherii*). These rat delicacies are rare on the main island. So far these reptiles have escaped the fate of less-fortunate island species, although an introduced skink is proving more successful than the native one. The 1918 introduction of black rats from the grounded SS *Makambo*, plus feral cats, goats, pigs, and hunting wiped out the Lord Howe boobook owl, Lord Howe fantail, vinous tinted thrush, robust silvereye, Lord Howe starling, and Lord Howe warbler, leaving only nine endemic bird species on the island.

North Bay

The Max Nichol's Track is the best way to get to North Bay, although the climb over the hill on a well-cut trail is steep both ways. Watch for exquisite emerald ground doves rooting among the leaf litter on the E side of the ridge—these non-endemic birds live up to their name. On north hill slopes the *Drypetes/Cryptocaria* rainforest merges with *Howea forsteriana* palm forests on the flats behind North Bay, with *H.*

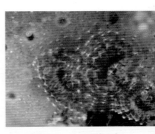

Coldwater-Tropical Combo

The palette of the coral reef combines coral species that drift down as larvae on warmer currents from the Great Barrier Reef with coldwater algae drifting up from the cooler south. Green, brown, purple, and blue soft corals (top left) can be distinguished from reef-building hard corals by their symmetry of eight tentacles. Blue xenia is a delicate sky-blue soft coral found in rock pools. Sea fans (above), and sponges (center right) all thrive under and around rocks and in rock pools. These are major new sources of pharmaceuticals and several thousand new Australian species have been identified in the quest for the next cures. The sea hare (center left) is carefully camouflaged but common. Look for a caravan of sea hares in the act of mating.

Sea urchins (lower left), slipper oysters (lower right), and crabs (below) add to 447 fish species.

Mount Gower

Guided Mount Gower walks leave several times a week. The summit can be fogged in, so go at the first opportunity of good weather. Be well-prepared with hiking boots, water, camera, and trail mix. You gain the camaraderie of Mount Gower trek achievers if you go, but bear in mind that Mount Gower is perhaps four times higher than the hardest walks on this island, except Goat House Track. Most regular walkers will find they can comfortably build up to the trek after a few active days on the island. Get in shape, otherwise exhaustion will prevent you from fully experiencing the stunning views, beautiful tangled forest, and rare birds. You need to examine the terrain of every step you make for safety's sake, and this will tax your concentration. Ropes are provided to haul you up the steepest parts. If you don't like heights, the guides will help you master the Get Up Place at 700m/2275ft which involves a very brief rock climb with fixed ropes.

belmoreana palms in the narrow gullies. The alternative to the ridge is to go around Dawson's Point at low tide, but neither time nor energy is saved as the boulders require careful navigation and there is little sea life to view until you get to the bay. If you paddle around North Beach by kayak or on foot in summer you can spot brown-camouflaged sea hares, sea fans, hermit crabs, and symmetrically beautiful soft coral polyps. But you have to stay still and watch for movement in the brown shallows dotted with green algae and green shrimp, and there are a few coral scatterings. If you want to snorkel, go with a guide, otherwise the North Bay appears barren.

Mount Eliza

Mount Eliza is a half-hour hike up a steep hill from North Bay. Sooty terns nest here. Masked boobies and black winged petrels fly very close to observers. The view and bird life are fantastic, but the walk is challenging as it involves two steep hills. Some boat trips allow walkers to miss the first hill.

DIFFICULT WALKS

Goat House Cave

For fit walkers, the views of this tough hike are very rewarding. Start south of the airstrip on Lagoon Road. Take the track east from unmarked Mosely Park and split south to Intermediate Hill (250m/718ft) altitude, to climb up Smoking Tree Ridge to trek half way up the eastern side of Mt. Lidgbird (400m/1,300ft) where fixed ropes are in place. Look out for Ball's Pyramid piercing the ocean blue. Several of the endemic species found on the Mount Gower hike can be found here also in the damper higher altitudes starting around 400m/1,300ft) including hot bark, mountain rose, Fitzgeraldii tree and *Dendrobium moorei* orchids. This orchid flowers year-round and has drooping small white flowers, some with pink dots. It grows as an epiphyte from tree branches.

Mount Gower

One of Mount Gower's draws is the challenge in getting to the top and back in one day (called "walking" but to the uninitiated it is climbing). The appeal is the Gondwanan animals and plants found in greater concentration as you ascend. Walkers pass through several unique habitats as they scale Mount Gower, including cliffs dotted with epiphytes, beautiful palm groves that change species with altitude, rainforests with Gondwanan hot bark (*Zygogynum howeanum*) and tree ferns (*Cyanthea howeana*), and, on top, a moss forest of 28ha/11acres where the flat part is just a bit bigger than your backyard. Relatives of Mount Gower's cloud forest species are found on damp mountain-tops mostly in New Zealand, with some in India, Australia, and New Caledonia.

What is incredible about Mount Gower and Mount Lidgbird's cloud forest is that they are so small, and there aren't others to exchange genes with for thousands of miles. Yet many species are endemic and are so primitive in evolutionary terms that they must stay above the cloud-line, or dessicate. This elfin world is all they know, yet it is a fully functional ecosystem. That is, with our help: rat bait stations can be seen occasionally, looking like

Mountain Walking Tips

On the way up, avoid burning out muscles by reducing stride length to a comfortable pace.

Use as much of the entire foot as possible to roll on and off the weight so toes and calves are not overtaxed.

Try to keep near the front of the group so that you get full use of rest periods.

Take even more care on the way down. This is when fatigue sets in, which makes for more injuries.

Island Floaters

Spiders have been found floating on air at 15,000 feet high in the atmosphere by plane traps in other regions. The enormous lift from a spider's gossamer thread may explain how many spiders—102 species—arrived on the island. About half of these have now evolved into distinct species. Some species came to this island during Gondwanan times when easy island-hopping was possible. (Lord Howe Island, however, was never joined to Gondwana directly.) Other species originated by obscure travel routes. This island has been waiting for colonizers since it was formed as a volcano 6.5 million years ago. Following the spiders and flying insects came a forest bat, the little cave eptesicus (*E. sagittula*), which evolved into the only endemic mammal still living on the island. Another bat, a new species *Nyctophilus howensis*, died out some time ago. Most plants came first as seeds in bird's stomachs when island-hopping was possible. Just 17% of plants floated here as robust seeds. Others got caught up on seabird feet, or were lifted into the atmosphere by cyclones. "Rain" of saltwater fish has been recorded in India after cyclones funneled them whole from the oceans and deposited them far inland.

Curly palm

Elfin Forest

30 fern species are found on the Mount Gower cloud forest, 27 more grow below it, and half of these are endemic. The beautiful filmy fronds of *Cephalomanes* and *Hymenophyllum* (below left) are found only on Mounts Gower and Lidgbird. The meter-tall *Blechnum howeanum* (below right) crowds Mount Gower's miniature plateau. Mixed with these are mosses, liverworts (top), crustal and foliose lichens (center right), and a sprinkling of orchids. *Calanthe triplicata* is a rare ground orchid you may see on Mount Gower and at Erskine Valley. Above 400m/1300ft find moorei orchid (*Dendrobium moorei*), a small endemic epiphyte with white drooping flowers year round (center left). At lower elevations this is replaced by big clumps of bush orchid (*D. macropus howeanum*) with its yellowish flowers.

The moss cushions on Mount Gower summit hide wingless moss bugs that pre-date modern insects. Their relatives are located only in cool Gondwanan habitats in South America, New Caledonia, New Zealand, and Australia. The Lord Howe Island Rise formed the outskirts of Gondwana with New Zealand until 80 million years ago. Until the Tasman Sea rose at that time, island-hopping species had an easier time colonizing new areas.

Endemic Palms
Curly palm (*Howea belmoreana*) (page 30) is found on slopes and has delicate curly leaf spikes. Kentia palm (*Howea forsteriana*) (top) is found on lowland flats. Its seeds are a major economic crop for Lord Howe Islanders. The seeds are grown by nurseries as house plants, particularly in cooler European environments. Little mountain or moorei palm (*Lepidorrhachis mooreana*) (center) is a dwarf palm with a robust trunk that is found on peaks. Big mountain palm (*Hedyscepe canterburyana*) (bottom) is found on the upper mountain slopes and has larger fruit. Relatives are found only in Southern Africa.

discarded plumbing. These protect several endangered species that surround you, although you may not be aware of them. Discoveries abound: recently identified are a new species of Talitrid amphipod on Mount Gower, and twelve new species of terrestrial isopods, organisms that pre-date insects. The "land lobster," or Lord Howe Island phasmid (*Dryococoelus australis*), a huge stick insect that recently disappeared from Mount Gower and was thought extinct, was confirmed alive with eggs on nearby Ball's Pyramid in 2001. Ancient wingless moss bugs burrow between the mossy filaments, their relatives located only in similar Gondwanan habitats in South America, New Caledonia, New Zealand, and Australia. You can see small endemic freshwater prawns (*Pratya howensis*) on the way up in the creek of Erskine Run. These flit in the shadows of lily-like Fitzgeraldii trees (*Dracophyllum fitzgeraldii*), whose lineage as a member of the Heath family is so ancient and rare that they stir quivers up a botanist's spine. Its Gondwanan relatives are found in Tasmania's cool mountains and are linked to the time when arid land species evolved on poor soils close to dominant rainforests. This set up a new collection of species ready for non-rainforest living as aridity increased.

Endemic land birds can still be seen on the island among the island's 129 bird species, largely due to recent conservation and rescue efforts, which have held the count at nine out of fifteen endemics extinct. There are 220 individual Lord Howe Island woodhens on the island, and you are almost guaranteed a sighting at the top of Mount Gower. People who don't want to climb have a good chance of seeing the woodhen on the Little Island Track, near picturesque Little Island. Listen for their low honks or their high bell-like territorial call. Their very existence is a major turnaround for they had declined to only 26 birds in 1975. The woodhen's decline was caused by hunting after 1788 and the effects of feral pigs and cats. A captive breeding program

Cauliflory is seen in the island's apple (bottom left) where flowers and fruit burst from the bark.

Rarest of Rare

The Lord Howe Island woodhen (top left) and Lord Howe Island currawong (lower right) are endemic. One third of island plants are endemic and are mostly found on damper slopes. These are thought to have originated shortly after parts of Gondwana broke up, since many are from New Zealand. These ancient relicts include rhododendron-like hotbark (*Zygogynum howeanum*), found on Mount Gower slopes. Its leaves have a refreshing peppery taste, since it is a member of the Winteraceae family, which produces the tasty oil of Wintergreen. Other Gondwanan endemics include the white wedding lily (*Dietes robinsoniana*) (top right) found around Mount Gower, Far Flats, and Goat House Cave. Its relatives are only found in southern Africa. The plump orange flowers of the pumpkin tree (*Negria rhabdothamnoides*) is also more ancient than many modern plants. The endemic mountain rose (*Metrosideros nervulosa*) has airborne roots, disk-like leaves and deep red bottle-brush flowers that are seen from Oct–Jan. Many Lord Howe Island flowers are green or white, but a few, like the unidentified Crowea (center left), are brightly colored.

was put in place and feral pigs and cats removed. This has brought the population back. Abundant endemics include the silver-eye (*Zosterops tephropleura*) and the Lord Howe Island golden whistler contempta (*Pachycephala pectoralis*). The Lord Howe Island currawong (*Strepera graculina crissalis*) is common around the southern mountains. Species that did not survive the hunting from maritime and whaling vessel food sorties include the white gallinule in 1844 and Lord Howe pigeon in 1870. The Lord Howe parakeet was shot to extinction in 1870, because it "ate settlers' crops."

DIVING, SNORKELING, & KAYAKING

Ned's Beach

Ned's Beach is often the first stop for reef snorkeling and is a short bike ride away from anywhere on the island. To get there, turn east at the powerhouse onto Ned's Beach Road and bear left. Just before the beach, you will pass

Endemic Cyanthea howea *tree fern*

Shrimping

This endemic shrimp (above) is found in streams, even high up Mount Gower in Erskine Run. It probably originated from east Australia where its ancestors are now extinct. Perhaps it came as an egg on the foot of a bird.

through Ned's Beach Common where you will see the nesting holes made by muttonbirds (flesh-footed shearwaters) among the tree roots. These shy muttonbirds collect offshore in rafts at dusk before coming to land to feed their nestlings after a day at sea. The trees are worth a quiet visit at dusk September–April, when these would-be rubber chickens pelt the branches, fall to the ground, then skitter like rats to each bolt-hole that leads to their chicks. This is a not-to-be-missed experience, although you may have to wait a few minutes in the dark until the action starts. Other muttonbird colonies are found at Middle Beach and the Clear Place.

Muttonbird is the colloquial name for a shearwater, which is more apt. Not only are shearwater wings designed to fly, but also to swim by cutting through water. After the aerodynamic bird dive-bombs the water surface, it uses oar-like wing action to power it around and down to 15-m/50-ft deep, hunting with excellent underwater eyesight. To feed their huge flocks, shearwaters are dependent on a cooperative arrangement with other hunters—dolphins—to drive fish shoals near the surface where shearwaters can dive to reach them.

By day, Ned's Beach is brimming with shoals of two species of tubby fish that wait expectantly for visitors to feed them, a fun tradition. You can check which fish species you are looking at by using the charts in the small visitor shelter, which also offers water and shade. Small tight black shoals of juvenile goatfish roll like a ball over the sand surface. Those near the sand grab food; the others scare away predators. And the threat is real: their barbles are poisonous to humans, even though these fish are only the length of your little finger, so don't stick your hand in the black cluster.

The reef extending from Ned's Beach is made up of a collection of coral patches that are not extensive, but are worth several snorkeling visits to explore their colorful diversity. As in many cases on the island, if you think small, you will be rewarded. The reefs at the southern end has some rare organ pipe coral (*Tubipora musica*) with green polyps. These mask the orange skeleton that is sought out for use in jewelry. Look here for the anemone-like soft coral, blue-gray *Xenia*, whose delicate polyps house symbiotic pale blue crabs that preen the coral of parasites.

The calcerinite rocky platforms on the south side may have the most species of any intertidal zone on the island, so check them out at low tide with a walking pole and closed-toed walking boots. The pincers of pistol prawns click as you walk. Calcerinite is a calcium carbonate precipitation responsible for cave stalagtites and stalagmites, and it can be seen here at sea level and on the bluffs. The difficult-to-walk headlands above this limestone are a great nesting site for several seabird species. These birds are not used to humans, so do not scare them by approaching too closely.

Middle Beach

Middle Beach is located down steps at the end of the signposted track starting at the northeast end of Middle Beach Road. The south beach is best at low tide where you can find shady urchins that camouflage themselves with bits of rocks and seaweed, and miniature coral gardens

Bubble Netting

Shearwaters are highly strategic hunters that work with dolphins to net their dinner. Dolphins work in communicative superpods, separating into small hunting groups once they detect a deep large shoal. Swimming aggressively, they force the fish upwards, away from the safer darkness and into the solid ceiling of the surface. The dolphins then cut off a splinter-group of panicked fish by blowing air to form an encircling "bubble net." The fish form a tight bait ball that is their only defense as they reach the surface. There, the dolphins are joined by huge numbers of shearwaters and other strategic hunters in a feeding frenzy. The benefit of the bait ball highlights new theories of evolutionary biology and mathematics, whereby it is an advantage for individuals to collaborate for the survival of the group, rather than compete solely for an individual's genes as Darwin proposed.

The bait ball is a tight mass of spiraling fish. To the predator, the bait ball appears to be a huge meal, but when attacked, it dissolves like a bead curtain into scintillating evaders. By confusing, the bait ball protects. In cooperative strategies, the group usually wins. Some fish are sacrificed to the inevitable, but a significant number of the fish in the group survive.

Strategic Fliers

Half the world's population of fleshy-footed shearwaters, or muttonbird (bottom right, nocturnal), is found on Lord Howe Island where large numbers breed in burrows. They pelt the trees after dusk as they land from far offshore and seek their chicks. You can also see wedge-tailed shearwaters at Muttonbird Point, Blackburn Island, and Signal Point. White terns (center left) nest on Lagoon Road. The shearwaters are among the 14 species of oceanic birds that use Lord Howe Island as a critical breeding ground, many of them unused to humans. Wedge-tailed shearwaters migrate from rich fish stocks in the Philippines to Australia for nesting every year. Lord Howe and Norfolk Islands are the only places in the world where the providence petrel breeds. The highest concentration of red-tailed tropicbird is located here, breeding along the northern cliffs west of Malabar, and on Goat House cliffs. Black-winged petrels nest at Ned's Beach (top) and perform wonderful courtship displays floating on the strong air currents. The most common nesting seabirds are sooty terns (bottom left), which nest at Muttonbird Point and Ned's Beach. Common Noddy (center right) nests at Old Gulch and Blinky Beach.

among the shallow snorkeling pools. Beware of the patterned oblong stromb shell and cone shell species because they have a spear that darts out several inches beyond their shells to spear their prey or unsuspecting humans. The toxin is lethal to those stung. Do not pick them up. If you want to examine them, use long tongs. Fortunately, these are nocturnal animals so it is unusual to find one active during the day.

North Bay

North Bay snorkeling is best done from a glass-bottom or punt-boat cruise rather than from the beach directly, in order to find the least sedimented reefs. In the summer Spanish dancers and other fantastic nudibranchs can be seen here, with sea hares, orange-tipped sea urchins, and plate and brain corals.

Herring Pools

Old Gulch is a short walk north from North Beach for daring snorkeling around the Herring

Pools on the east side of the Gulch. Or look at them on foot by walking over the boulder beach and east around the base of the Old Gulch cliffs at low tide. These pools are marked on the local maps, but they are really very small. There are other rock pools worth visiting first, unless you are a rock pool enthusiast. A pair of red-tailed tropicbirds nest on the west side, close to observers on the east of the Gulch. The parents and their chick can be seen better here than in places where larger numbers breed.

Sylphs Hole

Sylphs Hole is found by swimming out to the white buoy on the northwest side of Old Settlement Beach. This is a recommended site for turtle-sitings: keep your ear to the island's bush telegraph. Majestic green turtles, some older than you, browse attentively on the algae pockets growing from the reef walls, and they confer a wonderful experience to any divers fortunate enough to find them. Some species of turtles also eat poisonous jellyfish, unstung, probably due to their leathery skin. If you keep away so the turtles are not frightened, you can observe them for a long time.

The Lagoon

If you want to snorkel from Lagoon Beach, there is a very small patch of reef below the flagstaff at Signal Point and a couple of small bommies (coral clusters) out from there. But the recommended way to snorkel in the lagoon is from the small glass-bottomed boat cruises that offer dedicated snorkeling trips to Comet's Hole and Erscott's Hole on the seaward side within the southern Lagoon.

The reef fish are so scintillating at Comet's Hole you may forget to look at the sand below, but here you'll find the rays. The lionfish (*Pterois volitans*) is protected here,

Tideline

Pink flowers of a pea plant (top) colonize the sand, colored the same as the *Ipomoea pescaprae* vine (above, center). Nearby are beachcoming jewels (bottom). Fossil fragments of the terrestrial giant horned turtle (*Meiolania platyceps*) are found in calcerinite rocks, so keep your eyes peeled at the tideline. The turtle became extinct about 20,000 years ago. A complete replica from a full skeleton discovered on the island in 1971 is displayed at the new Lord Howe Island Museum. Take care what you pick up: the white and orange nocturnal textile cone shell is one of several seashells on Ned's and other beaches that have a barb that lashes out a few inches beyond the edge of the shell. Its toxicity is lethal.

Globetrotters

The globetrotter species of dragonfly has been found flying happily 1440km/900 mi from the mainland where it hatched. It can easily reach Lord Howe Island from Australia. One way it does this is through tissue engineering: it has evolved resilient elastic materials that minimize energy loss during each wingbeat. One of these materials is similar to resilin. Resilin has the properties of technologically ideal rubber. Yet it is a natural polymer. It is found in butterfly and locust wing joints. H. Randall Hepburn discovered resilin and found that an arid land locust like those chomping away in central Australia saves 96% of the energy required for each stroke, allowing them to fly long journeys without tiring. The globetrotter uses these types of advantages, and has wings that are aeronautically designed to maximize lift. No one quite understands how they do this so well.

and uses its poison spines to anchor itself inside reef holes when not swimming around, so take a look to see what lurks without putting your hand in any holes.

At Erscott's Hole the endemic double-header wrasse (*Coris bulbufrons*) may hang around for their needle-spined sea urchin dinner from the dive guide. Beware of urchins, as they may have toxic spines or toxic darts between the spines. 477 species of fish are found in island waters from 107 families; four percent of these are endemic. Divers are likely to see damsel fish, buttefly cod, *Pterois volitans*, school mackerel, silver bream, spangled emperors, and silver drummers. Relatively harmless reef sharks are sometimes seen, especially at night.

The coral and algae are fascinating. Look for green *Goniastrea benhami*, yellow sheets of *Acropora brueggemanni*, and pretty pink branching coral *Pocillopora bulbosa*. *Caulerpa sedoides* seaweed has green mulberry-like floaters found nearer rock pools, and the *Lithothamnium* alga that cements coral can be seen on the southern side of the lagoon too. Look for orange sea-star (*Ophidiaster confertus*) and seven-armed starfish too.

3
Fraser Island

Fraser Island

Access

Urangan Boat Harbour to
Moon Point car ferry.
Urangan Boat Harbour to
Kingfisher Bay.
Fast Cat passenger ferry.
River Heads to Kingfisher
Bay car ferry.
River Heads to Wanggoolba
Creek car ferry.
Inskip Point at Rainbow
Beach to Hook Point car
ferry.

Time Windows Drive Schedule

Allow a half day to drive
from Dilli Village to
Kingfisher Bay by 4WD,
depending on conditions.
Ideally, start at Cathedral
Beach to include the
Maheno wreck and
Rainbow Gorge, though
this adds two to four hours
with stops.

Forest Lakes Walking Schedule

The Forest Lakes walking
trail takes about five days to
complete, round-trip.

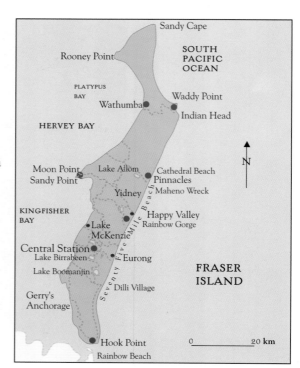

Fraser Island

Diverse and dramatic, Fraser Island is covered in scrubby woodland, heathland, and rainforest, brimming with stunning freshwater lakes. By day, most visitors cluster at a few key sites, including Lake McKenzie and Central Station. If you go elsewhere, you can find true wilderness here, including the beach at Wathumba Creek, above. Fraser, the largest sand island in the world, has evolved its own species. Endemic to the island and nearby areas are the aromatic herb Wide Bay boronia (*Boronia rivularis*), the underground Cooloola monster (a bizarre cricket) and a special species of skink that is now almost legless, to better burrow in the sand. Over 300 bird species are seen here, including the endangered red goshawk, beach stone curlew, and the very elusive ground parrot. The island's three sheltered creeks provide some of the only remaining refuges for relict rainforest trees and ferns originating before Jurassic times.

photo © Andrew Hedges

The rainforests here have a density of biomass that is the second highest in the world. Yet the sand underneath is pure silica, or silicon dioxide, laced with 2 percent of biologically inert zircon, rutile, and ilmenite minerals. The eastern edge of the island constantly builds whole ecosystems from scratch, reenacting the cooperative evolution of the last 400 million years. Dust and colored sand blowing from the mainland, visits from bats, birds, and insects, fungi, beach debris, plus upwelling freshwater systems have gradually built up a sustainable base upon which this diverse woodland has grown. And you'll soon find out that the masters of the island are not humans, but dingoes—wily and wild.

Wildflower Woodlands

Fraser Island is full of wildflowers year-round, though you may have to look for them. The highest density of wildflowers is found in the Wallum communities of the older western side of the island including the area around Kingfisher

Don't Miss

✤ Lake Birrabeen is quieter than Lake McKenzie.
✤ Wanggoolba Creek at Central Station
✤ Champagne Pools— old Aboriginal rock fish traps
✤ Lake Boomanjin is the world's largest perched lake.
✤ Rainbow Gorge
✤ Pile Valley

Banksia's Designer Nectar

The banksia colonizing the sand dunes (right) rely on a 65-million-year-old biochemical breakthrough. This resulted in the evolution of proteoid roots and led to the rapid parallel evolution of the honeyeater bird species. Honeyeaters' insect-eating mouthparts have adapted brush-tipped tongues for pollination and nectar gathering. But banksia and other Proteaceae went one step further. Unlike most flowers, Proteaceae blossoms have developed designer nectar spiked with proteins and essential amino acids. These supplements increase the time some honeyeaters can devote to pollination, removing the distraction of finding high-quality insect protein. This is a direct correlation: Proteaceae flowers not visited by honeyeaters lack amino-acid-enhanced nectar. Banksia probably originated in sandy areas similar to Fraser Island, outside the Gondwanan rainforests that dominated at that time. They developed roots that grow in clumps and use incredibly powerful phenolic acid solvents to pry off scarce phosphate molecules locked on the surface of sand grains. Phosphate is critical to growth, forming to transfer sunlight energy. Because Proteaceae evolved in poor soils, they were ready to thrive when Australia became arid.

Bay. Wallum is the name given by Aboriginal peoples to describe the nectar-laden banksia, *Banksia serrata* and *B. aemula,* that grew on the sandy soils of lowland Queensland. Wallum is now the name extended to the habitats where these banksia are found, areas now cleared from the mainland. Fraser's western Wallum is as diverse as the habitat is stunted, its nutrients locked away in an impenetrable layer of minerals. Perhaps this habitat is what prompted Matthew Flinders to report in 1802, "Nothing can be imagined more barren than this peninsula." Yet a riot of scented flowers is found in the Wallum, concentrated in the springtime but continuing year-round. You can easily get close to groups of brilliant scarlet, white-cheeked, and Lewin's honeyeaters among the banksias. Red-backed fairy wrens flit around the nectar-laden lemon-scented tea trees where lynx spiders wait for unsuspecting insect visitors. Look for exquisite rainbow bee-eaters sitting on paperbarks (*Melaleuca quinquenervia*) by the western beach. There are two groups of rainbow bee-eaters found here, a southern group from Victoria and New South Wales that nest from February to June in sand burrows (look for some at the Kingfisher gas station), and a second shift that comes from October to March from Northern Queensland and Papua New Guinea. Brilliantly colored sacred and forest kingfishers migrate here from September to March. You can spot their nests by the telltale vegetation sticking out of the top of termite nests on tree trunks.

Mixed Forest

The mixed woodland builds in height away from the coast until it becomes tall eucalypt forest. Lake McKenzie, Lake Birrabeen, and Lake Boomanjin are found in these habitats. Bright green foxtail sedge (*Caustis blakei*) is often found in place of understory grasses, for the sedge does not provide the equivalent nutritive value of grass, which accounts for why

The Legend of the Island

In the First Time, K'gari (pronounced Gurri) was a white spirit sent to help Yindingie. Yindingie had been commissioned by the Great Spirit in the Sky to build land and other things. K'gari got tired and Yindingie told her to sleep on some rocks that he had just made in the sea. When she woke up, she saw sandy beaches, little islands, a river, and a mountain. K'gari found them beautiful and wanted to stay. But Yindingie said that since she was a spirit from the sky she couldn't stay on earth. When she begged and pleaded, though, he relented. But he had to change her into something else first. So he asked her to go to sleep again, and while she was sleeping Yindingie clothed her with orchids, trees, and ferns. He made lakes for her eyes so she could look back up at her home in the sky, and her voice became the sound of the swift-flowing creeks. Then, he made animals and people and taught them procreation, enabling them to have children so that K'gari, Fraser Island, would never be lonely.

(Left from top) Wallum (Banksia serrata). Lemon scented tea tree (Leptospermum sp.) with lynx spider (Oxyopes sp.) Blady grass (Imperata cylindrica) with introduced honey bees (Apis mellifera), the grass stalks can be nibbled like sugarcane. (Right from top) Wide Bay boronia (Boronia rivularis) only found in Great Sandy region, with scented leaves. Guinea flower vine (Hibbertia scandens) with native bee (Trigona sp. or Austroplebia sp.) Native bees do not sting. They are major pollinators and build nests of wax and resin with pots to store honey. Termites (nest, bottom right) are essential collectors and recyclers of scarce nutrients.

Spotlighting

Most animals on Fraser Island are nocturnal. Spotlighting is a great way to see them, but there is a definite trick to do this successfully. What you are looking for is eyeshine reflected back from the retina of the nocturnal animal into your own eyes. In order to do this, hold the flashlight at nose level and look directly down the beam. If you do this correctly, you will see brilliant embers whenever an animal is looking at you, including green pinpricks reflected intensely from spider eyes. Unlike insects, spiders have eyes structured similarly to our own and have strong retinal mirrors. Sweep the vegetation with the light beam and you are on your way to finding possums, yellow-footed antechinuses, grassland melomys, sugar gliders, native rats, and many frog species. Experienced spotlighters can tell one species from another just by the color and intensity of the eyeshine. To avoid interfering with animals, restrict flashlight intensity to 40 watts. It is not ecologically necessary to use red light filters. Use a broad diverging single beam from a distance after an animal is sighted, rather than several focused narrow beams, as these can temporarily disorient the animal. Camera flashes do not interfere with animal vision provided pictures are taken at least a meter away.

there are no kangaroos and only eastern swamp wallabies found here. The few feral horses or Brumbies have a hard time finding high-quality food, and their hooves spread unnaturally on the soft sand. Large scribbly gum (*Eucalyptus signata*) and smooth-barked apple trees have huge blood-red gashes of sap caused by sugar gliders (*Petaurus breviceps*), squirrel gliders (*P. norfolcensis*), and feathertail gliders (*Acrobates pygmaeus*). Sugar gliders live in groups of up to ten and supplement the sap with nectar and insects. They can float for meters on their membrane parachutes that stretch from hand to foot. King parrots nest in the taller trees and use UV-sensitive eyes, unlike humans. This capability was possibly inherited from dinosaurs, which had more complex eyes than humans. The bloom on the fleshy fruits of the rainforest brightly reflects UV light, attracting these fruit-eaters. The male king parrot has a bright band of UV-reflective feathers on the nape of its neck to attract females and scare bird predators.

Rainforests

Tall eucalypts start to tower as you move inland from the island's coasts. At the center of Fraser Island are deep, nutritious gullies fed by freshwater streams, and it is in these wind-sheltered enclaves where Gondwanan rainforest communities replace the eucalypts and deepen the color of green. You'll cross the rainforest in several places on the island: at crowded Central Station, inland from Happy Valley, and on the walk that goes around Lake Allom, 9.5km/5.9mi from the spectacular golden sand formation called the Pinnacles.

Huge Fraser Island satinays (*Syncarpia hillii*) and fibrous-barked, red-limbed brush (*Leptostermon confertus*) dominate these rainforests, with taller hoop pines (*Araucaria cunninghamii*) and Kauri pines (*Agathis robusta*) stretching above the canopy.

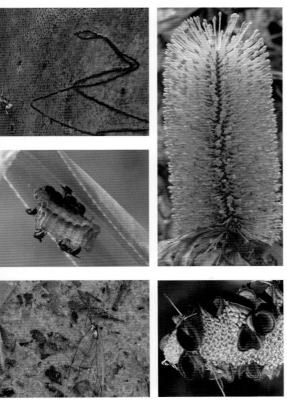

Why Do Gums Have Scribbles, Not Spirals?

Scribbly gum (*Eucalyptus racemosa*) (top left) and the higher limbs of blackbutt (*E. pilularis*) are decorated by scribbles created by a moth larva. Each tree sends sugar from different leaf areas in pulses down the trunk. The *Ogmograptis scribula* moth larva finds one of these, a sweet patch under the bark above the phloem, and tacks back and forth, turning when the sap turns thin and bitter. At the same time, the damage caused by the larva triggers a defense mechanism in the tree that releases additional sugars. If you look carefully, you can see that the tracks not only go from side to side, but also turn around at the top and return the same way, as the larva mines the extra sweetness exuded after its first visit.

Bus-busy Central Station is right in the middle of the island, bisected by Wanggoolba Creek. Huge-girthed Kauri pines (*Agathis robusta*) immediately greet you, moving you to the time of Gondwanan gymnosperm domination, 200 million years ago. You can walk 450m/1,471ft along the rainforest boardwalk deep beside Wanggoolba Creek for a magical look at the mossy vineforest decorated by tall thin Piccabeen palms (*Archontophoenix cunninghamiana*), tree Ferns, strangler figs (*Ficus* sp.), and a single patch of king ferns (*Angiopteris evecta*). These ferns are signposted just after the path reaches the creek, but you might miss them if you don't look carefully. The extremely primitive king fern has single bundles of vascular stem tissue instead of the concentric arrangement found in more highly evolved ferns. It also has simple, parallel leaf veins, which make it look similar to a palm frond.

Scribbly gum (Eucalyptus signata) and meat ant (Iridomyrmex spp). with metallic iridescent tail (top left) probably looking for honeydew exuded by sap-sucking bugs.
Paper wasp nest on Macrozamia (center left).
Ant pulling dragonfly wing to nest (bottom left).
Banksia serrata flower and seed pod (right, above and below).

Dingoes

Watching the dingo (*Canis familiaris dingo*) up close can be one of the thrills of visiting Fraser Island. They look like family pets but act like lateral thinkers who are past masters of the wilderness. In fact, dingoes have recently been found to be closer genetically to the Asian wolf than to the domestic dog. The island and gene pool are so large and isolated that Fraser Island is now the primary conservation area for these animals. The dingo came to Australia 4,000–5,000 years ago with humans, probably as a mobile food source, and this coincided with the time when Fraser Island started to be inhabited by Aboriginal people. The thylacine and Tasmanian devil, Australia's then-dominant marsupial carnivores, disappeared from the mainland after this time, possibly due to the impact of the dingo. Dingoes have a complex social organization and now work in packs to outwit bandicoots and small prey, or alone to grab crabs and insects. You can easily spot alpha dingoes because they show status by holding their tails curled above the backbone. Lower-hierarchy animals hold their tails low. Unfortunately, dingoes can become dependent on and aggressive toward humans if we feed them. A "Dingo Aware" safety brochure is available from www.epa.qld.gov.au

Despite its primitive engineering, these graceful fronds grow to be the longest of all living ferns. This is one of the three "fossil ferns" found associated with freshwater creeks of the island and mainland fragments. Even the palms and lawyer vines that hang from them are Gondwanan, coming from Indian palm stock 100 million years ago. The creek may appear to be so crystal clear above the pale sand as to have no depth or life, but look carefully, because you may see eel-tailed catfish that float by like Gond-wanan ghosts. You can continue along the walk to see the remaining Fraser Island satinays in Pile Valley (4km/2.5mi, total round trip). These and other flowering plants evolved from West African origins into unique Australian species after the island continent separated from Gondwana, which set loose the evolutionary ark of Australian rainforest 180 to 53 million years ago.

Coastal Pioneers, Coastal Destroyers

Fraser Island's eastern beach is continually forming, with new habitat pioneered by coastal plants that build a nutrient base. Some of these habitats are devoured by onshore winds, creating sand-blows that smother the vegetation and sweep westward. Tiny Lake Wabby is being consumed by the Hammerstone Sandblow, which dammed the original creek. This sits near the Stonetool Sandblow that you'll see with its wind-exhumed trees by Cornwell's Break Road. Great views of the Sandy Cape, the tip of the island, can be seen from the Binngih Sandblow at Waddy Point. Nearby is the not-to-be missed swimming hole at Champagne Pools that was used as a natural fish trap by Aboriginal people.

Time Windows Drive

To get a cross-section of species from the time windows that extend across 600 million years of

Bush Tucker

Aboriginal families visited Fraser Island seasonally for fish and its wide range of plant food stocks. The orange fruits of the screw pine (*Pandanus* spp.) look mouthwatering (top left). When cooked, the small seeds inside are an excellent source of fats and protein and were a major Aboriginal food. The pulp is dangerous to eat when raw. Blueberry ash (*Eleocarpus reticulatus*) (bottom left) has a floury taste when ripe, like tart apples. They should only be eaten when blue. The more palatable fruit of the geebung (*Persoonia virgata*) (top right) are as refreshing as watermelon once they fall from the tree. Several types of ancient Cycads are found on the island, including the endangered *Macrozamia pauli-guilielmi*. The female cones of one, *Macrozamia miquelii* (center right, male cone) is starchy and was eaten by the Aboriginals when carefully prepared to reduce its toxins by cracking, soaking, grinding, and baking. The seeds were stored underground. This food is similar to sago and tapioca, starches also prepared from non-Australian cycads. Aboriginal children made bubble baths in creeks using the saponin lather from soap tree leaves (bottom right). Banksia nectar was a delicacy for Aboriginal people who did not have much sugar in their diet.

Perched Lakes

Lake McKenzie (above) is among the 50% of the world's perched lakes that are found on Fraser Island. These are lakes where the water rests high above the water table. They sit on a waterproof basin of hard pan. Hard pan or "coffee rock" forms when decaying plant matter's tannin combines with the aluminum and iron salts in natural minerals to form impenetrable cement. When all these minerals have been stripped from the sand particles, pure white silica sand remains, providing the intense brilliance of some of the lakes on Fraser Island. At the edge of perched lakes, the hard pan prevents paperbark trees (*Melaleuca quinquenervia*) from reaching nutrient layers, so they grow in wizened shapes. Perched lakes are not the only water form-ations on the island. Barrage lakes like Lake Wabby are formed when creeks get dammed up. Window lakes including Ocean Lake near Orchid Beach are sculpted by unrelenting wind.

photo © Andrew Hedges

Australian evolution to the present time, drive from Dilli Village to Kingfisher Bay (45km/28mi). This can be completed as a loop from your camp or accommodation starting on the east or west coasts and taking a day. The sand tracks of the island require 4WD vehicles, which can be rented on the mainland or, more expensively, on the island.

Starting on the beach at Dilli Village, look for a toxic animal that evolved 600 million years ago: a blue Portuguese man o' war jellyfish. It has remained virtually unchanged across time. It is unlike other sea jellies you'll see, as it is part colony, part single animal. Each group of bluebottle animals specialize as organs in one bluebottle, collaborating as a colony to make stingers, tentacles, and a bubble sail. Most other jellies are single animals. Bluebottles originated during animals' first major expansion as complex beings from single cells, when atmospheric oxygen first built up to near current levels just after ATP originated in living systems. ATP is an energy-trapping molecule eighteen times more efficient than its predecessors.

You can also witness what it must have been like 400 million years ago when plants moved from the ocean to the land. You can glimpse a "hypersea" of mycorrhizal fungi that

Swampland

Long-finned eels *Anguilla reinhardtii* (top left) join the animal and plant Wallum swamp predators. Nonvenomous spotted python *Antaresia maculosa* (bottom right) has infrared sensors on its lower lips, fork-leaved sundew *Drosera binata* (center right) catches high-nitrogen insects on its protein-digesting sticky dewdrops, and bladderwort *Utricularia lateriflora* (top right) traps small bugs and nematode worms in below-ground cups. Listen for "wreeek" sounds of the Wallum tree frog *Litoria cooloolensis* (bottom left) on swamp banksia *B. robur* and other tree branches. Look for the emerald tree frog (left below center) and the Wallum Rocketfrog, *Litoria freycinetti* (left above center). Acid frogs have evolved to require acid waters from the tannin for tadpole development. Green tree frogs produce a neurochemical in their skin that is used in schizophrenia cases and to assist recovery from abdominal surgery.

extends the reach of plants and gathers scarce nutrients from nutrient-poor sand in exchange for plant sugars. Minute filaments of the fungi can be seen draped around exposed roots on the foredunes connected to pioneering plants several meters inland.

Some of the earliest plants that evolved at that time can still be seen around Dilli Village and its Wallum surroundings. Look under trees for the hard leaves of foot-high lycopod club mosses unchanged since they evolved 400 million years ago when Pangea was still attached to Gondwana in a single world continent.

Only 30 million years later, animals joined plants on land when the lungfish clambered out to dry. Queensland lungfish are only found in the rivers that flow into Hervey Bay. All land vertebrates including humans descended from an ancestor shared with one of these fish.

Wanggoolba Creek

Umbrella moss (below) decorates the mossy banks of Wanggoolba Creek. The water flows silently over the sandy bottom. Ghostly eel-tailed catfish swim with the current under Gondwanan relict king ferns and thin, tall Piccabeen palms. Sulfur-crested cockatoos (above) screech on the palm fruits above.

Right page counter-clockwise: rainforest canopy, lace monitor, king fern, strangler fig.

As you move away from the ocean, the sand ages from around 500 years old at Dilli Village to eucalypt forest on 1,500–5,000 year-old dunes under the large freshwater lakes inland. As you move into the forest, you pass through 200 million years of evolutionary progression from primitive land mosses, ferns, and liverworts, to the tall tree ferns that surrounded the dinosaurs. The dark football-sized mud nests you can see on the trees are made by termites that evolved at the end of this time, 230 million years ago, after a single termite made a favorable association with a group of bacteria in its gut. Since then, these cellulose-digesting, vitamin-creating bacteria have never left their termite hosts, and are passed from one termite generation to another by termites taking material from the anus into the mouth.

Be sure to take your swim gear with you to Lake Boomanjin and Lake Birrabeen to experience their 200-year-old vintage waters. One lake is blue and the other copper. Both are irresistible.

After you leave Lake Birrabeen, you suddenly enter the rainforest, a Gondwanan tapestry nurtured by 120,000 year old dunes. You will enter Central Station where there are several interesting walks. Look on the rainforest

floor to try and spot the beautiful emerald ground dove gleaning fallen fruit from these trees. Ground strewn with fresh blossoms can alert you to good places to see canopy nectivores and frugivores including lorikeets and sulphur-crested cockatoos, screeching as always. At night, flying foxes flap over from the mainland to cluster on the rainforest fruit trees, animals that sound in their day roosts like squabbling monkeys. In fact, they've now been found to be more closely related to primates than other bats, perhaps explaining their intelligence and quizzical nature. Their flight to Fraser from the mainland re-enacts the time when they island-hopped from Asia 5–10 million years ago. They came with the ancestors of the native rats that you may see around Fraser's swamps.

Below Lake McKenzie a hard-pan layer of impenetrable minerals starts to form, stunting the paperbarks on its shores. From here to the coast, the nutrient layer drops below the reach of plant roots. At this point, you'll experience a series of time windows stretching from 10–2 million years ago when the rainforests withdrew to remnant gorges as Australia became increasingly arid, to be replaced by eucalypts and Wallum Proteaceae. The older Wallum woodland species evolved on marginal sandy

Timber History

Fraser Island was a major center of the timber industry. The native Kauri pines (*Agathis robusta*) were logged from 1863, when Fraser Island Aboriginals were moved off the island. Cooloola goldmining needs then spurred logging, which became the area's primary economic resource. The main Fraser Island species that were logged included hoop pine (*Auraucaria cunninghammii*), blackbutt (*Eucalyptus pilularis*), and tallowwood (*Eucalyptus mycrocorys*). Fraser Island satinay (*Syncarpia hillii*) was logged from 1925 when it was found that its turpentine oils resisted the Toredo marine borer worm, a pest that attacks most ocean timbers. As a result, Satinay wood from Fraser Island was used for the piles in the Suez Canal and the London Docks at Falmouth. Ancient satinays can still be seen in Pile Valley up to 40m/130ft high with a girth of up to 12m/39ft, though many more have been logged. Timber logging ended on Fraser Island in the early 1990s after several mostly-unsuccessful attempts were made at reforestation, and pressure to halt the logging increased from conservation groups. In December 1992, one year after the last logs were removed from Fraser Island, it was listed as a World Heritage area.

Siberian Wanderers

You can often see whimbrels (with down-turned bills) and Eastern curlews (with upturned bills) wading on Fraser Island beaches September to March, on their way from Siberia to South Australia. These birds use various tools, including seeking out the infrasound created by thermals. They can hear the infrasound up to 5km away, a sound below the threshold of human hearing. Once on the thermal, they build height to find jetstreams to assist them toward their destination. They navigate using complex systems including magnetic brain particles, the ability to find the sun using polarizing light filters, and genetically embedded homing instincts that may predate some tectonic movements of the earth's continents.

*Coastal pioneers include salt-spray tolerant spinifex grass, pigface (*Carpobrotus glausescens*) (bottom right) and goatsfoot (*Convulvulus sp.*) (top left) that associate with mycorrhizal fungi (second from top left) to colonize sand. Pigface has delicious fruit that tastes like kiwi fruit. Needly she-oaks (*Alloca-suarina sp.*) (center left) fix nitrogen with their roots, and banksias (center right) grow from fire-triggered seeds using their phosphorous-sponging proteoid roots. Prop roots of pandanus (bottom left) stabilize the sand.*

photo © Andrew Hedges

areas outside the rainforests 65 million years ago, producing nectar-filled banksia, grevillea, and hakea flowers of the Proteaceae family associated with honeyeaters. The scribbly gum eucalypt community took 30 million more years to evolve from their Myrtacae ancestors. And both eucalypts and wallum were pre-adapted to withstand the fires that increased when Aboriginal peoples came to the mainland 120,000 or so years ago. The dunes on the western side of Fraser much older than this, 700,000 years in actual age, somehow staying intact through changing sea levels, and the last great polar ice melt, which occurred 10–16,000 years ago.

The Time Windows drive ends at the Kingfisher Bay Resort complex, where the excellent architecture brings you up-to-date. This major ecolodge has won numerous awards for its world-class stature, ecoexploration activities, sensitivity to cultural issues, and ecofriendly policies.

Hypersea

On the dunes of a 120-km/ 75-mi long beach, you can just discern fine fungal threads draped around exposed spinifex roots. These mycorrhizal fungi stretch meters beyond root tips into bare sand where they take phosphorous and nitrogen from individual sand particles and exchange them for sugars with fused plant root cells. 80% of land plants depend on this association, which stretches back to the time when plants moved onto land, 400 million years ago, creating what McMehamins has called "Hypersea." This moved the majority of the world's biomass above sea level, and continues on Fraser Island and worldwide today. Mycorrhizal fungi are so dependent on plants that they die when separated. Plants lacking mycorrhizal fungi germinate poorly, grow more slowly, and are less drought resistant. Not surprisingly, commercial preparations are available for conservation and horticultural use. Some scientists are even pursuing the theory that plants themselves are a fusion of structural fungi (roots, trunks, and branches) and photosynthetic algae (leaves and flowers). Some intriguing clues support this idea, including the fact that plant roots have ended up with the fungal enzyme chitinase, otherwise used by fungi to digest the skeletons of insects and crustaceans.

Meet Uncle Ed

The Queensland lungfish shares a common ancestor with all land vertebrates, including humans. Yet there are only two people in the world directly charged with overseeing their future. This overlooked celebrity is found in the Mary and Burnett Rivers, which feed Hervey Bay. The lungfish has four strong flippers that help it walk over rocks as well as paddle. It has fully developed air-breathing lungs in addition to gills, though this species does not leave the water. The lungfish's omnivorous mouthparts are as soft as a cow's lips, and its skin plates feel leathery and smooth. Five species of lungfish remain alive today, found also in Africa and South America, but the Queensland lungfish is closest to the original ancestor from which we evolved. Juveniles are now rarely found, indicating an aging and challenged population. You can occasionally spot adults of up to 30kg/66lbs and 80 years wallowing lazily under home river bridges of these rivers in the late afternoon.

Hervey Bay

Huge humpback whales (*Megaptera novaengliae*) visit Platypus Bay, part of Hervey Bay, between July and October. Each whale stays a few days in this sheltered bay on its 5,000km/3,100mi journey from Antarctica's icy krill banks to warmer nursery waters in the north around the Great Barrier Reef, waters suitable for breeding and suckling their young. During this time, don't miss the whalewatching trips from Kingfisher jetty on Fraser Island or Urangan boat harbor on the mainland. Or you can walk to Platypus Bay (now closed to vehicular traffic) from Orchid Beach township at Waddy Point (10km/6mi one way). You can also see smaller minke whales (*Balaenoptera acutorostrata*) from Kingfisher jetty or the lookout. Pods of bottlenose dolphins (*Tursiops truncates*) and common dolphins (*Delphinus delphis*) often accompany boats to and from Fraser Island, riding the bow waves while leaping and spinning. Fraser's sandy beaches provide habitat for breeding populations of green and loggerhead turtles, opposite the largest green turtle nesting ground in the world at Bundaberg. The World Heritage Site of Fraser Island includes the seagrass beds and seabird mudflat havens of Great Sandy Bay but does not extend beyond them into Hervey Bay, where commercial overfishing is significant, and agricultural run-off is polluting the waters. Fish with nationally important populations around Fraser Island include the endangered honey blue-eye (*Psudomugil mellis*) and oxleyan pygmy perch (*Nannoperca oxleyana*). On rare occasions, you may see a dugong (*Dugong dugong*) near the seagrass beds, perhaps a mother with a calf riding on her back. The dugong population was hit hard, though, by two 1992 cyclones that silted up the seagrass beds. Now the dugongs are rebuilding their numbers as the seagrass recovers.

4
Queensland Wet Tropics

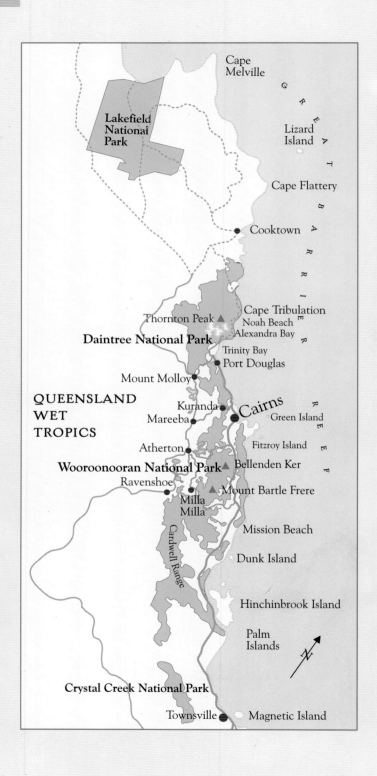

Queensland Wet Tropics

The Wet Tropics contain some of the highest species diversity of any area in Australia. For this reason alone, the Queensland rainforests are fascinating to explore and should be high on your destination plan. But more important, they are also the closest living experience to what it must have been like during Jurassic times. In fact, it has now been found that some ancient rainforest species may have originated here when part of dinosaur-filled Gondwana, rather than being later imports from Asia as was previously thought.

"The outstanding significance of the area," stated an official of the Wet Tropics Management Authority, "is that it contains many taxa representing long, distinct lineages and therefore preserves a greater degree of evolutionary heritage" than other world rainforests with more abundant species. Even the Amazon has fewer primitive flowering plant genera than found here.

Don't Miss
✤ 4WD night-spotting safari or self-guided rainforest walk
✤ Atherton Tableland: Crater Lakes Drive
✤ A walk in the rainforest at Noah's Beach
✤ Coastal drive to Cape Tribulation
✤ Kuranda Scenic Railway
✤ Kuranda Butterfly Sanctuary

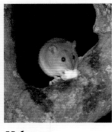

Melomys

The grassland melomys (*Melomys burtoni*) (above) is a mouse-sized native mosaic-tailed rat that eats a lot of sugar cane (above) with buddy canefield rat. Photographer John Young is working with farmers in a win-win situation to re-introduce nesting sites for masked owls, grass owls, and barking owls. Owls keep rat populations down and are now an economic advantage to farmers. The owl populations were previously decimated by toxic rat bait, to which the rats became resistant.

This ancient gene bank includes relict birds and flowers from several different earth periods, including the flightless cassowary from 180 million years ago; "modern" rainforest species like the macadamia nut that evolved here 65 million years ago after Gondwana split up and flowering plants boomed; and "recent" Australian species like the spectacled flying fox that were exchanged and re-exchanged when Asian island hopping started 10–15 million years ago. The platypus and echidna represent snapshots of all mammals' origins and remain relatively unchanged egg-laying monotremes. But evolution has not stopped in the past for all rainforest life: significant genetic changes may occur in some species within the span of a few years as habitats change, as described in Jonathan Weiner's *The Beak of the Finch*.

Where to Go

At first glance, there are two primary rainforest regions to visit in the Queensland Wet Tropics: the coastal Daintree and the tropical tablelands around Atherton. Both of these are within this UNESCO-protected World Heritage Area, a large collection of outstanding tropical rainforest patches that are like pastry slivers left after cutting out the rich pie crusts of agricultural land.

But, these two well-oiled destinations are not the only choice. Once you cross the Daintree River by ferry and go north beyond the usual tourist stops, you begin to enter a region where the words "remote" and "wilderness" take on a whole new set of meanings, demanding a self-sufficient and highly prepared approach. There are new options for adventure and wildlife expeditions opening up throughout the entire area. The rainforest, mixed with eucalypt forest, wetlands and scrub, extend inside and outside the World Heritage Area all the way North to the tip of Cape York Peninsula and South to include the important Bellenden Ker area near Cairns and Townsville. But start with the Daintree and Atherton Tablelands to see distinct types of rainforest, plus the Lamb Range for sclerophyllous eucalypt species. Then expand to a Bellenden Ker trek, or to a rugged wilderness safari through the remote Cape York Peninsula.

Cassowary Country

The best place to find Southern cassowaries on your own is at Mission Beach. Mission Beach is 2 hours south of Cairns on the Bruce Highway. Turn east at El Arish to Mission Beach (11 km/6.8mi).

Cassowaries

If I were a cassowary
On the plains of Timbuctoo,
I would eat a missionary,
Cassock, band, and hymn-
book too.
—Bishop Samuel Wilberforce

The Southern cassowary's presence feels more like that of a lizard than a bird. For one thing, it roars rather than chirps. In fact, its genetic origins are closer to lizards than most birds. It is a ratite, a Gondwanan group of roaming, flightless ostriches, rheas, kiwis, and emus. Bulking out at up to 85kg/187lb for females and 35kg/77lb for males, this 1.5m/5ft bird can leap its own height when threatened, and slash lethally with the talons of both feet at once. The styrofoam-like casque on top of its head is probably an indicator of dominance rather than a crash helmet. This bird is a keystone species that eats 115 species of fruit, the most of any fauna. Many of these fruit depend entirely on the cassowary for distribution and seeding, as the cassowary's digestive system leaves the pits intact. You can find evidence of cassowary activity by looking for dung that looks like brown pizzas decorated with huge olives.
Birds may have evolved flight twice, once in the ratites, which later lost this ability, and a second time in the ancestor of modern bird families.

Cassowaries can occasionally be seen from the road and in the rainforest patches all the way from Mission Beach to Cape Tribulation. Many cassowary deaths are due to auto accidents on the coast road, so drive slowly. The best times to observe cassowaries are just after dawn and at dusk. Do not approach cassowaries on foot as they can jump 1.5m/5ft and lash out with their lethally sharp outer talons of both feet without provocation, especially when the male is looking after his young. If threatened, hold a camera or bag over your head to increase your apparent size, and stay still.

If you want to see a cassowary and are in the Cairns area, the Kuranda-based Carrawong Fauna Sanctuary Night Wildlife Spotlighting Tour (07-4093-7287) is an excellent choice. Their fun jungle cooking hut area (complete with collectible memorabilia) is often visited by wild cassowaries. The two safari choices that the company offers continue on by 4WD to a variety of spontaneous wildlife discoveries around the Wet Tropics and are among the best spotlighting expeditions.

The Daintree

The Daintree rose to international stature in 1983 when protesters blocked the creation of a major road from Cairns to Cooktown via Cape

A male Southern cassowary rears its young after incubating the mixed-pair-parent clutch of eggs. (Above and opposite page, top.)

Tribulation because it would open up pristine rainforest and destroy it through increased erosion. Although the road was eventually built, the resulting public support for conservation overtook state government opposition and snow-balled into an even larger vision: the establishment of the Queensland Wet Tropics World Heritage Area. Some local wilderness guides wince at the marketing hype surrounding Daintree with its limited access walks dotting the Coral Sea coast, narrow ribbon-road to Cape Tribulation and dusty 4WD road north of Cape Tribulation. The area may be operating at capacity, with rainforest zoos being the only way some speedy travelers see the birds and fauna of the area since finding wildlife can be challenging. But this is still an astounding area with good safari guides ready to show you living relics in what is one of the oldest rainforests in the world. And with the help of this chapter, you can go it alone and be amply rewarded.

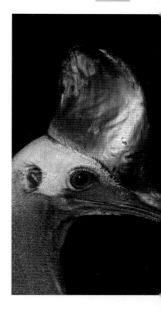

Port Douglas

Port Douglas is an upmarket resort village that was developed as the ecotourist destination for discriminating reef and rainforest travelers, away from the crowds of Cairns. Personalized rainforest safari tours and charters leave on regular schedules from Port Douglas, just as they do from Cairns. Dive boats of all sizes leave the port for the Great Barrier Reef. There are also a collection of competitive wilderness rainforest lodges scattered around the Port Douglas area. The Silky Oaks Rainforest Lodge near Mossman is a highly recommended nature lodge at the top price-range, and the welcoming hosts at Red Mill House in Daintree Village offer a wonderful bed-and-breakfast for discriminating birders and naturalists at the other end of the price scale, complete with a breakfast balcony on rainforest timbers from times past. When comparing accommodations, check the access arrangements as some require extra planning.

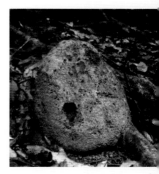

Bird Diversity

Northern Queensland is the most diverse in all of Australia with 370 species. One third of these can be seen in the closed rainforest. Look for the beautiful noisy pitta on the ground, plus pied monarch, red-necked crake, and little kingfisher. You may see the long white tail feathers of the buff-breasted kingfisher sticking out of the hole in its converted ground-level termite nest (above).

Gaps for Growth

Silky Oaks Rainforest Lodge rises on tall stilts to the canopy above the sound of the Mossman River. The lodge is located on the edge of Daintree National Park. Part of the surrounding rainforest used to be cleared hillside, but the rainforest is reestablishing itself. Disturbances are a key element of this forest's diversity. The question is how varied these disturbances make the light. Some scientists feel that diversity in gap size and their light angles are the primary driving forces behind the heightened variety of the most diverse tropical rainforests, including the Daintree. Some micro-areas are cyclone-prone, such as under the rainforest skyrail. This looks more consistent, reflecting the way that cyclones cut a path through the forest, reducing light choices.

Restoration Rainforest: The Human Story

"People often say they like nature," says Stephen Kaplan, a medical researcher, "yet they often fail to realize that they need it." A line of dramatic research studies by E. O. Moore, R. S. Ulrich, and S. Verderber show that access to even a window view of nature (as opposed to a view of a brick wall) can significantly reduce the incidence of illness among healthy people, or shorten hospital stays and improve the results of surgery among the sick. About this, Kaplan says: "Nature is not merely 'nice.' It is not just a matter of improving one's mood, rather it is a vital ingredient in healthy human functioning." Kaplan has developed a theory called "directed attention" to explain some of these measurable restorative effects.

So, for a boost to your physical and mental fitness, take a walk on the wild side while you are in the rainforest. One way to help you do this is to take a moment to focus intently on what you see, hear, smell, and touch in these natural surroundings, and even try to taste some of the edibles. Savor the moment as you watch a sunset or step into the midst of the playland of some dingo puppies.

If you go on a rainforest safari, the guide may shave a curl of wood that smells like apricots, provide the delectable tastes of tropical fruit on the way, or offer a dip in a river pool. Here, you may feel jungle perch nibbling your toes as you relax to the whistle of sulfur-crested cockatoos beneath the green canopy. When you return home and during times of stress, it can help to switch into a restorative mode by savoring the memory of the most inspiring moment in nature that you experienced. Photographs help too.

A small nerve connecting the brain and the heart has been recently discovered that may account directly for this calming result. When calm, we are more likely to be aware of "out-of-the-box" solutions. And this may also be associated with immune-boosting mechanisms, although none of this is clearly understood.

For some people, being in nature may be a stressful experience associated with danger, rather than a place to unwind. This can reverse the beneficial effects. Make sure that you are wise about the ways you seek renewal. Look where you put your feet and hands while you enjoy being a part of your heritage.

Santa's Pioneers

Many rainforest leaves are red or purple when young, like holiday season decorations. This is particularly common on Mount Lewis. *Syzygium* species often have these dazzling displays. Possums like to nibble them. The color comes from anthocyanin, which turns purple or red (above) according to the acidity of the leaf. Research by Sharon Robinson shows that the anthocyanin acts as a sunscreen to protect undeveloped chloroplasts from damage by the intense tropical sunlight. The pigment remains until the leaf matures and starts photosynthesizing. During mature photosynthesis, chloroplasts absorb red light and store the energy as sugars.

The black tree fern (above right) and Rebecca's tree fern are two of 240 beautiful fern species found in the Wet Tropics; 46 are endemic.

Mossman Gorge

You may see the largest butterfly in the world in Mossman Gorge, the female Cairns birdwing. You are more likely, though, to spot the blue Ulysses butterflies that burst like lightning into canopy spaces. The surrounding rainforest is true tropical canopy forest, but Mossman Gorge is not deep enough to be a gorge, nor are there accessible waterfalls to swim in despite claims to the contrary on many maps. In fact, most rainforest of the Mossman Gorge and the slopes of Mount Carbine and Mount Windsor tableland in this 56,500ha/219mi-square section of the Daintree is inaccessible except to experienced bushwalkers who know the area, or guided night and day safaris operated by licensed leaders. You can take an interesting guided walk lead by the knowledgeable Kaku Yalanji Aboriginal people. (To book, call Mossman Gorge Community Rangers at 07-4098-1305.) To reach the public trail, go to Mossman township, and turn west to the Mossman Gorge parking lot. The rainforest trail starts on the south side of the Mossman River after the Rex Creek swinging bridge. On the other side of the river, the Silky Oaks rainforest resort has its own network of rainforest trails, guides, and explanatory brochures for residents and visitors who sign up for their safari programs.

You may see several possums and gliders at night. The miniature long-tailed pygmy possum sips nectar from flowers including the cauliflorous bumpy satinash (*Syzygium cormiflorum*), and dines on pollen and insects. If you can find one of these trees with white puffy flowers bursting through its trunk, wait at dusk and see what stirs among its blossoms, using a flashlight. The elegantly curled tail is prehensile, and the possum may use the tail to hang from a branch to explore, and then change its mind and turn around to crawl back up its own tail to safety. You may find this possum anywhere in upland and lowland forest from the Daintree to the Paluma Range, and also in New Guinea. The striped possum eats insects, plus some flowers and fruit. It uses its fourth finger, which is twice as long as the others, to delve into rotting wood for grubs, which it removes with its long tongue. Look and listen for claw and teeth gnawing activity on ripped logs for signs of this possum.

On the way north to Mossman or Port Douglas, stop off at Hartley's Creek Crocodile Farm (07-4055-3576), which provides a lively, close-up interaction with estuarine crocodiles. 37km/23mi north of Cairns (19km/11.8mi south of Port Douglas) on the coastal highway opposite Wangetti Beach.

Mount Lewis

The paradox of Wet Tropics wilderness history is experienced on Mount Lewis. The older granite of the mountain has a greater diversity than the newer volcanic Tableland, despite granite's poor nutrient levels. But Mount Lewis can be a bleak, damp mountain for a visit and at first you may not notice what is diverse or different about it, compared with lowland rainforest. Its ocean-wind exposure and altitude give clues to what makes the area so important.

Oskars & Nurse Trees

Many rainforest canopy trees have seeds with only six weeks' viability; only a few are viable for over a year. Still these climax species can grow in low light. Their spindly saplings can stay in a state of suppressed growth under the canopy, ready to shoot up as soon as light levels increase after a tree or branch falls. A 1m/3ft climax tree can be in suspended growth mode for 20–30 years. These are called Oskars after Gunter Grass's fictional boy who did not grow up.

Pioneer species like the hairy-leaf stinging tree (*Dendrocnide moroides*) respond differently. Their seeds remain dormant for long periods, waiting for bright light, as they cannot survive in dim conditions under a canopy. As soon as scorching tropical sun hits, they grow rapidly. They can withstand hotter conditions and sink their roots deeper than climax species. This provides necessary shade and stability, plus branches on which seed dispersers sit, spreading climax species seeds. In this way, Oskars establish themselves during the second phase.

Crocs & Co.

Salties can grow to be 115 years old in captivity. They are found in freshwater rivers as well as in estuarine areas. They are highly territorial. Males mature at around 16 years old, females at 12. Nests are built November-March, then watched over by the female after eggs are laid. If it gets too hot, she will splash the nest with water from a purpose-dug pool nearby. Temperature determines the sex of the young. Males result from incubation at 31.6° C, females a few degrees lower or higher. Contrary to evolutionary theory about brain development, which correlates the evolution of maternal instincts with brains of a higher order of animals than reptiles, female crocodiles are strongly maternal. As they hatch, chirping juveniles are gently lifted out of the nest and placed by the mother into a shallow waterway. She looks over them for a few weeks before they leave on their own. Only 1% survive to maturity. There are about 100,000 salties in Australia, and since 1971 these have been protected from hunting. They are growing in numbers again now after the population and average age were significantly reduced by trophy hunting. Aboriginal communities have rights to collect wild crocodile eggs, which are raised on crocodile farms, and to hunt wild crocodiles at controlled levels.

Juvenile estuarine crocodile on the Daintree River

During dry periods in Australia, ancient species of plants and insects that had not evolved drought tolerance retreated to this humid peak. This made it a unique evolutionary refuge for rare rainforest species, a special collection shared with Mt. Bartle Frere. And the reason you don't see many rare species is that they are just that—rare and hard to find, even though the overall species variety is deep and rich. It is better to go with an expert guide to Mount Lewis, and go first to lowland rainforest around the Daintree to compare the two. If you prepare for the trip, you will appreciate Mount Lewis all the more. There are two types of rainforest refuge: those suited to later-evolving "dry" rainforest types such as found on the Atherton tableland and scattered all across northern Australia, and a much more restricted handful of refuges suited to more ancient "wet" rainforest species. Mt. Lewis, Mt. Bartle Frere, Thornton Peak, and lowland Noah's Creek are examples of these much rarer "wet" refuges.

If you know what to look for, observant visitors relatively new to the Wet Tropics will notice a few differences on Mount Lewis. You may spot the Mount Lewis blue crayfish, which can grow to a huge size. You will see more species with new red or bronze leaves here than in the lowland rainforests of the Daintree. The familiar Alexander palm (*Archontophoenix*

alexandae) of the Daintree is different on this mountain, with purple under the fronds and larger fruit, probably evolving right now into a new species. Australia's *Rhododendron lochae* is found sprawled on peak ridges of this and close mountains, its only relatives being in the Himalayas, linked by Gondwanan heritage. The easy-to spot walking stick palm (*Linospadix* sp.) found in the Daintree understory, with bright red fruit drooping at eye level, has different-looking cabbage-like suckers on Mount Lewis that form a clump, often called "cabbage palm." A beautiful fern-leafed tree is found high up, *Stenocarpus davallioides*, not seen elsewhere.

Mangroves

The 6,000 year-old mangrove community of the Daintree River (above left) and coastal beaches are critical to rainforest survival. They capture and raise the level of soil sediments, detoxify pollution, provide breeding grounds for commercial fish species, and stabilize the coast-line. Mangroves have pneumatophore roots to reach oxygen above waterlogged mud: stilt roots (top) reduce wave energy above mud: red mangrove. Knee roots (left) are kinked stabilizing pneumatophores in the orange mangrove. Kneed buttress roots (tree left) in cannonball mangrove. Viviparous seed of red mangrove (*Rhizopora stylosa*) (second from top right).

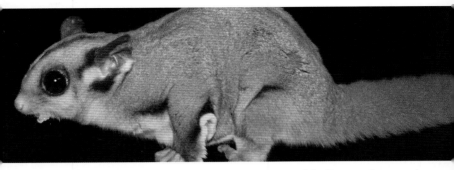

Look outside your veranda at night and you may spot a sugar glider (Petaurus breviceps)
(above), one of four gliders in the area. You can just see the furry skin flap on which it
glides. Even when wild, these creatures may be tame enough to let you pet them. They feed
on wattle and eucalypt sap, nectar, and insects.

Bizarre Incubators

The Australian brush turkey (above) is found from New South Wales to Cape York and is common in closed forest.

The orange-footed scrubfowl is from an ancient Gondwanan family. It is more of an ugly duckling than a rainforest jewel, but it is well-loved. It is found in Northern Australia, New Guinea, and the Phillipines.

The males of both these species build huge leaf mounds to incubate eggs in hot, decomposing leaf matter. They control the temperature by sticking their head in the leaf mass to measure the heat, then scraping in or out as much litter as required to adjust the temperature to the right level for the eggs.

Bunya pines (*Araucaria bidwillii*) scatter the west side, and at lower levels the beautiful-flowering *Grevillea baileaya* has bronze undersides to its leaves, which are lobed when juvenile. A large relict Gondwanan stag beetle (*Sphaenognathus queenslandicus*) is found only on two of these cloud peaks, and its closest relatives are found in South America. You will see many kinds of tree fern, some endemic to this peak. At night, rare possums and gliders may be spotted at this higher altitude that are different from the species found in the lowlands. One of these is the lemuroid ringtail possum (*Hemibelideus lemuroides*). Its eyeshine lights up at night with two very bright silvery gold reflections to a flash light, which can be used by a licensed, trained guide to identify it. The non-tapering tail is used as a rudder when it jumps between trees in a series of free-fall semi-gliding leaps, unique among possums. The forward-facing eyes are more stereoscopic than in other species, to nail their landings. Around Mount Lewis, this possum is mostly chocolate colored, but on the nearby Carbine Tableland, one third are white.

To get to Mount Lewis, turn onto winding, climbing 4WD Mount Lewis Road from the Rex Range Highway north of Julatten before Mossman. You will need permission to access the full route. Wait-A-While Tours are the only licensed safari outfit to travel to Mount Lewis. This is a premiere night-spotting safari company

with a strong environmental education history. It is one of the longest-established outfits in the area and offers several fascinating safaris to choose from.

Daintree River

The Daintree River is renowned for the numerous rare birds in the headwater including golden bowerbirds, and also for the lower mangrove swamp estuary that is home to many fascinating species including nesting black bitterns. The headwaters of the Daintree River are home to several rare plant, bird, frog, and insect species. The Daintree River ringtail possum (*Pseudochirulus cinereus*) is only found on three peaks in three separate populations: Thornton Peak, Mount Windsor, and Mount Carbine Tablelands. It eats the leaves of short-lived pioneer species, clearing the way for long-living "oskars" to burst through.

Small Daintree River Cruise boats leave from a dock about 1km/.6mi south of the Daintree River Ferry at regular intervals throughout the day and traverse the lower part of the estuarine river. Dawn boat tours are recommended, though they may not be running during the wet season. Ask your accommodation hosts for the latest nesting or birding news before you go, so you can make sure to choose a guide who can include the latest seasonal news. Each boat has an owner or guide with a different wildlife specialty, so ask around to suit your own. Make sure the specialist leads your trip, rather than

Cycad Scents

Throughout the rainforests you will see palm-like cycads (left) with dark green leaves and very short stems. Cycads evolved before flowering plants, palm trees and conifers. Cycads and beetles probably originated one of the first animal-plant pollination system, using cycad scent. Australian and African cycads are pollinated this way, reflecting their shared Gondwanan heritage. Beetles, especially weevils, are attracted to the male cone and plant by the musty odor. The beetles lay their eggs in the cone. The larvae eat parts of the cone but not the pollen. When the larvae become adults, they chew their way out and get dusted with pollen. Some remain to mate and lay eggs, others hunt for the perfumed female cone and plant, attracted by her perfume. Fertilization requires a recreation of the watery habitat in which cycads evolved. The pollen dusts a droplet of water exuded by the ovule. The pollen grain moves into this droplet and creates a pollen tube that penetrates into the egg region. The fertilization process takes up to 5 months, unlike the few hours in flowering plants. Conifers take a year. The pollen then releases two sperm, the largest among plants, visible to the naked eye at a half a millimeter in diameter. The motile sperm cross a moat of water surrounding the egg in order to complete fertilization.

Sunspecks

"Sunspeck species" have dark green leaves that switch on photosyntheis as soon as a sunfleck appears, and do not switch off until a long time after the light has moved on. Most other rainforest species switch on more slowly, and switch off immediately and cannot survive on the dim forest floor. The characteristically glossy leaf surfaces and "drip tips" found on rainforest leaves help keep surfaces drier and thereby freer of the network of colonizing lichens and algae that otherwise would compete for light.

substituting another guide. You are likely to see an estuarine crocodile or two on the river if it is cool.

The area on the immediate North side of the river is lower in mammal and bird species than the southern side of the river, though higher in insect diversity. The Daintree River area itself combines several "edge" habitats and therefore increases species diversity beyond the closed forest, which is why it is a birdwatching and wildlife focus. Birds in the rainforests here are not as varied or common as in Amazon rainforests. The closed forests of this area have a concentration of about 40 species and 250–300 individuals in a 20ha/50acre area. In the Amazon, the same area would contain about 300 species and 1,000 birds.

Rhizophoraceae is a mangrove family that evolved about 30 million years ago in Australia from the common ancestor of the eucalyptus tree and spread worldwide. Mangroves are now critical to world ecology in many ways. For example, one third of all commercial fish stocks worldwide are hatched in mangroves. The mangroves around the Daintree River provide a fascinating view of this community, and boardwalks by the beaches are good mangrove sites too. Cottonwood, or river mangrove (*Hibiscus tiliaceus*) prefers fresher water, and has delightful large yellow blossoms. Keeled mangrove seeds of the looking-glass mangrove (*Heritiera littoralis*) can be seen as their little hulls catch the wind to sail to new lands. Red mangroves (*Rhizophora stylosa*) exhibit pre-sprouted green shoots, or vivipary, from the brown fruit while still attached to the parent (see picture, page 67). Vivipary is rare outside the mangrove family. Under highly saline conditions, these seedlings float horizontally for long distances, turning upright when waters become less salty near land. In this way, the sprout can swiftly get carried across the ocean like a kayak, and just as quickly touch down and root as soon as it reaches a sweet water location, signalling land. Mangroves have evolved to withstand

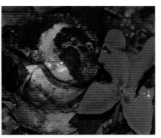

ocean salt, some excreting salt crystals on their stems. Some of the arid-land plants of central Australia are likely to have evolved from mangroves, as this was once an inland salty sea. The physiological ability to withstand salty conditions is the same as for drought conditions, so these early mangroves were pre-adapted for drying out.

Cape Tribulation Section, Daintree

The Cape Tribulation section of Daintree park is special because it is here that many of Australia's rainforest species are thought to have originated, shared with its then-neighbors of S. America, S. Africa, India, and Antarctica. The origins of the rainforests in southeast Asia are quite different. The forests around Noah's Creek and Cooper's Creek are two of these evolutionary cradles, identified by their enormous peaks in biological diversity, with about five times as many tree species per acre than found in temperate forests. To get there, travel north from Cairns along the Cook Highway across the Daintree River Ferry, 104km/64.5mi, and start exploring along the road from there. Large flightless cassowaries cross the road in several places and are prone to

Dino Snacks

Once, fern-allies such as the beautiful zamia fern (*Bowena spectablis*) (below left), dominated the world. This one can be seen at Marrdja. Zamiads and cycads were the dominant plants 200 million years ago. The much-later transition from a world greened by non-flowering conifers to the kind of tropical forest found worldwide today was made possible by the evolution of angiosperms, or flowering plants. Most rainforest trees are flowering plants, as are palm trees. The Daintree is unique in the world in that 13 of the 19 families of primitive flowering plants identified worldwide are found in the area. Most of these are located it two peak areas of diversity around Noah Creek and Copper Creek. The primitive flowering plant, ribbonwood (*Idiospermum australianse*), (fruit, above right with green bull oak seedling) is one of these. The woody fruit inside ribbonwood's fleshy hull fits together like a five-piece Chinese puzzle.

Bull oak, a member of the proteaceae family, is a rainforest ancestor of some of Australia's dry sclerophyllous species that later evolved to thrive in the Red Center. The scent of this *Gardenia actinocarpa* (top left) pervaded during dinsaur times. Now, a few dozen plants remain.

Color Capacity

Many butterflies have colored scales (top) on their wings. Others diffract light waves into intense colors when a sunbeam hits them at a specific angle, rather like a prism. The common eggfly shows the color difference when a circle of apparently black scales around a white patch are lit up (bottom) or unlit (center right).

Color vision dates back at least 370 million years, as shown by color-causing cells in the scales of *Groenlandaspis*, an armored fish found fossilized in Antarctica. These cells created a silvery mirrorlike reflection, and an actual red pigment layer above this reflector was preserved intact. The type of diffraction grating used by butterfly scales to produce color has been dated back at least 350 million years by a University of Sydney researcher of the seed-shrimp *Myodocopid ostracod*. These Australian marine shrimp create iridescent rainbow colors on their body to communicate their mating intentions. Top, territorial orange cruiser (*Vindula arsinoeda*); center left, red-bodied swallowtail (*Atrophanaura polydrons*), which competes with Cairns birdwing (on opposite page).

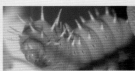

Butterfly and Moth Memories

When you spot the intense blue of the swift Ulysses butterfly (*Papilio ulysses*) (bottom right) darting from the canopy into the spaces left by fallen trees, consider this: lepidoptera evolved in apparent anticipation of a future need. The scaly-winged ancestors to butterflies evolved before flowering plants. These early insects were found among the Gondwanan podocarps, conifers, ferns, ginkgos, and cycads that emerged 208–245 million years ago. Some cycads had evolved to produce nectar by that point. The nectar may have evolved from the process where cycads exude water droplets in imitation of the first watery habitats, to capture pollen during fertilization. The cycad-pre-butterfly connection prepared for the flower-butterfly/insect boom that followed, entirely changing world vegetation. Many evolutionary leaps have evidence of this type of preparatory framework whose significance can only be seen in retrospect.

Some large rainforest butterflies, moths, and bees can remember where distant tropical trees are. They can relocate them up to ten miles away over a lengthy flowering period. 62 percent of Australia's butterfly species are found in the Wet Tropics. Some of the largest butterflies and moths in the world are found here including the daytime Hercules moth (*Coscinocera hercules*) (right, center), which has a 22cm/9.5in wingspan. This is the largest female moth in the world and has a pale blue-green larva (above right) that can be found on bleeding heart trees. Australia's largest butterfly is the Cairns birdwing (*Ornithoptera priamus*) (mature butterfly above, and larva, top right). Birdwing larvae feed on native pipe vines like *Atistolochia tagala*, but die on introduced pipe vines on which eggs are laid. Restricted-location butterflies include purple brown eye (*Chaetocneme porphyropis*) and Australian hedge blue (*Adara tenella*). Ecotravellers are likely to spot the four o'clock moth, also called the bumble bee moth, hovering like a hummingbird above the vegetation, a stunning and beautiful sight.

Many butterflies and moths control their food sources interactively. The moth *Hypsipyla robusta* attacks red cedar (*Toona australis*), a common tree that ecotravellers can learn to identify fairly easily. But it only targets trees that are not under the rainforest canopy. The larvae tunnel into the terminal shoots, which causes the cedar to produce a multibranched tree. Look for bushy examples of cedars affected by this moth. Palms outwit insect attack by growing rapidly in insect-scarce cooler months. The moth *Eudocima salaminia* eats the vine *Stephania japonica*, but it does this selectively. At first, it eats the plant leaves except for the apex or stem tip, which is where the plant hormones that stimulate growth are produced. Only as the moth pupates does it remove the apex, severely stunting growth.

Aussie Monkeys

Flying foxes are a keystone species in the Wet Tropics due to their clever tricks. The spectacled flying fox (*Pteropus conspicillatus*) is the only rainforest flying fox on the mainland. This is a major pollination and seed dispersal agent, taking a large variety of rainforest seeds up to 25 kilometers from the originating plant, including fruit too large for their mouths (above). This effective dispersal arises from the flying fox's sneaky behavior. Raiders invade territories that are well established by other bats. These newcomers are eventually driven off, but not before they steal fruit. The seeds are too large for the raiders to eat (except for figs) and so they drop the seeds after alighting far away and eating the pulp. This is an essential ecological role of this bat. As with other flying foxes, a scent from their penises is smeared on male neck ruffs and rubbed onto branches to mark territories. In the spectacled flying-fox this is bright red in color, giving them red-tinged manes. They can withstand huge temperature changes of ±40° C without changing metabolic rate, unlike other bats and mammals.

traffic injuries. The road from the automobile ferry to Cape Tribulation winds through dense rainforest and there are several short walks that introduce the rainforest and beach mangroves as you travel to Cape Tribulation. From Cape Tribulation to Bloomfield you will need a 4WD vehicle. The area is often closed during the wet season, December to April: call RACQ (4033-6711) for conditions.

Jindalba and the Daintree Rainforest Environmental Centre

An unguided walk in mature rainforest can be a daunting task when you are just starting to be comfortable identifying the life around you, so start with a self-guided walk or with a guide.

The Daintree Environmental Centre is a good place to do this. On Cape Tribulation Road, 11km/6.8mi north of the ferry, turn right onto Buchanan Creek Road toward Cow Bay and follow the signs.

Here, you can choose between a looped 700m/.4mi brief rainforest walk, a short vertical climb up a tree stairway to the canopy, and a 2.7 km/1.6 mile hiking trail. You will soon become familiar with the buttress shapes, bark texture, and flower and fruit debris that are identifiers for the most common rainforest trees. And palms soon fall into groups of thorny wait-a-while climbers, elegant palm trees, and fan palms. The matchbox vine snakes down in zig-zags among the lianes, and a cycad or two. Plus there are four main epiphytic ferns: bird's nest, elkhorn, basket, and endemic strap fern. You will become attuned to the whip-cracks of the Eastern whip bird, the cat-wails of a local bowerbird, the spotted catbird, and a few more bird-calls that catch your interest. After that, you are an expert, more or less, because even the experts don't know their way around all of the species in the area.

The plant you're wondering about could be the cause of the next pharmaceutical gold rush, estimated to be worth $2 billion a year from

King Fern Angiopteris evecta *has the longest fronds of all ferns, yet it is one of the first ferns to evolve. Seen on the foot bridge to the Daintree Rainforest Environmental Center.*

Australia alone. In the late 1990s, the Queensland Pharmaceutical Research Institute started major expeditions to find previously unidentified species that might have medical uses. They investigated an un-named plant used by Aboriginal peoples with pain-killing properties that exceed morphine. And the locally common tree, the black bean, or Moreton Bay chestnut (*Castanospermine australe*), made early headlines as an AIDS and anti-viral drug that attacks viruses by bonding to their sugar-studded surfaces. Look for its bean-like pinnate leaves and pea-like orange or red flowers.

One of the more interesting eco-activities involve spotting and watching the fruiting and flowering trees, because it is in these menageries that most of the canopy bird and bat life takes place. In fact, it is for this interaction that these lofty flowering plants evolved: 84 percent of Queensland rainforest trees bear fleshy fruit and depend on finely adapted fruit-eaters, or frugivores, for dispersal. To find the hot spots, look on the ground for signs of recent flowerings, brightly colored new fruits, and ripe figs. Listen for the screeches of spectacled fruit bats and king parrots, the "my name is wompoo" call of the very plump jade, gold, and purple wompoo fruit-doves high in the canopy, and the call of the

Sap-Suckers and Symbiosis

Imagine eating maple syrup, and nothing else, for a lifetime. Not only would you get tired of it, you'd probably die of dietary deficiencies. The same is true for aphids and other rainforest sap suckers. They need tryptophan and leucine, essential amino acids that are rare in plant sap. 200 million years ago, buchnera, a bacteria, infected a prehistoric insect. But instead of killing it, it allowed the hungry host to stick around and suck more sap as opposed to using more energy to look for a more varied diet like its sisters and brothers. Buchnera synthesizes an excess of these amino acids from scratch, providing the sap sucker with its needs. This union resulted in the first aphid, an insect that was a billion times more successful than its generalist parent. Now, neither the aphid nor buchnera can live alone. Buchnera are inherited maternally. They have evolved so buchnera inject themselves into the next aphid generation from the female aphid line. When the aphid's eggs are fertilized, the maternal colony of bacteria that is enclosed in a bacteriocyte home near the aphid's ovary forms an inoculating tube that pierces the aphid oocyte, or early embryo, and injects bacteria, which then form a new bacteriocyte in the developing embryo.

Rainbow Lorikeet
This popular lorikeet with brilliant colors has become comfortable around towns and cities and can be seen around the edges of the Wet Tropics. It is an appealing tourist attraction. Its social display behavior has been studied in-depth, because it takes part in complex displays of solidarity, romance, distraction, and alarm.

superb fruit-doves. Wompoo fruit-doves live in the canopy and rely on four pivotal species that are critical to their survival, including Eleacarpaceae. You will soon start to appreciate this essential world of the frugivores, which includes even rainforest fish.

True avian frugivores have digestive systems that lack the grit or harsh digestion of seed-eaters that otherwise destroy some seeds. Instead, they have delicate guts that massage off the fruit pulp while leaving the pits intact. This leaves the seed to sprout new food-producing trees for them later on. It's a cooperative system: everyone thrives with help from everyone else. The cassowary might be the only frugivore with a mouth large enough to disperse the biggest rainforest pits into successional areas, now that moas have left the scene. Keep an eye out for cassowary pancakes, dark piles of semi-digested pits and nuts from 115 species and 46 families, the most variety of any frugivore, ready to sprout into spindly new "oskars." Although the diet is broad, some species such as *Lauraceae* are critical to the cassowary's diet. The Torresian imperial pigeon distributes and eats 37 species and 20 families. All frugivores are dependent on the rotating seasons of year-round fruit, and may travel over long distances to find them. Fruiting species have evolved in concert to make this year-long plenty possible, with few gaps. Some frugivores, such as parrots, pigeons, and hornbills, are nomadic or migratory. Cassowaries and arboreal possums are not.

Fruit is poor quality food if it is the primary food source, as it is low in protein though high in carbohydrate. Hardly any species feed their young entirely on fruit. The fruit pigeons of Asia and the Pacific, like all pigeons, produce crop milk for their young that is high in protein to supplement the fruit diet. The chicks lap the milk from the parents' open gullets.

Cape Tribulation was named by Lieutenant James Cook in 1770 who ran aground on the shallow coral reefs before finding a way through them to sail north.

Fruit dispersal by bats and birds is so effective that if the frugivores disappear, the rainforest trees are more likely to become extinct than if the species-intact habitat were to be diminished in size into a limited patchwork by habitat reduction alone. This research-based observation challenges the prevailing view that species diversity declines in direct proportion to loss of habitat, and points to the limitation of focusing on individual species rather than on the relationship webs of a habitat. It is critical to restore the network of interacting and keystone frugivorous plant and animal species in damaged habitats. Ecologists are now working to make sure these ecosystem's seed distribution participants remain viable, so that small and connected rainforest areas can thrive as representatives of much larger forests, now lost. Bat House is shoring up one of these critical links.

There are about 2,500 tropical fruits in the world that people can eat. Only fifteen of these aromatic, silky varieties are available commercially in the world's markets. So, make sure you delight your palate while you are in the tropics. Ecotravellers are recommended to stop at the Daintree Ice Cream Company about 14km/8.7mi north of the Daintree River for ice cream made from local rainforest fruit (07-4098-9114), or Scomazzon's for exotic fruit and a nursery (07-4098-2446), Daintree Road 3km/1.8mi north of Mossman.

Palms

The black palm is a common Daintree palm. The Kuku Yalanji Aboriginal people cleft the wood into thin strips that they sharpened, and then hardened in a fire to make spear-heads.

Oriana Palm is found at high altitudes below the canopy and its trunk is surrounded by spiraling roots from nearby trees. These originally sought the high-nutrient debris accumulated at the large leaf base which was at ground level when the Oriana was young.

Wait-a-while (*Calamus sp.*) are climbing palms whose barbs are backward-facing to grip onto foliage. Its vine-like trunk is used to make rattan furniture.

The fan palm has circular fronds and is a beautiful and important endemic palm of the area.

Alexandra palm (*Archontophoenix alexandae*) is a pale green slender palm that is very common below the canopy here. Aboriginal people ate the hearts of palm from this tree.

Palms were among the earliest angiosperms, or flowering plants. They probably came to Australia via India, reaching Australia about 100 million years ago. Fourteen of the fifteen Daintree palms are endemic to Australia and probably evolved within Australia from early palm ancestors.

The Homeless Herbivore

The green ringtail possum is a rainforest endemic that you are likely to spot during the daytime because it sleeps out in tree branches. Found high in trees in a ball during the day, gripping with its hind foot, it conserves energy by sleeping in the daytime and eating at night. This way, it conserves energy while surviving off the low-nutrient poisonous leaves of figs, laurels, and the stinging tree. Found in the Wet Tropics from the Atherton Tablelands up to the headwaters of the Daintree River, it has very waterproof fur so it can stay out in the rain without relying on a nest. Black, yellow, and white hairs give the possum a green sheen. These creatures have developed a selective capacity to digest toxins. The best way to see rainforest herbivores is on a night hike with a strong flashlight. Australian marsupials probably originated on the Antarctic side of Gondwana, then evolved considerably when Australia cast off on its island voyage. South American possums share common ancestors with Australian possums. Later, Australian possums entered New Guinea and continued their evolution there 15 million years ago when land bridges or close islands re-formed several times. Some marsupials like the cuscus re-entered Australia from New Guinea later on.

Pied currawong, brown cuckoo-doves and white-headed pigeons are important seed dispersers, though they are not true frugivores. These have grit in their digestive systems and grind up some of the seeds. Pied currawong are important establishers for some rainforest seeds in grassland areas. In this way, the rainforest can take over new territory. Other distributors stay within the closed rainforest and so don't help break new ground. Solitary tree perches are used by pied currawong and are key sites for seed dispersal. Honeyeaters, brown cuckoo-doves, king parrots, and crimson rosellas also use these perches. Perches in trees without fruit are more likely to be a site to spread seeds, as brown cuckoo-doves vigorously defend fruiting trees and eat their fruit. As a result, they can keep seed-diversifying dispersers away. Once rainforest begins to grow and pioneer species begin to be replaced by long-living climax species, pure frugivores, rather than these seed dispersers, become key.

Cooper Creek

Cooper Creek spills over the small, beautiful Alexandra Falls into the dense rainforest and is another rare center of rainforest diversity. The best way to experience Cooper Creek is with Cooper Creek Wilderness Walks, which has a telephone booking system by the side of the road for early passers-by, or call (07-4098-9126). Another choice is the Cooper Creek Wilderness Cruise (07-4098-9052). Turpentine Road goes along the creek, but there are no public trails accessible from the road. The Daintree Entomological Museum and Gallery is found at the beginning of Turpentine Road. Check for opening times before arriving (07-4098-9045). Turpentine Road runs west after driving 22km/13.6mi north from Daintree ferry.

Marrdja and Noah's Creek

It is worth taking the 45-min Marrdja boardwalk

at Oliver Creek and Noah Creek to see examples of the world's early flowering plants. Critical flowering plants of world importance are identified by signs and their evolutionary context is explained as you walk through the rainforest and mangroves. The flowers of these plants look like those of modern rainforest trees and bushes, but many are in fact very primitive. Unlike conifers, mosses, and ferns, which look the same as their ancestors, flowering plants evolved rapidly from their origins as woody herbs, into a wide diversity of beautiful forms. One reason for this great variety has been flowering plant's co-evolution with insects. But once they made the change, flowering plants left little trace of their originators, unlike conifers. Therefore, botanists are fascinated to learn more about the characteristics of any primitive flowering species they can find in the world. You can smell the perfume of some of these early species, indicating that right from the start, these flowers evolved to attract and interact with insects. And from these ancestors and their relatives that evolved 130 million years ago in west Gondwana (the part that became west Africa and the northern part of South America), all other flowering plants evolved. The reason that you can find these ancestors here is that the vast rainforests of Gondwana retreated to this humid corner of Australia when new icecaps dried up the water from Australia's rainforest center, 5 million years ago. As a result, these plants have been able to survive without evolutionary pressures in a relatively stable, closed rainforest system, unchanged.

Noahdendron nicholasii is frozen in time as one of these first flowering trees to evolve. It is found at Noah Creek and has long trailing pink flowers that smell wonderful, with young leaves colored pink with an early sunscreen. From the Marrdja Boardwalk you can see a specimen of ribbonwood or idiot fruit (*Idiospermum australiense*), the only representative of the

A Pademelon is Not a Fruit

At dusk you can sometimes see small kangaroos emerging from the rainforest to browse on leaves and fruit. They are about 50cm/1ft6in when sitting on their haunches. These are red-legged pademelons (*Thylogale stigmatica*), a name that probably comes from an Aboriginal word. They are intensely social animals with a network of communications. When two or three browse, a group of facilitators keep watch, scout, and play bush telegraph with outlying members of the group. So you are only seeing a very small part of a large pack of intelligent creatures whose every move is carefully choreographed and re-examined from moment to moment. During the afternoons, musky rat-kangaroos (*Hypsiprymnodon moschatus*) scuttle around the deep undergrowth of pure rainforest. The Lake Eacham area is a good start if you want to find one, where they are locally common but otherwise rare. 25cm/9in in long, they walk on all fours like huge rats. These are a 20-million-year-old genetic link representing primitive kangaroos in the stage between the possum, from which they evolved, and the kangaroo that we now associate with gum trees.

Spiders that Learn

One jumping spider found in these Wet Tropics is *Portia fimbriata* (top right), an incredible mimic that captures other spiders as prey. Portia's behavior suggests that even small brains can do an enormous amount of "figuring." Portia is up to a half-inch in length and takes on each spider species differently. Portia combines trial and error with instinct. It lures some victims by tweaking their webs with precise messages that urge them into the open. It walks the fine line between pretending to be prey in order to lure the other spider out for an investigation, and calming or slowing down the target so the intended victim does not rush out so fast that it overwhelms Portia instead. It approaches long-legged *Pholcid* spiders obliquely for a good swipe, switches tactics to try other approaches if its victim loses interest, uses wind as a vibratory smokescreen to speed its attack, and even masks its approach by creating faint vibrations that mimic leaf fall. Portia does all this with planned intent, mapping out complex circuitous routes.

Other spiders fight back. An orb spider (*Argiope appensa*), "pumps" its web back and forth to bounce Portia out. But Portia is a step ahead, assessing the situation and moving to a higher spot where it can swing down on its lifeline parallel to the orb spider's web, going for a direct body blow without touching the web.

Euryattus is a jumping spider with a local Wet Tropics population that has learned to recognize Portia's approaches. The female defends its rolled-up leaf nest by head-butting Portia, which then runs away. *Euryattus* found living outside *Portia fimbriata's* region has not learned this behavior.

Portia also stalks free jumping spiders on the ground, pulling in its characteristic mouthparts and using an odd hunched posture so it don't give itself away. It freezes when the victim turns around. Portia's advantage is that it can jump four to six inches, skillfully using its silk lifeline as a lever to swing it where it wants to go. It has superb eyesight. Its eyes are at the second smallest retinal receptor theoretically possible for light. They use a non-compound structure that is similar to ours, can focus by moving inward or outward, and can turn around to concentrate on a specific point of attention up to 40cm/1ft4in away. Jumping spiders, including Portia, can also turn their breast carapace over 45 degrees as they look around, a bit like a tank's gun turret. You can see this yourself if you encounter Portia or another species of jumping spider, for they will often carefully inspect a camera lens by swiveling their eyes and heads like a curious pet. Portia have not been found to be dangerous to humans.

Very poisonous spiders to humans include funnel-webs. Avoid "T" or "X" shaped webs in trees, or webs of "dirty socks"under logs, representing homes of two of these locally-rare species. The Wet Tropic's other 300 spider species include the flower spiders that are side-ways walking crab spiders that change tone to match their flower's color, swift wolf spiders that carry their eggs on their backs, huge golden orb weavers whose gold-slimed webs are strong enough to catch birds, adobe-sculpting trap door spiders, and nocturnal giant huntsmen which have exquisiely patterned, flattened bodies to squeeze under bark.

Spiders in all shapes and sizes, from top: Portia fimbriata, *web-lined closed door of trap door spider* (Idiopidae or Nemesiidae), *northern jeweled spider (*Gateracantha *sp.), leaf-curling spider (*Phonognatha *sp.) furled in the middle of its web.*

Red-tailed black cockatoos

Idiospermaceae family. This tree was discovered after its fruit poisoned local cattle. Other examples in the area include a small bottlebrush ancestor, *Xanthostemon formosa,* found around Little Cooper Creek, a vine *Australbaileya scandens* with green waxy flowers and one with the oldest type of pollen, the beautiful *Gardenia actinocarpa,* and a she-oak ancestor dating to 50 million years ago, *Gymnostoma australianum.*

For campers there is a small National Park campground by Noah Creek, with self-registration available at the site or from a ranger. Follow the highway north past Cow Bay Village until you see the signs for Marrjda on the right, about 27km/16.7mi north from the ferry.

Dubuji, Kulki, and Cape Tribulation

At Cape Tribulation you can view the beach at the end of the 400m/.25mi boardwalk from the Kulki picnic area, and then walk southwest over the saddle to Myall Beach. Myall Beach has a 1.2km/.75mi interpretive boardwalk taking about 45 minutes. This can also be accessed from the Dubuji parking and picnic area. It is probably less crowded if you park at Dubuji, walk across the boardwalk and then to the beach, walking south along Myall Beach to view the Coral Sea and Cape Tribulation from there.

Delightful little crabs can be seen among the mangroves and on the beach. Leaf-eating graspid-type crabs are very common, and quickly dispose of leaves and seeds in their small burrows. Mud-sucking ocypodid-type crabs

Plant-Insect Defenses

Many plants produce tannin to protect themselves from browsers. Tannin, used for human generations to preserve leather, renders plant protein indigestible to grazers, is sticky enough to glue insect legs together, and can be rapidly produced by plants in response to attack. For example, if leaves are chomped on by a swarm of caterpillars, the leaves increase their tannin levels and may release ethylene gas into the surroundings. Ethylene is a trigger that boosts the production of tannin among any "eavesdropping" plants, which collectively fume "not in our backyard," collectively repelling insect attack. Plants stressed by poor growing conditions conserve energy and shut these defenses down, attracting the bulk of insect pests away from the healthiest gene carriers. Rainforest trees in the middle of gaps sacrifice the production of insect repellents for rapid growth and are often peppered with chomp-holes.

Plants also call in ants and wasps to protect themselves from herbivores. The combined aroma of caterpillar burp and the new-mown smell of damaged plant cells alerts passing wasps to remove the threat.

Fruit Lovers

The white-tailed rat is a seed disperser with drawbacks. This rodent is restricted to the Wet Tropics and to coastal Cape York Peninsula. It eats nearly every palatable hard-shelled seed it can find, making holes in the nuts from trees like yellow walnut (*Beilschmiedia bancroftii*), creamy silky oak (*Athertonia diversifolia*), and hairy walnut (*Ednandra insignis*). Look for holes in candle nuts (center) to find evidence of this rat's activities during your walks. This makes reproduction difficult for these trees, perhaps putting evolutionary pressure toward making the fruit less edible. The rat also carefully stores some uneaten seeds under a couple of leaves and a stick. The white-tailed rat also eats beetles from rotting logs. Look for claw-marks on trees to signify the tree hollow in which it rests during the day. Spotted quolls, owls, and dingoes are rat predators, as are feral cats.

Top: Strangler fig (Ficus sp.) fruit shown both intact and split open to show internal flowers. These fruits are prolific and feed large numbers of rainforest birds and animals.
Center: Candle nut husks chewed by white-tailed rats.
Bottom left: Blue Quandong is poisonous. Cassowaries disperse its seeds.
Bottom right: the common black bean or Moreton Bay chestnut pods (Castanospermum australe). A major AIDS and anti-viral drug called a sugar-mimic is obtained from these seeds. Aboriginals used to detoxify these seeds by leaching them before eating them.

leave little balls of sand and mud after straining edible slime off the sand grains through their mouth hairs. You can easily spot the Darwin red legs fiddler crab (*Uca falammula*), an ocypodid, soon after high tide. The males wave an enormously enlarged red claw that is used actively for ritual communication, the smaller claw being used for feeding. Fiddler crabs are so sensitive to the tides that their body shells get paler or blue at low tide, even if isolated in a non-tidal aquarium. In wetter mangrove mud, loud popping sounds are characteristic, caused when the pistol shrimp snaps its pneumatic claw joints. Forward-walking soldier crabs corkscrew into the mud if there is a threat. Large mud towers several feet high (up to 75cm) are made by nocturnal mud lobsters, which share their roost with Polychaete worms.

Visitors should try to volunteer for a day at Bat House opposite Myall Beach and learn more about these cute, intelligent creatures (07-4098-0063). "Look! A bat's clinging onto my T-shirt!" The spectacled flying fox is a keystone species on which many plants depend. These cute yet awkward creatures have three-foot wingspans. Many have been wiped out by an epidemic paralyzing disease and some are being re-habilitated successfully by human intervention. The disease is an example of what can happen when an ecosystem gets out of balance. The vector is a tick that climbs up low-lying branches, which used to be left alone by bats. However, the bats changed their behavior and moved closer to the ground after a foreign tobacco was introduced to the area, with low-lying blossoms the bats like. In the process, they got infected by the tick and its virus. Bats carry several diseases that can endanger humans.

The complex interaction between bats and seed germination is seen in the case of *Cecropia obtusifolia*, a pioneer neotropical tree found in the area. The germination of this tree is triggered by its phytochromes. Active phyto-chromes are proteins capable of switching on

Sippers

The Northern blossom-bat (*Macroglossus minimus*) is a frugivore important to the dioecious fig (*Timonius* sp.), which it is able to swallow as the fig is soft and has no large pit. It then disperses the seeds, which remain intact after exiting the gut. Several rainforest plants add laxatives to their seed pulp. This increases the percentage of germinating seeds, by reducing the time they are attacked by digestive juices. This blossom-bat is a major pollinator along with the common blossom bat. It pollinates durian trees, so look for lots of bats near these. It is also found around the blossoms of *Syzigium*, a native cauliflorous tree. Cauliflory is a rainforest adaptation where trees burst flowers from their trunks, beneath the canopy, probably as a way to compete better for the attention of pollinators at a different height. Bumpy satinash is effectively pollinated by the blossom bat (*Syconycteris australis*), even though it also self-pollinates and is visited by bird pollinators. Somehow these are less effective than the bat. Pollen is caught on the specially-adapted fur of the bat, which hovers or lands near flowers, lapping nectar with its tongue.

Diggers Boost Forest Yields

The long-nosed bandicoot (*Perameles nasuta*) (right) is commonly found in rainforest and woodland. It digs conical holes in the topsoil and lawns with its paws and sticks its nose into them. Listen for its grunting squeak at night. It nests on the ground, with closed entrance. Solitary and common with a high reproductive rate, it eats succulent plants and insects. The northern bettong (*Bettongia tropica*) is a small, similar-looking but rarer marsupial that eats bulbs, roots, and fungi, and disperses truffle spores. Truffles depend on bettongs to disperse their spores: passage through the bettong gut improves germination and does not digest them. Since truffles are important fungal decomposers in this rainforest, bettongs help ensure forest fertility. There is a problem in the Atherton tableland near Kuranda where bettongs have a major colony. Recently, foxes have followed rabbit populations into Atherton. These threaten the bettong population and thereby the interactive forces that hold the rainforest's fertility in balance. This is important because many of these truffles are mycorrhizal, transporting critical nutrients directly into root cells of rainforest plants in exchange for sugars. Inoculation of soils with mycorrhizal fungi significantly increases yields.

germination or flowering. The phytochrome is switched to an active form under the red light that is found in gaps between the canopy that are suitable for new pioneer growth, and is inactivated by the far red light that is found under the shady canopy that would not allow seedlings to thrive. Passage of cecropia seeds through bat guts enhances their light sensitivity, because this thins the seed coats and increases the transmission of light to the seed, and thereby amplifies the "go" signal.

Cairns

Cairns is the bustling gateway city for rainforest and reef travelers, with a well-connected airport. Reef boats and rainforest safaris pick up from hotels and backpacking accommodations in Cairns, and you can rent camping gear and tents from a couple of outdoor-specialist stores.

Cairns is a routing city, not a primary destination in itself, except that it is also a birding hot-spot. Cairns Esplanade is famous for offering shorebird photo opportunities. Late afternoon from August to November is best for photos, especially when high tide moves birds within range. Asian shorebirds plus spoonbills, ibis, and rare terek sandpipers can be seen. The mud skipper fish flipping around in the mud below the Esplanade are the staple food of juvenile saltwater crocodiles. Double-eyed fig-parrots, rufous night-herons, varied honeyeaters, and New Guinea friarbirds can be seen in nearby fig trees and gardens. Centenary Park is superb for rufous owl, papuan frogmouth, red-necked and white-browed crakes (look at the forest near Centenary Boardwalk at dusk), latham's snipes, bush thick-knees, double-eye fig-parrots, little kingfishers (by salt lake, not freshwater lake), graceful, yellow, and brown-backed honey-eaters, mangrove robins (central channel mangroves) and metallic starlings. In Mount Whitfield Environmental Park look for buff-breasted paradise kingfishers, noisy pittas, fairywrens, and pied monarchs.

Atherton Tropical Tableland

The Atherton Tropical Tableland farming plateau is an easy hour's drive inland from Cairns. To reach the small town of Atherton, go south from Cairns on the Bruce Highway and turn west on the Gillies Highway at Gordonvale up the hill and across the farmland to Atherton, a total of 87km involving a steep switchback road for part of the trip. The alternate drive to Atherton is via activity-rich Kuranda: north from Cairns on the Cook Highway, turn west on the Kennedy Highway up the switchback to Kuranda, 22km/13.6mi, then on to Atherton, for 88 km/44.5mi total. You can also reach Kuranda with world-class views from the Kuranda Scenic Railway (07-4052-6249) up the steep Barron River Gorge from Cairns, or the Skyrail Rainforest Cableway over the rainforest canopy (07-4038-1555) from just north of Cairns.

The tableland's richer basaltic soils support a more easily spotted array of rare possums, birdlife, and carnivorous marsupials than the granites of the more ancient Daintree lowlands, because larger populations thrive on the volcanic minerals. You can also find the rare holly (*Ilex arnhemensis*), the earliest-evolved flowering plant, or angiosperm, alive in Australia. Greatest species diversity, though, is found in the poor granite soils of the Daintree, as these 120-million-year-old rainforests retain more ancient lineages intact than the 4-million-year-old volcanic tableland. Even so, it is simply often harder to find what you are looking for in the

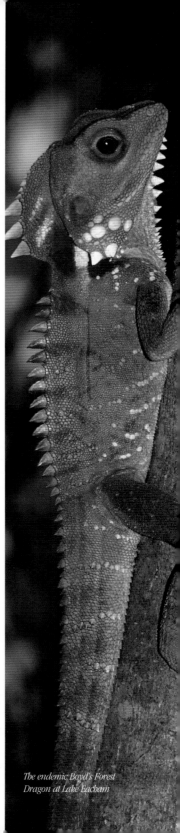

The endemic Boyd's Forest Dragon at Lake Eacham

The 120-Decibel Forest

One of the most spectacular experiences is to immerse oneself among a group of active 120-decibel northern double drummer cicadas (*Thopha sessiliba*), found around Australia's eucalypts. Double drummers are the loudest insects on Earth. The second loudest are the greengrocers. The large greengrocer cicada (*Cyclochila virens*) is found from Mossman to Townsville in mountain rainforest. One's ears feel as though they are being tortured with sandpaper as the sound waves interfere with one another. Most cicadas throw their voice so that a bank of white noise confuses a predator's ability to locate them. The double drummer uses a directional mating call. Cicadas have good hearing, yet just before males sing, they shut off their auditory nerve to their tympanums with a muscle. Perhaps their feet or knees sense the vibration necessary to keep in unison. Cicadas sometimes respond to people who whistle tremulously or clap their hands. The male cicada's body is a hollow sounding board with its vital organs restricted to a strip along its back. Its sound is produced by two membranes either side of the back that click when popping back into shape.

Green whizzer cicada (Macrotristria intersecta) (top left). Empty cicada pupae (top right, bottom left). Double-drummer (Thopha saccata) (bottom right).

Daintree. Wildlife can be found in several types of rainforest patches surrounding Atherton's many lakes or in the dry sclerophyllous eucalypt forest of the associated Lamb Range, so you have more places to look on the tableland. Immersion in the total rainforest experience is possible if you stay at one of the rainforest ecolodges on the tableland or are prepared to camp, and also take at least one spotlighting tour, either on the tableland or in the Daintree, starting from Cairns, Kuranda, or Port Douglas.

The Crater, Mt. Hypipamee Park

An enormous volcanic gas explosion punched out the vertical granite walls of Crater Lake. The altitude is high enough that the cooler climate has shifted some of the ecosystem from tropical to sub-tropical. Victoria's riflebirds, golden bowerbirds, spotted catbirds, and toothbilled bowerbirds and their bowers can be seen here, and you can also find Lewin's honeyeaters. Several types of rainforest are found, depending on whether the soils are poorer granite (near Dinner Falls) or richer basaltic (near the bridge) loams. The lake ridge is fringed by sclerophyllous eucalypt forest. A looping 800m/.5mi trail meanders in the direction of the Barron River to an observation platform overlooking the Crater Lake (24km/14.9mi south of Atherton on the Kennedy Highway).

Lake Eacham, Crater Lakes Park

An excellent 700m/ .4mi self-guided walk about rain-forest species can be taken around part of Lake Eacham, with illustrated brochures available in a box at the start of the walk near the lakeside parking lot. The trail ends at the district office. You will find several rainforest types, starting with the smaller, unbuttressed trees of the "pole forest" of less fertile metamorphic soil. The main trail is 4km/2.4mi around the lake, accessed halfway along the self-guided walk. Around most of the aquamarine lake you'll see maidenhair ferns in the rich basaltic soils under buttressed trees carrying an enormous load of epiphytes and vines. Look on the ground for pale, upturned leaves placed daily on a circular area by the tooth-billed bowerbird. This dully-spotted bowerbird imitates other bird songs beautifully.

The lake itself is an underwater treasure, but most people will be unaware of this as they walk above it. Recently, after a species of fish unique to Lake Eacham became extinct due to the introduction of predatory non-native fish species, a collector was able to re-supply the fish from his own aquarium. They are now reestablished in their native home. To reach Lake Eacham, go to Lake Barrine on the Gillies Highway going south, continue toward Malanda for 3km/1.8mi then turn left on Wrights Creek Road and follow Lake Eacham signs for another 3km/1.8mi. On the way back north from Lake Eacham, visit the giant red cedar tree by turning right off Wrights Creek Road onto Gadgarra Road 3km until you reach the Gadgarra State Forest. Then bear left along a short unsealed section. It is a short 600m/.3mi walk to the tree and back.

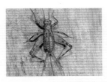

The Hedge Grasshopper

Valanga irregularis (above left) lives in open forest and gardens of Queensland and North New South Wales. Grasshoppers can escape spiders by thwacking the web with their legs, while spitting out digestive juices that can dissolve the silk, both resulting in the grasshopper breaking through. Female tree trunk cricket (*Tathra* sp.) (above) on a tree trunk where it is commonly found. The males make most of the night's rainforest noise. A bunch of caterpillars has evolved a way to look larger to predators: they fan out at the slightest external movement to imitate a bottlebrush. The spinifex termite (*Nasutitermes triodiae*) (nest, below) is found in the eucalypts across much of N Australia. Soldiers defend the nest by squirting noxious glue from a head nozzle.

A Hair's Breadth

The northern leaf-tailed gecko (above) is a nocturnal tree-dweller with exquisite camouflage and primitive characteristics. Geckos stick to surfaces, sometimes upside down, through what are known as van der Waals forces. These are weak but significant bonds formed between close-by molecules: in this case, between the molecules on the minute branched hairs of the gecko's feet and the molecules of the walked-on surface. The gecko's hairs are so microscopic that they literally penetrate the electrostatic forces of the outside world.

The amethystine python (*Morelia amethistina*) (center) of Cape York Peninsula constricts small wallabies, flying foxes, birds, and possums. This is one of the most beautiful snakes you can see. The color appears to shimmer disconnected above the scales. The eastern brown snake (*Psuedonaja textilis*) (right, held by Ian Gynther of the Queensland Parks and Wildlife Service), has the ninth most neurotoxic venom of the world's snakes.

Lake Barrine, Crater Lakes Park

Rainforest surrounds the brilliant blue lake that has formed in a volcanic crater, 8km/5mi northeast of Yungaburra on the Gillies Highway. A 5km/3mi walk goes around the lake and you can take a relaxing boat ride with the Lake Barrine Rainforest Cruise and Teahouse.

A pair of huge Kauri pines (*Agathis* sp.) are next to the lake path, a species of true pines that, with other Southern Hemisphere pines, have long flat leaf blades rather than needles. Lake Barrine brings you as close as you can get to what it was like in the dinosaur age. Kauri pines used to dominate the rainforest across Australia and other Gondwanan areas in Jurassic times, starting 300 million years ago. Several modern species of this Kauri pine forest are surprising matches to a fossil Jurassic forest from 175 million years ago found in New South Wales. Triassic southern pines, also known as podocarp conifers, grow with Kauri pines, then as now, accompanied by the Cycad *Pentoxylon australica* (then) and *Lepidozamia hopei* (now).

Pollen and charcoal samples from Lake Barrine, Lynch's Crater on the southwestern

Self-Guided Tableland Driving Tours

The picturesque 16km/10mi Waterfall Circuit Drive starts at Millaa on the southern part of the tableland. From Cairns go south on the Bruce Highway 95km/59mi. Then take Palmerston Highway west 64 km/39.7mi to Theresa Creek Road in the direction of Millaa Milla Falls, and continue around to Zillie Falls and Ellinjaa Falls. If you want more than a photo-op, a driving and walking tour that opens up the rainforest, bird, and marsupial life is the Crater Lakes Drive to Lakes Barrine and Eacham, continuing to Malanda Falls and the Crater in Mount Hypipamee National Park. Go south from Cairns on the Bruce Highway 31km/19.2mi, west on the steep Gillies Highway to Lake Barrine about 30km/18mi, which also offers a boat cruise around the rainforest perimeter and an interesting rainforest walk around the lake. Continue south and turn left onto Lake Drive toward Lake Eacham where you can walk around its perimeter or take the separate self-guided walk. Then go south to visit Malanda Falls and the information center, and take the Upper Barron Road via the fascinating Bromfield Crater to the Crater in Mount Hypipamee National Park where you can walk through bowerbird and bird-of-paradise territory and several types of rainforest. Upper Barron Road can get rough for driving; an alternate route is via Atherton. The Wongabel State Forest Botanical Walk offers more in-depth identification of rainforest trees. At night, a spotlighting trip to any of these locations can theoretically reveal up to 13 species of possums and gliders due to the proximity of rainforest and eucalypt habitat. Possums are not that numerous so you will need patience. Worth it, though, for the coppery brushtail possum, for example, is only found in the tableland rainforest. It has large triangular ears, unlike ringtails, which have small ears. They occasionally scavenge around picnic areas. It has digestive enzymes adapted to the rainforest toxins so it can eat poisonous leaves without keeling over.

Quolls

The spotted-tail-quoll or tiger quoll (*Dasyrus maculates*) is a striking example of a large marsupial that isn't a kangaroo or a possum. It is the largest marsupial carnivore on the mainland. Its call is like a blast from a circular saw. Nocturnal, it eats wallabies, other mammals, birds, carrion from dingo kills, and insects. It lives on the ground but can climb. Probably becoming extinct on the mainland, its Tasmanian numbers are increasing. Declining habitat and cat and fox competition, plus traps and poisoning for feral animals are killing it off.

The northern tiger quoll (*D. m. gracilis*) is found on the Lamb Range, Mount Windsor, Mt. Bartle Frere, and Bellenden Ker with sporadic sightings between the Daintree River and Cape Tribulation. The northern quoll (*Dasyurus hallucatus*) is another uncommon quoll of the area. The Eastern quoll (*D. viverrinus*) (below) is repopulating habitats as a result of a captive breeding program conducted by Earth Sanctuary.

*Northern dwarf treefrog (*Litoria bicolor*) (above) is found in grassy areas in northern Australia and New Guinea, including the non-rainforest patches in the Wet Tropics of northern Queensland. This frog is a delicate little beauty not much bigger than a thumbnail. Listen for its high-pitched whirring sounds. The rainforest has plenty of frog food (below) in the form of insect larvae. You are likely to spot this one,* Dysphania fenestrata, *feeding on Carallia leaves. It develops into a beautiful rainforest moth with window-pane black and white wings and yellow spots, and a wingspan of 85mm/3.5in.*

tableland, and offshore from Cairns have shown the major effect that the introduction of Aboriginal fire stick farming and, more importantly, mega-fauna hunting, probably has had on rapidly amplifying the natural switch of the entire continent from rainforest to arid land. When man entered the Australia with fire stick and spear in hand, he probably created a quantum-shift in the rainforest vegetation from an increasingly dominant "dry" *Araucaria*-type rainforest to fire-dependent eucalypt forest. This triggered a man-made climate change that compounded naturally increasing aridity.

You can spot the signs of this immense shift on the tableland. You can see several examples of hoop pine (*Araucaria cunninghamii*) on the tableland by the roadside on farmland, and popping out of rainforest. You can identify it from a distance by looking for a classic pine tree shape, with what appear to be powder-puffs of mid-green needles in dense clusters along the branches. Hoop pines are Southern pines, and are the earliest pines of all found in Australia, just preceding flowering plants. Wet rainforest species are currently dominant in the Wet Tropics, and consist of the more-familiar dark green broadleaved trees that cannot survive any drought or fire, but previously dominated Australia when wetter climates prevailed. According to Tim Flannery and other researchers chronicled in his important book *The Future Eaters*, what appears to have happened is a series of changes in which man and nature rapidly adjusted to each another, with dramatic results. As Aboriginal peoples spread across Australia, 60 species of megafauna

Frog-Watch

In the 1990s, three Wet Tropics frog species disappeared and others suddenly declined—a crisis that also occurred worldwide. High-altitude stream-based species in pristine areas were most affected. This puzzling observation indicated that lack of conservation was not the primary cause. An Australian team has found evidence and proof linking this global population crash to a chytrid epidemic carried on hiking boots and soil. Other factors such as increased UV light affecting egg development, climate changes, and pollution have not been ruled out. Frog species that float eggs in water, though, all have a small black dot on top to protect the eggs from UV damage. The northern gastric-brooding frog, nursery frogs, and whistling frogs do not have tadpoles but either brood them in their stomach or lay and care for eggs in mud.

*The best way to identify frogs is not so much by their appearance but by their call. Their colors vary both within species and within an individual over a period of hours. The green-eyed treefrog (*Litoria genimaculata*) (top) is colorful, measuring up to 65mm/2.5in, found in the Wet Tropics and New Guinean rainforests. It looks like it has been draped with lichen. It calls "toc." The stony-creek frog (*Litoria lesueuri*) (above right) whirrs gently and the male turns lemon yellow at night during the breeding season. The Australian woodfrog (*Rana daemeli*) (above left) quacks reedily and can leap 2.5m/8ft in one bound, the longest frog leap in Australia. The Northern barred frog tadpole (center left) is a major rainforest leaf recycler. The stealth-bomber-shaped adult (center right) will reply to human imitations of their "waaark" sounds. All of these are sought by a sleek collection of venomless green tree snakes (*Dendrelaphis calligastra*) (below) which are hard to spot in the rainforest vegetation unless you have an alert eye.*

Killer Critters

You may spot the predatory marsupial yellow-footed antechinus (*Antechinus flavipes ruberculus*) (above) darting rapidly along branches and rocks. It eats insects voraciously, plus a few flowers, mice, and birds. Watch for the telltale signs of prey turned inside-out after eating. An evolutionary quirk allows antechinus babies to survive their predatory fathers. Finding a mate is such work for the aggressive and territorial males that their immune systems pack up, and they die at about a year old. This allows the female to rear her young in peace. The Atherton antichinus is a secretive species that is rare and limited to the Atherton Tableland. It is large and rat-sized. It eats insects, slugs, and spiders but little is known about it.

This red cedar (Toona ciliata) *(no relation to European cedars)is the species that originally brought Europeans to settle the area. Now there are only a few left, but they can be seen in many ecotravel sites, loaded with epiphytes.*

species were hunted to extinction. This man-made extinction occurred on other continents, too, for the same reasons. In Australia the percentage of wipe-out, however, was larger than on other continents. One theory is that Australian animals were so unused to human beings that their fear reflexes had not been developed, unlike in Africa where man evolved side-by-side with the alert megafauna that they hunted. In Australia, Flannery contends that the vegetarian food of these hippo-sized beasts quickly became a tangle of fire-prone overgrown thickets, once the munchers disappeared. So, when lit by Aboriginal fire sticks or natural lightning, much hotter fires dominated for a time. Man's hand can be seen in the fossil record of Lake Barrine, which shows a huge increase in soot charcoal from the fires when Aboriginal people arrived 38,000 years ago (65,000 years ago and more in other pollen/soot core samples), correlating with a major change in plant pollen species found in the same core of mud that confirm Flannery's view. The only tree species that could grow back from these searing fires were the eucalypts, which became dominant everywhere except in the fire-sheltered rainforest refuges that the Aboriginals couldn't get to, such as those found here on top of mountains and on steep, sheltered slopes. But the eucalypts are not good at retaining moisture in the soil or seeding the atmosphere with rain, unlike the dry rainforest species, which enrich the soil, reduce water run-off, and foster damper, rain-prone air. As a result, not only did the vegetation shift in composition, but the new sun-trees switched the climate itself from a drier to a parched weather pattern. This closed the door to the dry rainforest, which otherwise would have continued to do well across the continent, even as it dried—if the megafauna had continued to roam. After their disastrous experience with the megafauna, Aboriginal peoples carefully adapted their approach to conserve what was left, a move that successfully saved many mid-sized mammals from extinction. Aboriginal fire management stimulated a patchwork of interconnected bushland for themselves and for wild animals, while maintaining rainforest borders intact at fire lines. These rainforest refuges became important seasonal sources for hunted game, starchy staples, and fruits.

Wongabel State Forest Botanical Walk

You will find the Wongabel State Forest 8km/5mi south of Atherton on the Kennedy Highway. A 45-minute 2.6km/1.6mi walk around this tableland rainforest reveals an abundance of carefully research, numbered, and labeled trees. In fact, the best way to get familiar with some of the tropical forest trees is through guided walks like these, as identification of rainforest species is challenging without the real thing in front of you. There are so many species that it is better to focus on five or six common trees first. Detailed notes about each species that correlate

Monotremes with X-Ray Ears & Noses

The oldest evolved living mammal species in the world, the platypus and echidna, can be found in the Wet Tropics. Their origins are so ancient that they have lived half their existence alongside dinosaurs. These two monotremes still lay eggs, but their food-detecting senses verge on ESP.

Platypuses sense electromagnetic fields emitted by underwater prey. They do this through their "bills," even in mud.

The best time to see a platypus is at dusk on any of the many waterways in the Wet Tropics. The best way is to go with a guide who knows where to find them. Platypuses live secretively at the end of long burrows with underwater entrances.

Echidnas have spines. Their ears can detect the sub-sonic sound made by worm guts churning sand. Worms and termites are favorite foods.

They are widespread and successful, found snuffling the dirt all over Australia, even in suburbia, to which they have rapidly adapted. The best way to see one is to stay alert to one crossing your path: you can't go looking for them. They are exceptionally strong and can break through refrigerator doors. Females lay their eggs directly into their pouch by curling into a ball.

Ant Plants

Staghorn fern, elkhorn fern, basket fern, crow's-nest fern, and locally common endemic strap fern are epiphytes. Their inverted umbrella design captures falling leaves which nourish them. The epiphytic ant plant (*Myrmecodia* sp.) is a small flowering plant with ant-proof white blossoms, found on paperbark trunks. It has pseudobulbs occupied by the ant *Iridomyrmex cordatus* which develop large colonies. Specialized plant cells digest and absorb nutrients from the ant waste. Ants actually carry their waste to chambers lined with these cells. Phosphorous is absorbed from these chambers and ends up in the leaves within hours of ants captururing phosphorous-rich prey insects. This is a scarce mineral in the rainforest and so the relationship helps the plant grow, while giving the ants protection. This ant plant also houses Apollo jewel butterfly larvae. The ants provide the larva with nitrogen and phosphorous-rich ant-plant leaves in exchange for honeydew from the larva. When the larva transforms into a butterfly, it escapes the predatory jaws of the ants by sprinkling the ants with angel dust in the form of millions of slippery scales from its new wings. Ants introduced to Australia are now replacing *Iridomyrmex* in these ant plants, killing the butterflies and depressing plant germination.

with their numbered specimens are available from the Natural Resources Office in Atherton, at Box 210, 83 Main Street, Atherton QLD 4883 or (07-4091-1844).

Around Wongabel you may see pioneer species growing on disturbed land. These are important shade plants that help establish the first steps of a rainforest under sun too hot for canopy seeds to sprout without pioneer help. The candle-nut tree (*Lantana camara*) and *Solanum mauritianum* were both introduced into the area and their seeds are dispersed by honeyeaters, king parrots, and brown cuckoo-doves. Once these pioneer species have established growth in the cleared area, these are overtaken by insect attack from butterfly and moth larvae. This brings light into the secondary species whose seeds can grow in their shade, the canopy specialists that eventually displace them and last for thousands of years. Once the transition from pioneers has been completed with insect help, there is an insect exodus and a new green area is attacked by this sudden insect boom.

Kuranda

Kuranda is located at the northern end of the Atherton Tableland and is the stop for art, a crush of people, and some natural history diversions. The township offers a butterfly sanctuary, two aviaries, a wildlife noctarium, and a colonial-era train station filled with a wonderful tropical rainforest flower display. To drive to Kuranda, take the Captain Cook Highway north from Cairns and turn west on the Kennedy Highway up and across Saddle Mountain to Kuranda (22km/13.6mi). You can also take the exceptional Kuranda Scenic Railway (07-4052-6249) up the steep Barron River Gorge from Cairns, or the Skyrail Rainforest Cableway over the rainforest canopy (07-4038-1555) from just north of Cairns.

Walk through the Barron Gorge National

Mural Artists

Bowerbirds are the only animals besides human beings to woo their mate by displaying collections of inanimate objects. These birds of Gondwanan origin are found only in Australia and New Guinea. They seem to have transferred some of their plumage colors and nest-building anxiety into aesthetically attractive bower-building activites that show the female which male has the best survival instincts. Most alpha males build complex bowers consisting of a cleared display avenue plus a twig sculpture, all decorated in precise locations with objects of a particular color. It takes about seven years for apprentice birds to watch alpha males and learn how to build the architecture, from painting the twigs with brightly colored lichen-laced spittle to aligning the bower with the morning sun for maximum feather brilliance. Lots of practice bowers are built until they perfect their technique. At that time, the male dons his adult plumage. The dullest species have the most elaborate bowers, perhaps so that the bright colors can attract the female without making the male a target for predators. In fact, bower ornaments often contrast with the bird's plumage. In the Wet Tropics highlands, you may find an example of a "maypole bower" of two towers of sticks propped up by saplings and joined by a perch. This is carefully built deep in the rainforest by the golden

bowerbird, which uses it as a display arena, not as a nest. Females only select males that can build the bower, sing, maintain the decorations, and feed themselves. Successful males live much longer than similar-sized song-birds. Wait-a-While Safari Tours may show you one of these bowers. Further south, in Lamington National Park outside Brisbane, you can see the other type, the "avenue bowers" built by the satin bowerbird and the black and gold regent bowerbird. A small patch of satin bowerbirds can be found south of Cairns, but the major population is found in southern Australia. Blue-black satin bowerbirds choose rainforest gaps and stack twigs in exact parallels on a platform decorated with blue and green items such as plastic straws, bottle tops, and blue rosella feathers, chosen to contrast with the male's own violet eyes. Some bowerbirds feed the female with fresh berries from the bower's decorations. The untidy-looking great

Satin bowerbird bower.

bowerbird can be found across all of northern Australia including the Queensland Wet Tropics, though it chooses tropical savanna woodland rather than rainforest in which to build its large avenue bower, often decorated with shells. The mealy-colored spotted catbird and tooth-billed bowerbird are bowerbirds that do not build twig bowers, though the tooth-billed bowerbird clears a stage on which he places fresh upturned leaves. The male offers the female a bouquet of these leaves when she shows interest. You are likely to come across them in the Atherton tablelands. Listen for their unmistakable, loud wailing sounds reminiscent of a cat or an infant. Or look for very pale leaves arrayed underside-up around a cleared oval "stage" on the forest floor.

The land mullet is twice the size of a large rat. But because it is a reptile with a body temperature the same as its surrounding, its food consumption needs are much lower than a mammal's.

The spice clove is a member of the Syzigium family. Bumpy satinash and other Syzigiums are common in the Wet Tropics. They exhibit cauliflory (cluster fig, above), where fruit and flowers burst through the trunk to attract another level of pollinators.

Park by taking the track south from the train station along Barron Falls Road to Barron Falls Lookout, about 2 hours return. Or continue along Barron Falls Road to Wrights Lookout Road until you reach Wrights Lookout. The small Penda's Circuit Track is a 15-minute detour around two huge rainforest trees. Find the clay track by going southwest from Barron Falls Road opposite the National Parks Sign, 500m/1,635ft above Barron Falls Lookout.

Kahlpahlim Rock, Lamb Range

The Lamb Range is sclerophyllous forest in the northern area of the Atherton tableland. The forest has several interesting possum and quoll species that may be seen at night, so this is the destination of one of the spotlighting safaris. The 11km/6.6mi, challenging wilderness trail to the Lamb Range's highest point goes through open eucalypt woodland, casuarina forest, and rainforest with good views of Davies Creek. A permit for road access is required and a map is provided. Take the Kennedy Highway road north out of Mareeba toward Kuranda and at 14km/8.4mi turn onto Davies Creek Road. The trail is 14.5km/8.7mi along this 4WD track.

The white-kneed king cricket (Penalva flavocalceata) is common in the rainforest. This is related to the huge New Zealand weta.

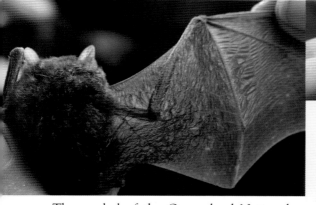

The symbol of the Queensland National Parks and Wildlife Service, the Herbert River ringtail possum (*Pseudochirulus herbertensis*) is found from the Lamb Range to the Seaview Range near Townsville. This is a black-and-white possum with a prehensile tail that it uses to climb and to grab nesting twigs.

You can often find small colonies of the large-footed myotis (*M. adversus*) roosting under culverts and bridges beside roads on the tablelands. These bats use the toes of their large hind legs to comb for insects and fish above water. This genus is found widely around the world, but Australia is probably too arid for more species of this genus to have evolved within the continent, for it is not strictly a rainforest bat. Males breed by collecting a harem and establishing a territory by fighting aggressively. Unlike other bats, the young of dark-colored large-footed myotis and bleached-looking ghost bats (*Macrodermia gigas*) train with their mothers for about four weeks after weaning, to learn how to find food. The ghost bat is a rare bat found within and without the rainforest. It captures prey from the ground using vision combined with echolocation, taking bitten prey to a favorite rock. Fossils of this bat and its prey have been found in Riversleigh, North Queensland, which suggests that this bat used to be much more widespread before Australia became arid.

Microbat Soundings

Microbats (above) have such accurate echo location that they can snatch golden orb-weaving spiders without touching the web. The tensile strength of this particular spider silk is strong enough to catch small birds and bats if entangled, and yellow slime compounds the error by increasing the captive's flight weight.

Fruit bats and other megabats can easily be heard squabbling when they roost in trees during the day. In contrast, the unrelated microbats have high frequency calls that often are too high for our ears, though we may hear "beats" that are like scraping sounds as the pitches interfere. Each microbat species has a distinctive call. This helps researchers survey for different species using wavelength-reducing amplifiers that bring the calls into audible range. When these amplifiers are used, two peaks of bat activity become evident: after-dusk and midnight. The bat above is sounding with an open mouth to assess an escape route after being caught temporarily for a survey conducted by O'Reilly's Rainforest Lodge and the Queensland Conservation Corps.

UV Trails

Crimson rosellas (above) are gorgeous parrots tame enough to sit on hat tops. Several rosellas and parrots have a band of UV-reflecting feathers on the nape of their neck. This may be to spot one another in the canopy, or to flash and scare away predators at a last resort. Hawks use their UV-sensitive eyes to spot prey. Not only do they see UV-reflective feathers, they also look for the urine trails of mice and other prey. Urine actually glows under UV light, and sunlight has enough UV to lead hawks to the nests and runs of their prey.

Tolga Scrub

The Tolga Scrub is a tiny sliver of rainforest a few meters either side of the road just north of Atherton. Malanda Falls Information Office offers a low-tech self-guided description of a handful of common rainforest tree species found around three driveways along here. Go if you are interested in botany and don't mind being in the middle of busy traffic while you sort out one tree from another.

Hasties Swamp

Small but worth a birding and herpetology visit, this unsignposted wetland is in eucalypt forest and is a delight, offering sightings of magpie geese, brolgas, and whistling ducks. Take the Kennedy Highway south of Atherton toward Heberton and turn east onto Hastie Road just out of Atherton, then south on Koci Road to the swamp.

Malanda Falls

The roadside Malanda Falls Conservation Park is just west of the township of Malanda. The information center is a key stop for collecting the self-guided walks and other pamphlets to the area. Two very short trails enter two types of rainforest: the tulip oak walk through the dry northern type of rainforest and, across the road, the Johnstone River walk through the wet southern rainforest among black bean and Queensland black walnut trees. There is a platypus viewing platform on this side, which is best entered at dusk. Next driving stops after Malanda are Bromfield Swamp, a left turn just west of Malanda Falls, on the rough Upper Baron Road, and from there to the Crater in Mt. Hypipamee National Park. Bromfield Swamp is a good wetlands observation site for bird life.

Cathedral Fig

This celebrated *Ficus* sp. is loaded with epiphytic ferns. Several fig species in these rainforests sprout high up in a light area on another tree, then uses their air roots to connect with the ground before out-competing the hosts. From Cairns take Gillies Highway south and, as you reach the plateau, turn right onto Boars Pocket Road for 5km/3.1mi. Access is easy and short. In addition, there is a 2-hour, difficult 4 km/2.5 mi return walk along an early explorer's trail called Robsons Track. It starts from Gillies Lookout near the cathedral fig. Rainforest, creek, ridgeline, and granite boulders are encountered. The track is reached by turning off Boars Pocket Road just north of the cathedral fig tree, northeast along an unpicturesque old forestry track for 4 km/2.5 mi.

Bellenden Ker and Bartle Frere, Wooroonooran National Park

These two mountains offer wonderful alternatives to the much-visited tropical forests of the Daintree for wilderness travelers. Bellenden Ker is 45 minutes' drive south of Cairns. Mount Bartle Frere nearby is Queensland's highest peak.

The Bartle Frere skink (*Leiolopisma jigurru*) has been found near the summit of Mount Bartle Frere around exposed boulders. The discovery was exciting because this creature, now stranded on the peak's cloud forest, was the first temperate vertebrate "relict" species found

ID-101 for Tropical Forest Trees

Eight-hundred species of trees have been identified in the Queensland rainforest, many of them endemic. One hundred of these species have buttresses. Half of the tree species are found in the oldest rainforest near Cape Tribulation. You can identify some major rainforest trees by the shape of their buttresses as they meet the ground, the texture of the bark, and any seeds or old blossoms that decorate the forest bed. Gray bollywood (*Acofitsea dealbata*) (above) has leaves with silver undersides and no buttresses. White cedar, Queensland maple (corky), and red tulip oak (*Argyrodendron peralatum*), which used to be used for polished floor boards, have fissured bark. Buttress figs have large plank buttresses.

Glow-in-the-Dark

There are more interesting fungi in the Wet Tropics than the usual bracket, puff-ball, and toadstool collection that are important recyclers. You can locate the star-burst stinkhorn (top right) by following the bad-breath odor to its source. Elegant coral fungi (below) can be found gracing rotting logs. But the most interesting are the several fungi species that you can spot glowing in the dark (top left). You are only likely to find these during the wet season and by going to the shadiest, wettest microhabitat within the rainforest. It is worth a trip to find what will look like a Milky Way extending from your feet in all directions. Conditions are so perfect for fungi in the Wet Tropics that it is surprising that everything isn't veiled with fuzz or goo. The way this is managed is that the community controls fungi and microorganisms, and also selectively moves these around.

Some rainforest leaves carry small mite shelters called domatia, especially on quandongs (*Eleocarpus* sp.) The mites in these pouches, found at main vein junctions, vacuum fungi off the light-sensitive leaves in exchange for shelter. This has been going on for 40 million years.

in the region with prior Gondwanan connections to cooler lands. A blue crayfish, deserted the same way on this mountain has yet to be named. And you may see the microhylid frog (*Cophixalus neglectus*) on the Bartle Frere Summit and the associated Ballenden Ker Range above 900m/2,943ft, its only habitat. The ecological isolation of these mountain peaks has been long and yet stable enough to retain relicts such as these. Not surprisingly, then, Mt. Bartle Frere is a significant refuge area for these types of "wet" rainforest species. Rainfall is above 10m/392in a year. Botanical treasures only found on these few mountain peaks include an unnamed flowering Proteaceae family species, a giant-leaved *Stenocarpus cryptocarpus*, and an unnamed mountain silky oak (*Orites* sp.) Easier to identify, and scattered in niches of the wider upland rainforest here, you are likely to spot the purple-trunked blue Kauri pine (*Agathis atropurpurea*), red-trunked paperbark satin ash (*Syzygium papyraceaum*) with iridescent purple fruit, and the ivory silky oak (*Hicksbeachia pilosa*) common above Bobbin Bobbin Falls, 50m/55yds north of the Bartle Frere Trail 2km/1.2 mi from the Tableland start. Ivory silky oak has large compound leaves and pink flower streamers that burst from the trunk and twigs.

The strenuous 15km/9mi Bartle Frere Summit Trail to the cloud forest, 1622m/5,304ft at the summit, can be approached from Josephine Falls from the east (from sea level) or the easier western route starting from the Atherton tablelands. Both take about two days. Signposts and orange triangle markers help you find your way through difficult boulder areas. Spectacular views of the tablelands can be seen from a boulder lookout near the trail at the northwest peak, 5km/3mi from the western trailhead, and again across to Bellenden Ker and Mulgrave River by scrambling on top of some more boulders at 6km/3.6mi. Spend time here rather than later on the summit, where the vistas are less stunning. Josephine Falls at the other end is in Wooroonooran National Park and is located by taking the Bruce Highway 71km/44mi south of Cairns and turning west at Pawngilly along the road by the Russell River. There is a registration booth at the trailhead, with three campsites en route. Dense tall rainforest, dwarf rainforest, mossy cloud forest, sedgeland, boulder creeks, and paperbark swamp are some of the habitats experienced across the whole route. Golden bowerbirds have display platforms on the way. Australia's only native rhododendron (*Rhododendron lochae*) is found here, its nearest relatives located in the Himalayas where these two lands were once joined. *Leptospermum wooroonooran* is a dominant yet otherwise rare species forming a low, dense canopy on the peak. Take good raingear, extra food, and water supplies to deal with wet summit weather. More information can be obtained from the Ranger, Josephine Falls Section, Wooroonooran NP, Box 93, Miriwinni, QLD 4871.

Other activities include the 19 km/11.4mi Goldfield Trail walk through the Wet Tropics across a saddle extending between the northern Mt. Bellenden Ker area and Mt. Bartle Frere.

Insects Among the Flowers

The pink dendrobium orchid (above) is similar to (*Dendrobium phalaenopsi*), Queensland's state flower, which grows in isolated spots on the coastal ranges. But if you look among the flowers, you may see more than plants. Some plant-insect relationships are bizarre. The orchid of genus *Cryptostylis* is pollinated by the Ichneuominid wasp (*Lissopimpla excelsa*), which mistakes the flower for a female wasp. This is how you can recognize them both. The wasp pollinates the flower as it tries to mate with it. Invisible leaf insects (*Phyllium siccifolium* and *P. frondosum*) have leaf-like extensions and form "procryptic" species that are hard to spot. But look carefully and you might see one.

This takes about 9 hours one way. There are two camping sites; get permits at Josephine Falls.

Rough maps and guides to all these Wet Tropics trails can be obtained from the Queensland National Parks and Wildlife Service, 1 Moffat Street, Cairns, QLD 4870 07-4053-4533 for Cairns or 07-3227-8185 for the main Brisbane office.

Eubenangee Swamp National Park is near Josephine Falls and is one of the best regional bird-watching sites for waterbirds and rainforest species.

Cape York Peninsula

Cape York Peninsula parks offer intense remoteness and the opportunity for extreme wilderness adventure. These are rewarding ecotravel destinations for those willing to camp and survive in rugged terrain. Only experienced wilderness travelers should consider going. Estuarine crocodiles are found throughout the waterways in this area. Roads are seasonally impassable during the wet season. Yet this is a way to visit a New Guinea habitat and explore its rainforest origins.

The far northern peninsula includes rainforest, heathland, paperbark forest, and open woodland. From here, you also can reach the far northern section of the Great Barrier Reef. The farther north you go along the Queensland coast, the greater the species exchange is with lowland Papua New Guinea. Some of these are bird species, including the palm cockatoos that fly over each year, continuing a connection established when the two regions were connected via the Torres Strait, relatively recently in geological time.

Jardine River National Park

The Heidewald forests in northern Cape York Peninsula Jardine River Basin match those of New Guinea. These forests are intermediate evolutionary remnants of a step toward a drier forest that orignated 30 million years ago. Later steps resulted in the evolution of 500 eucalypt species, which evolved from the Gondwanan family of Myrticae.

This "wet desert" near the tip of the peninsula covers most of the catchment of the Jardine River, which runs year round. Cypress pine rainforest, eucalypt forest, and heathland perch on sandstone ridges above the bogs and swamps of the croc-happy Jardine River. Look for pitcher plants and other plant carnivores. Birds restricted to northern Cape York Peninsula include the yellow-billed kingfisher and the fawn-breasted bowerbird. Get camping permits at the Heathlands Ranger Station, PMB 76, Cairns Mail Centre, QLD 4871 (07-4060-3314, or fax 07-4060-3301 7–11am and 5–10pm fax time). From Coen take the new road to the east of the rougher old Telegraph Line Road to Jardine River, where there is a gas station. The road continues to the tip of Cape York Peninsula and Pajinka Wilderness Lodge north of Bamaga, a specialist destination for birdwatchers looking for New Guinean species. The lodge is run by Aboriginal hosts who offer a variety of guided wilderness exploration options.

Iron Range National Park

Captain William Bligh landed here after the mutiny on the *Bounty* in 1789. The Iron Range is a place where the Kuuku Ya'u Aboriginal peoples lived until the 1920s. It is the largest lowland tropical rainforest in Australia, located in far northern Cape York Peninsula 130km/80.6mi north of the Archer River Roadhouse. Several bird and animal species seen are also found in Papua New Guinea. You may find a quaint possum called the spotted cuscus, plus green python, eclectus parrot, fawn-breasted bowerbird, and red-bellied pitta. Pitcher plants and sundews are found in the heathland in the western area. Gold was mined

Sunbeam Dancers

Birds of paradise are Gondwanan, and benefit from the abundance tropical fruit to the point where males have time to develop complex display rituals. Victoria's riflebird is a bird of paradise common in this and other northeastern areas of Australia, and if you observe it from the right angle during its courtship dance it is a fantastic display bird. Its brilliance cannot be reproduced. It is iridescent black, with metallic lilac, yellow, and gold feathers that glow intensely when they catch sunbeams. In spring and summer the male calls from a tree with a "yaah" call and then performs a rhythmically swaying dance on tree stumps. He fans his glinting wings out in an incredible round-heart shape. Sometimes he will envelop the female in his fanned wings and sway and dance with her in courtship. Several females are included in the alpha male's breeding group.

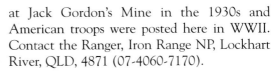

Leeches

Warmth and vibration signal leeches there is a human around. These rainforest creatures drop on you from the trees above or from the tips of vegetation near paths. Harmless and virtually painless, a leech can be removed with a sprinkling of salt. If you pull it off or use a match, it is more likely to exit so hastily that it leaves a gash that bleeds for hours.

The hirudin anticoagulant in leech saliva is a major heart medication used as a prescription medication. Leech teeth (its mouth is at its thinner end) are neat surgical tools: leeches are also used, live, in many Western hospitals for wound care in difficult cases.

at Jack Gordon's Mine in the 1930s and American troops were posted here in WWII. Contact the Ranger, Iron Range NP, Lockhart River, QLD, 4871 (07-4060-7170).

Lakefield National Park

The North Kennedy River basin spreads across the second largest national park in Queensland. A remote wilderness area, it is still popular because it is more accessible than other Cape York Peninsula parks. During the dry season, wildlife clusters at the permanent billabongs left on the vast floodplains. Tropical savanna, gallery rainforest, and sandstone escarpment scrubland are habitats experienced here. A large range of bush campsites are available and should be booked 12 weeks in advance by communicating with the Ranger, Lakefield NP, PMB 29, Cairns Mail Centre, QLD, 4871 (07-4060-3271). If you bring your own, boating is a good way to see wildlife; there are a couple of boat ramps. Take the Peninsula Developmental Road to Laura, 315km/195.3mi north of Cairns, 5–6 hours. Turn north to the New Laura Ranger Base. During the dry season, regular 2WD vehicles can reach Lakefield Homestead and Hann Crossing within the park.

Never touch any heart-shaped leaves in this rainforest. Two varieties of stinging trees (above) inject a toxic bundle of three alkaloids, producing extreme long-lasting pain. Yellow-spotted honeyeaters eat the stinger-free berries, and green ringtail possums eat the leaves, toxins and all.

Central leaves of epiphytic basket fern (*Drynaria rigidula*) are designed to capture

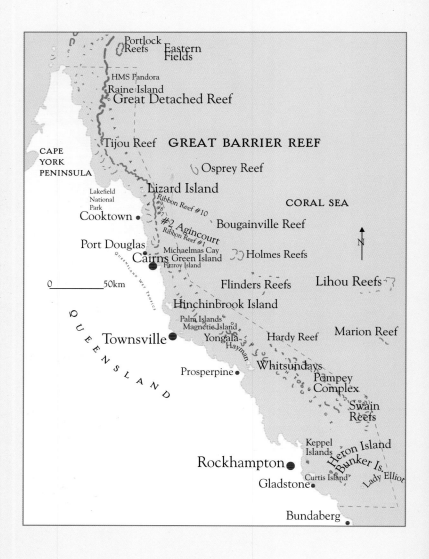

Portlock Reefs
Eastern Fields

HMS Pandora
Raine Island
Great Detached Reef

CAPE YORK PENINSULA

Tijou Reef   GREAT BARRIER REEF

Osprey Reef

Lakefield National Park
Lizard Island

Ribbon Reef #10
#9
#8
#7
Cooktown
Bougainville Reef

#2 Agincourt
Ribbon Reef #1
Port Douglas
Michaelmas Cay
Cairns Green Island
Fitzroy Island
Holmes Reefs

CORAL SEA

0   50km

QUEENSLAND WET TROPICS

Flinders Reefs
Lihou Reefs

Hinchinbrook Island

Palm Islands
Magnetic Island
Yongala
Hayman
Hardy Reef
Marion Reef

QUEENSLAND

Townsville

Prosperpine
Whitsundays
Pompey Complex

Swain Reefs

Keppel Islands
Heron Island
Bunker Is.
Rockhampton
Curtis Island
Lady Elliot
Gladstone

Bundaberg

N

5

The Great Barrier Reef

The Great Barrier Reef

Ecotravelers should not miss the world-class Great Barrier Reef. This exquisite panorama provides the ultimate other-worldly experience. Viewed from a plane, its coral cays look like turquoise frisbees scattered on a crisp blue surface, and ribbon reefs meander like a two-year-old's brown crayon scribbles parallel to 2,000km/1,250mi of coastline. The best destinations are on the outer edge of the reef—the barrier—far from Australia's northeastern coast. This edge of the continental shelf is 40–80km/25–50mi from the mainland yet only an hour-and-a-half by jet-powered catamaran. Edge sites offer superb snorkeling and scuba diving, because deep ocean currents mix with shallow coral waters to provide the greatest variety of life, while being far enough from the mainland to remain genuinely pristine.

The crystal blue waters immerse snorkelers and divers in a brilliant universe of 50-year-old turtles, fish that change sex and color within minutes, and corals pigmented by symbiotic dayglow algae. Nearly all the nutrients are contained in the thin living laminate of coral suspended in a "nutrient desert." Corals thrive in this niche. If you increase the nutrient gradient, coral calcification and growth rates halve, coral fertilization rates plummet up to 90 percent, and the interconnected coral microcosms get choked out by fast-growing algae. Inner reef sites have records of dioxins and the herbicide diuron, plus problems with heavy metals, nitrogen, and phosphorous. But fortunately, the outer reef does not suffer from mainland agricultural runoff or urban effluent, which puts it among the world's most untouched reefs, and likely to remain so. The remote outer northern reef is exceptionally wild. The Great Barrier is particularly special for other reasons, too. Half of the world's reefs are located in the Indo-Pacific center of coral

Butterflyfishes

The beaked coralfish (*Chelmon rostratus*) (left) is a butterflyfish that plucks at coral polyps using its tweezer-tipped snout. It strongly defends its coral patch and is found in pairs near the coralline seabed. This fish and threadfin butterflyfishes have a false "eye" spot near their dorsal fin, which distracts predators from their more vulnerable head. To the delight of snorkelers, many varieties of yellow-patterned butterflyfishes with eye-bands are active during the day in shallower waters. At night and during high stress, butterflyfishes turn black. Black night coloration is also seen in the Moorish idol (*Zanclus cornutus*), an unrelated fish that to the uninitiated looks similar to a longfin bannerfish (*Heniochus acuminatus*) (below). The Moorish idol, though, has a black tail and its eye is in a different location. Longfin bannerfish juveniles clean larger fish for their dinner scraps, and adults eat zooplankton. Bannerfish are related to butterflyfishes and to angelfishes. Angelfishes are differentiated from bannerfish and butterflyfish by a long spine near their gill.

diversity and lineage, including this one. Of these, only Micronesia, northern Papua New Guinea, and the Great Barrier Reef have coral reefs in areas unpopulated enough to be conserved as lasting world treasures. All the rest have signs of overfishing, sedimentation from coastal development, unregulated tourism, subsistence food gathering, and pollution-generating mining practices. Tourism within this area is concentrated in a few locations where there may be some coral damage. But discriminating ecotravellers can move beyond these to the untouched dive sites, where you can celebrate truly isolated beauty.

Symbiosis Trebles Growth

Nowhere is the importance of cooperation as a mechanism for survival and evolution more apparent than on the Great Barrier Reef. Here, five million zooxanthellae algae cram into each square centimeter of coral animal polyp to photosynthesize and exchange sugars in return for protection by the coral's skeleton (see sidebar, page 111). This symbiotic mechanism evolved 150 million years ago, close to this very area. The relationship enabled this reef to grow two to three times the alga-free rate, despite nutrient-poor waters. As ocean waters rose between ice ages, this reef grew fast enough to keep close to the surface and to essential sunlight. It is now the largest living system in the world. The reef has regrown on limestone left from fluctuating sea levels that previously produced reefs across a

Coral Bommies

Coral bommies, or bombies, are isolated domes of coral that rise from the sandy sea bed. They support an enormous diversity of corals, algae, fish, eels, and invertebrates and provide an excellent focus for many dives. Bommie comes from the word "bombora," an Aboriginal name for a submerged reef or group of rocks.

Can't identify all that you see around a bommie? That's not surprising, as many juvenile fish, including the emperor angelfish (*Pomacanthus imperator*), are colored differently from their adult kin. Emperor angelfish young are patterned with pale blue and white concentric ripples. Adults have blue and yellow stripes. Many adults have several color forms, and can change within minutes. There are between 1,500 and 2,000 species of fish on the Great Barrier Reef.

probable timespan of 18 million years at the reef's northern end and 2 million years at the southern. The reef grew in the niche left open by the stromatolites that dominated ocean life until 360 million years ago.

The symbiosis with zooxanthellae is not only shared in corals. Sponges, sea squirts, giant clams, and bryozoans all share cell space with bacteria and algae, exchanging essential food compounds and bizarre by-products. The bryozoan (*Bugula neritina*), which creates mossy mats under boats, has symbiotic bacteria that have been found to produce a pharmacologically active compound now being used in the experimental drug Bryostatin. It makes chemotherapy drugs, including Taxol and Cisplatin, much more effective by interfering with the DNA of cancer cells.

These complex compounds and the nematocyst stinging cells produced by corals make life difficult for divers. Even ordinary coral cuts may be difficult to heal and keep uninfected. The sharp coral skeletons can inject these compounds into the skin with the slightest graze. So, scrub coral abrasions in pure warm water and dress carefully.

Plate Coral

Seasons to Visit

Reef-lovers will not want to miss the annual coral spawning event around the full moon in November or early December.

Green turtle, hawksbill turtle, and loggerhead turtle court at times ranging from August to November in bays and estuaries, or in coral lagoons. Females then swim to nesting beaches, and eggs are laid about fourteen days after her arrival. In southern rookeries they lay eggs October through February. Female green turtles lay about four to six clutches every two weeks.

Snorkel near dwarf minke whales around the Ribbon Reefs of North Reef between March and October, particularly in June and July. Watch humpback whales pass the Whitsundays, North Stradbroke Island, and Hervey Bay in September.

The cyclone season from January to March can be an unpredictable time for a visit, though the corals are just as fascinating, and bad weather is interspersed with perfect weather and calm seas.

Where to Find Reef Highlights

Mainland ports provide access to five regions of reef. The north has a profusion of pristine coral reefs but these can be difficult to reach. The south has a greater number of resorts designed for reef and vacation activities, but the water can be rougher and with lower visibility. Although coral diversity generally increases as you go north, the types and variety of coral reef systems change more dramatically as you go west to east from the coast. Coral bleaching is more common nearest the mainland due to freshwater river runoff, which increases bleaching effects when waters are too warm. Most reefs preferred by divers have not suffered from much bleaching, or recover quickly, which

Coral Symbiosis

Coral growing in shallow seas resists excess ultraviolet by using its own sunscreen. This was discovered when reef corals were found to glow. Special pigments in the coral's zooxanthellae were converting UV-light to unharmful light of a different color. Zooxanthellae, brown algae of various colors, cram into the coral animal polyps. The algae give the coral polyps UV-protecting color, oxygen, and 95% of the sugars they produce. They do this in exchange for a calcium carbonate skeleton protection, useful nitrogen and phosphate waste products from prey captured by coral stingers, and carbon dioxide. The coral does not have to wait for the sugars: special enzymes make the algae "leak" nutrients.

Coral also produces acetate waste, which is transformed into waxes by the zooxanthellae. These return to the coral and are packed into coral eggs, providing a packet of compact energy for the coral larva's colonization journey. When bleaching occurs, although corals may survive, the viability of spawn may be affected by damping the production of these important secondary metabolites.

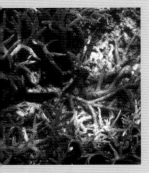

Coral Quirks

The annual growth-rings in boulder coral layers of living porites colonies on the Great Barrier Reef have been dated back to 1479, though individual polyps only live for six years. X-ray and fluorescent band studies of these seasonal rings are being used to estimate the tropical sea surface temperatures and rainfall of the past. These rings show that growth peaked during 1769–98 and 1940–60, indicating higher temperatures that stimulated faster growth. Since 1745 there have been cyclic temperature fluctuations about every 14 years, including twelve major temperature swings. Porites are one of three types of reef-building corals, amounting to 350 species here that have branching, plate, and boulder forms.

Branched or staghorn coral is created by coral polyps budding into branches. *Acropora pulchre* is one of many species that has pointed staghorns. The second coral form includes boulder, brain, and stone corals that are created by polyps splitting into two over and over again, expanding exponentially. *Acropora sarmentosa* is an abundant true stony coral with short branches stumpier than staghorns. *Acropora surculosa* is a tabular form of true stony coral colony. So, one genus can give rise to several different coral forms. The current and sun intensity also determine coral shape variation. Most coral polyps only come out at night, so a night dive can reveal wonderful colors invisible to daytime divers.

Massive coral (Porites lutea) (above and top left) form smooth-surfaced boulder-like communities. Acropora coral species take various forms, including spiky staghorn coral (second from top) in white, purple, brown, yellow, and orange, knobbier finger coral (third from top) and plate coral (bottom) with thin, flat veneers. Many other species look very similar, such as needle coral (Seriatopora hystrix) with pink pointed staghorns.

The reef surfaces are cemented together by another form of coral: encrusting corals. These take the shape of rocks onto which they laminate themselves, and can have prominent polyps arrayed in honeycomb patterns. Many corals that appear to have soft forms are actually hard corals. They puff out beautiful shapes but have a large hard skeleton underneath. These include hammer, daisy, bubble, and fleshy corals (right).

In addition to the reef-builders, solitary corals are actually a huge single polyp, sometimes with many tentacles. Examples include mushroom coral (*Fungia fungites*), which can move so fast it can free itself from a layer of sand in 5 hours, and solitary coral (*Fungia actiniformis*).

Non-reef building corals include several beautiful species of red, blue, and black corals, which are from a different coral group than hard corals. They have beautiful fine branches and live in strong currents as filer-feeders. They should not be handled. The colored skeleton of red coral is masked by its living tissue, and is used for jewelry.

Exquisitely-ornate soft corals such as alcyonarians are the most recently evolved coral type and are common here. They even dominate the reef in some areas, including Agincourt. The tentacles are multiples of eight, unlike hard corals. Gorgonian sea fans and sea whips are varieties of soft corals with fan-shaped horny skeletons that grow far into the current to sieve food particles.

The earliest corals to evolve were the stinging corals, such as hydroids (right), delicate, hairy corals with a merciless sting.

Some anemone-relatives are easy to confuse with soft corals. Mushroom anemones or corallimorpharians, (*Discosoma* sp.) (below), are false corals related to anemones. They may have a flat disk or tentacles. Button polyps (*Zoanthus* sp.) have collections of fleshy umbrellas coming from the main base and are also related to anemones. Anemones can be difficult to identify: sea cucumbers of the beach ball type sometimes hide their bodies in the sand, their protruding tentacles looking like sea anemones.

Waving hand coral (Xenia *sp.*)

Stinging coral

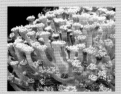
Daisy coral (Goniopora *sp.*)

Hammer coral (Euphyllia *sp.*)

Bubble coral (Plerogyra *sp.*)

Meandroid brain coral

Coralimorpharian (Discosoma *sp.*)

Fleshy coral (Acantha *sp.*)

Giant Clams

Don't miss giant clams (above, among soft coral, by Lizard Island), burrowing clams (*Tridacna* sp.), and horseshoe clams (*Hippopus* sp.) The fantastic colors seen in giant clam flesh are made more brilliant in three ways: zooxanthellae produce some of the color, iridescent Tyndall effects from within the clam's own mantle create intense blue and green spots, and hyaline organs maximize the tissue color and translucency. Unlike corals, giant clams eat their zooxanthellae by vacuuming these algae from their tissues through their bloodstream into their gut. Giant clams are not found south of the Pompey Complex.

is an advantage of the Great Barrier Reef compared with others reefs. To reach the outer reef, you will need a boat or a reef island from which to dive. Do not attempt to swim the few segments of coastal reef close to the mainland, due to the danger of estuarine crocodiles and box jellies: the jellies spawn large numbers in the estuaries and are very toxic.

From Port Douglas

The reefs accessible from the tiny resort town of Port Douglas include some of the best diving sites with the most intense variety. There are dense outer reefs closer to the mainland in this section, because the continental shelf is narrower from Cairns to Cooktown.

Ribbon, No Name, and Yonge Reefs

Distant outer Ribbon Reefs to the north offer true wilderness diving. These reefs drop off into the Queensland Trough on their eastern side, which deepens as you travel north. This abyss is so deep that scuba divers can't reach the bottom. The outer ribbon that dots along the edge of the continental shelf from Cape

Tribulation all the way north to Torres Strait is so significant that the ribbon can be seen from outer space. Several dive-boat companies offer single and multi-day expeditions to the Ribbon Reefs (see page 144). The coral cay Green Island near Cairns and the rocky remote Lizard Island both have resorts from which to dive in the mid-shelf section, halfway between the mainland and the outer reef. These resorts offer additional expeditions to the Ribbon Reefs on the outer shelf, which ecotravellers should consider as their primary dive destinations.

The Ribbon Reefs are fascinating because of the crystal clear waters that well up from the depths, creating a highly diverse "edge" ecosystem. Huge numbers of fish gather at the edge of these reefs during spawning season, attracting predators. Dwarf minke whales are found here in June and July. There are several dive points. Cod Hole is one of the better-known, accessible from the mainland or Lizard Island. It is located at Cormorant Pass, a gap in the outer coral reef through which the outer ocean can flow in and out of the reef. The coral is not particularly good at Cod Hole, because of strong currents, but it offers close proximity to thirty 135-kg/300-lb potato cod, plus giant Maori wrasses, coral trout, and red bass species. Unfortunately, fish feeding has caused disease and changed behavior. The unnaturally trained moray eels were removed after they severely injured a dive leader who habitually fed them. Pixie Pinnacle, Giant Clam Beds, and Manta Ray Point are other Ribbon Reef dive sites visited by multiple-day dive boats.

No Name Reef is an outer reef site with some interesting gullies as it drops off to a depth of 20m/65ft. Because it borders the Coral Sea on the outer shelf there is more hard coral here than many dive sites inside the reef lagoon (60 percent and more). Coral bleaching and crown-of-thorns starfish have not been a problem to date. Fascinating plate corals dominate the scene, among staghorn and boulder corals.

Echinos

Common blue sea stars (*Linckia laevigata*) (above) glow with a natural UV-sun-screen in shallow waters. Echinoderms evolved animal's first locomotion. They have pentaradiate symmetry including pincushion starfish, sea urchins, brittle stars, sea cucumbers, and primitive many-branched feather stars or crinoids.

The abundant Black Sea urchin (*Diadema*) and its relatives have light-sensitive skin and can rotate their needles toward any lurking threat. Slow-motion film show that they can "dance" and move very strategically toward their prey. The flower urchin (*Toxopneustes pileolus*) has highly toxic pedicellariae, or pincers, between spines. Crinoid ancestors dominated the oceans 300 million years ago.

Coral Bonds

"The bricks of a reef are laid by the corals, but the cement which binds the bricks into a homogenous rampart comes from a very different source," said C. M. Yonge in 1930.

Coralline algae create up to 80% of the sand that fills reef gaps and dominate exposed reefs. Here, sand is made of calcium carbonate, not silicon dioxide.

Lithothamnion is a form of coralline algae or nullipore that is very primitive. It creates nodular or short encrusting branches of pink- or mauve-colored calcium carbonate. Their cementing and binding action holds together exposed living and dead coral polyps with sand. The red encrusting algae *Paragoniolithon* and *Porolithon* form purple surfaces that are the signatures of the Great Barrier Reef.

Foraminifera or forams produce round and flat usually-microscopic calcareous disks, stars, and spindles that create ready-made sand particles for coral isles. These include the larger *Marginopora,* which have disks that are used for necklaces.

Halimeda, a green seaweed, secretes calcium carbonate that is as fine as that of forams and as cement-like.

Pomacentrus damselfish, fusiliers, parrotfish, surgeonfish, and sharks are commonly seen.

For the same reasons as No Name Reef, Yonge Reef is also fascinating and offers another way to look at high coral levels and fish variety. Both reefs share many of the same forms and species, with more snappers at Yonge.

Agincourt Reef

Agincourt Reef is a major site on the best side of the Great Barrier Reef. A shallow, huge outer-shelf coral reef, it provides scattered sites for several pontoons used by snorkelers and divers. Glass-bottom boats, reef "submarines," and other reef-viewing alternatives are available. This reef can be accessed quickly by day-trip jet catamarans from Port Douglas and Cairns. Agincourt dive boats offer the opportunity to rent high-quality underwater macro camera equipment with flash, but reserve in advance.

This is the place to see the beautiful forms of tabular *Acropora* coral that dominate the scene. These stand among staghorn *Acropora* species and plenty of soft coral. Brain and boulder coral dot the scene, and gorgonians can be found on one flank of the reef. Overall, hard

Acropora species in various forms.

This Blue Lagoon beach, Lizard Island, consumes as much carbon dioxide as a tropical rainforest canopy. These beaches are alive with so many photosynthetic microorganisms that they form a "carbon sink." A recent discovery has shown that the algae and bacteria in the sand create cements that stick sand particles together with complex sugar-based glues. These adhesives are made by trapping carbon dioxide and releasing enormous levels of oxygen.

coral coverage is high, about 35 percent, so there is plenty to see, and little, if any, of the coral has been bleached so far. Crown-of-thorns have not yet appeared in surveys. Look for commensal shrimp in anemones and mushroom corals. Colorful parrotfish chomp on the coral, which is lit up by fast-moving shoals of fairy basslets, surgeonfish, fusiliers, barracuda, sweetlips, and yellow-striped snapper. Around the sand and rocks, sea cucumbers and moray eels lurk, and giant clams glow blue and violet on the sandy bottom.

Agincourt Reefs have many visitors, and so the 1.5-hour voyage out or back may be more like being on a car ferry than a remote diving expedition. And the moored pontoons tend to be above damaged coral, even though dive instructors teach no-touch diving. So, dive a bit away from the immediate options and crowds, or book a side-trip. Agincourt is still an excellent high-quality choice if you do not have many days to visit the reef. It is worth adding the private marine biologist selection to the price of the jet-catamaran trip. If you do, you can take a small boat and go off with a few

Damselfishes that Flash Colors

Damselfishes sprinkle color all around reefs. Blue-green chromis (*Chromis viridis*) uses colored iridocyte cells to create blue color, plus diffraction gratings on the surface of its scales to split light wavelengths holographically into bright blues and greens. As a result, they look different colors from different directions. But not all damselfishes are strikingly colorful. Yellow-tail demoiselle (*Neopomacentrus azysron*), very common here, is a bland-looking brown damsel with blue spots and a yellowish tail. The more striking damsels include the successful all-blue Australian damsel (*Pomacentrus australis*), *P. lepidogenys*, *P. wardi*, and neon damsel (*P. coelestris*). The neon damsel (locally called blue damsel) has a blue body and variable yellow tail (above right) and is found over rubbly areas. These can turn their iridescent neon blue glow on and off at will. They are extremely territorial, fighting off intruders and raising their blue dorsal fin when aggravated. White-belly damselfish (*Ambly-glyphidodon leucogaster*) is common, and staghorn damselfish (*Ambly-glyphidodon curacao*) are found above branching corals. Dick's demoiselle (*Plectroglyphidodon dickii*) is a very pretty fish with orange and mauve spots. It is territorial above its *Acropora* coral home.

enthusiasts to a secluded location once you arrive. This way, you may experience the peace of swimming in mirror-calm waters that extend horizon to horizon above a thin laminate of untouched, profuse life, which changes form and color every time you make a stroke.

Snake Pit and More

Other reefs often visited from Port Douglas for day-trip diving and snorkeling include mid-shelf Batt and Tongue Reefs, Turtle Bay, Snake Pit (yes—it's a hole where sea snakes gather), and Low Islets, which offers a reef, cay, lagoon, and low-tide reef flat for fossickers very close to Port Douglas.

At Osprey Reef at the North Horn, research is going on into the lives of the prehistoric shelled Nautilus octopus, grey reef sharks, and silvertip reef sharks. Ecotravellers can participate. Marine biologists are looking at individual sharks that have been identified. Hammerhead schools are also found here in the winter. Octopuses are the most intelligent mollusk, and their problem-solving abilities can rival vertebrates.

North and South Opal Reefs are excellent boat-accessed dive sites with fantastic hard and soft corals and giant clams. On the north inshore side, dugong graze on the profuse seagrass beds. These are also frequented by estuarine crocodiles, so take care not to put yourself in danger.

Lizard Island

Lizard Island, or Jiigurru, is a very small rocky island in the northern section of mid-shelf reef accessed by light plane from Cairns. It is prized by researchers because it is the only island stopping-off point to the far northern reef and itself offers nearby pristine, thriving, and crystal-clear coral and fish life that is typical of the more varied northern region. The island so far, however, offers only the extremes of ecotraveller accommodation: a rather overpriced resort, or a bunk house for anyone enrolled in field trips at the Australian Museum Research Station. Or a minimalist campsite by a mangrove swamp and beach. Nothing in between. Four new tourism accommodation sites are planned for the island, in response to the demands of ecotravellers to open up the northern region of the reef to easier and better access.

Captain Cook named the island for the 1–2 meter-long Goulds sand monitor (*Varanus gouldii*). These can be seen poking around the dry vegetation or standing tall on two legs looking for giant insects that sun themselves on the rocks and sand. The island's appearance is scruffy and arid.

The Lizard Island Resort is located on a private bay to the southwest and is known for black marlin fishing. These huge game fish with dragon-like dorsal fins are so expressive they appear to have been invented by Disney animators. In addition to fishing and diving from boats, there is colorful snorkeling over

Reef Sharks

Sharks use electromagnetic fields to sense prey, have light-gathering adaptations within their eyes to perceive dim regions, are highly sensitive to thrashing vibrations, and yet are cautious predators. Their aerodynamic shape has survived almost unchanged for the last 100 million years. Most sharks are pelagic (roaming the open sea) and are not reef-specific, but three common shark species are associated with corals: black-tip reef shark (*Carcharhinus melanopterus*) (below), white-tip reef shark (*Triaenodon apicalis*), and epaulette shark (*Hemiscyllium ocellatum*). The reef sharks are nocturnal feeders that are sluggish during the day, sleeping in grottoes and lagoons. These reef sharks are much less dangerous than the most lethal great white shark that is extremely rare in the area near open waters and drop-offs. Divers are eight times as likely to die from a scuba diving accident as from a shark attack, and ten times as likely as from a croc attack. However, sharks are learning to expect bait food from humans. This is occurring at shark-feeding dive sites southeast and outside of the Reef, and this may create very dangerous learned "feeding frenzy" behavior that these sharks bring with them when they migrate hundreds of miles away.

Commensal Relationships

Cooperative dependencies exist between different kingdoms and species. The long-spined sea urchin has a close association with commensal siphamia fish and pairs of stegopontonia shrimp. Seven anemonefish species hide among anemone stingers. The fish are covered in a special type of mucus that prevents the stinging cells from being triggered. As a result, the anemone protects them from less-adapted predators. It has recently been found that the anemonefish returns the favor: anemones denuded of their resident anemonefish are quickly eaten by predators. Clark's anemonefish (*Amphiprion clarkii*) is rare here but you may see it in lagoons and reefs on a variety of anemones. It is black and white with a variable amount of orange or yellow. Sooty orange dusky anemonefish (*Amphiprion melanopus*) with a white priest-like neck band is common and prefers *Entacmaea* anemones. In the Coral Sea it may have no white band. Barrier Reef anemonefish (*Amphiprion akindynos*) (above right) is associated with 45 species of anemones and is common. Anemonefish can change sex to balance out need. When the alpha-female dies, the next male-in-line becomes female, and the largest immature fish becomes male.

giant clams a few steps from resort guests' rooms. The architecture of the cabin-style resort is plain vanilla and the experience may not be as luxurious as other resorts in the same price range, but the diving opportunities from the island and by resort boat are fantastic.

The small campsite with pit toilet is located at one end of a pretty sandy beach (the resort is at the other end). Reach it from the airstrip by climbing up a tiny footpath, Chinaman's Walk, over a rocky hill and across a mangrove swamp inhabited by a colony of squealing fruit-bats (about 45 minutes with gear). The campsite is usually quiet because of the cost of plane access, and the resort is closed to camping guests. Some research, cruise, and dive trips for the northern and far northern reef use a bay on Lizard Island as their access or stopping-off point, although there are no piers. Once on the island there are no opportunities to join dive boats unless you are with the resort or have made private arrangements beforehand.

The research station, run by the Australian Museum, is located on the exquisite Blue Lagoon on the eastern side. In the Blue Lagoon and on its reef edges you can see giant clams, rays, and soft and hard corals with no apparent coral bleaching. The island's hard coral cover is relatively low compared with nearby Ribbon Reefs, but soft corals abound. Surgeonfish, sharks, parrotfish, coral trout, and sweetlip are found but also at low levels. Crown-of-thorns are occasionally seen, but were not affecting coral levels at the time of writing. One flank of the island offers interesting dive features including bommies, overhangs, gullies, and swim-throughs. The Clam Gardens is known for one of the densest collections of these gorgeous bivalves that can live to 50 years old. Their incredible blues, greens, and other hues come from zooxanthellae, controlled by the giant clam, which can grow to 5 feet across. These alone are worth the visit if you like exquisite pigments. Watson's Bay offers more island reef diving beyond the sandy beach. This is below Captain Cook's Look, reached by a steep walk to where the navigator searched for a way through the reef in 1788.

Lizard is located near the major dive sites of Cormorant Pass and Cod Hole. Vik's Reef, Palfrey Hole, and the Ghost Beach on Palfrey Island and other fantastic dive sites are accessible from the island by boat.

One of the most exquisite and thrilling animals to encounter when diving anywhere on the reef is a comb jelly. I saw it making its own light show near Lizard Island. The brainless predator is not much more than an open, transparent cube, yet it pulsates with brilliant rainbow flashes along its fiber-optic edges. It should not be confused with a dangerous box jellyfish that may look similar: there are no hanging stinging tentacles in the surface species of comb jelly and it is not toxic to humans. It's so delicate that it is almost inconceivable that this illuminated animal exists near the wave surface, let alone captures prey in its bell. Its fragility is one reason why not much is known about it, and it is only now being studied by marine biologists and major aquariums. Research subs are discovering them in the deepest marine trenches, some glowing red, others with long trailing nets of up to 36m/120ft long that trail to catch copepods.

The way the comb jelly twinkles is what is fascinating. It diffracts sunlight into rainbow colors using fluttering prisms along its edges. These prisms are flagellae or whip-like cell

Rock Dwellers

Australia has no true lobsters, but its temperate-water crayfish can weigh up to 7.7kg/17lbs. In the Great Barrier Reef, several crayfish species from the Palinuridae and Scyllaridae families can be found lurking among the rocks. Scyllarids have no claws, and Palinurids have claws but their pincers are all more-or-less the same size, unlike in true lobsters. The Moreton Bay bug (*Thenus orientalis*) is a crayfish delicacy found in Queensland waters. Moray eels are generally not harmful to divers unless habitually hand-fed, when they can attack viciously without provocation. Honeycomb moray (*Gymnothorax favigineus*) (below) is found in holes on outer reef slopes, eats fish and can grow to almost 2m/6ft6in in length. The smaller snowflake moray (*Echidna nebulosa*) eats shrimp and other crustaceans at night, and lives among rock and coral-strewn seabeds.

Venomous Stickers Can Heal

The firefish or cobrafish (*Pteriois volitans*) (above right) avoids divers, but lurks in coral holes. When threatened, it flicks its spines forward, injecting venom. Very hot water can help ease the pain. This treatment is also useful for stingray barbs and scorpionfish (above left). Many reef cone shells are prized by shell-collectors. But do not pick them up. The nocturnal geographer cone (*Conus geographus*) harpoons fish with a venomous barb reaching inches from the shell. A quarter of the stings in humans have been fatal. Yet this venom is being used as a new painkiller. The brand-new drug Prialt contains ziconotide extracted from geographer cone venom, a major pain treatment that is 50 times more potent than morphine. It blocks pain messages at the spinal cord without interfering with the brain, so has no opiate side-effects. Sea snakes rarely release their very toxic venom during defensive bites. They may wrap themselves around a diver's leg in an attempt at mating: keep cool! The blue-ringed octopus is small and lethal. Don't collect empty shells or bottles from the beach in case they contain this little killer.

extensions that are probably ancestors of spirochete bacteria. Evolutionary biologist Lynn Margolis proposes that these bacteria probably cohabited with other cells early on in their evolution to create a symbiotic union that survived as a new species. She feels that this was so successful that all animal and plant cells have traces of spirochetes.

Specifically, the spirochete-flagellae may have eventually turned into the neurological fibers of our eye retina, brain, and nerves in the case of most higher animals, sparkling flagellae in comb jellies, and centrosomes used by all cells during cell division. One piece of evidence for this is that our neurological tissue has the same types of rare compounds found in free-living spirochetes. So, due to evolutionary lineage emanating from the same source, the scintillating whips that may catch your eye in a comb jelly may also have origins that enable you to see the comb jelly's beauty with your own eyes.

In another twist, comb jellies have been found to be bioluminescent, not just collections of prisms lit up by sunlight. In the darkest depths or at night, they can light up when they want to. How they determine when to switch on without a brain is unclear, but jellyfish have now been found to have light-sensitive organs spaced around their transparent bodies. This bioluminescence has recently been found to be exhibited by the vast majority of deep-sea life, not just a few animals as previously thought. Some deep ocean animals squirt out bioluminescent fluid to distract predators with a pyrotechnic display, others concentrate luminescence in a lure, as in the anglerfish, to catch inquisitive prey. The process of making "cold light" is an enzymatic one using up oxygen and energy. This was thought to be an early evolutionary answer that organisms came up with to try to stabilize and reduce the excess oxygen being produced by the stromatolite cyanobacteria reefs. At that time, oxygen was toxic. It took millions of years before organisms evolved to use oxygen to release energy in a valuable way to the organism, using mito-chondria, another bacterial hitchhiker that proved beneficial.

Torres Strait and Far Northern Great Barrier Reef

Torres Strait and the Far Northern Great Barrier Reef have top rating for pristine wilderness and diversity. Warrior reefs form wide mud flats edged to the east by coral, and there are deltaic and dissected reefs that protect a series of fascinating inner islands and cays. Many of

Upside-Down Swimmers

Razorfish (*Aeoliscus stigatus*) hide vetically among sea urchin spines, particularly the needle-spined sea urchin (*Diadema setosum*) which is a common urchin with long thin black spines. The razorfish is related to pipefish and has armor plates instead of scales over its body. They swim upside down even when not among the protective spines.

Bluespine unicornfish Naso unicornis *browses on brown algae, often in relatively shallow water.*

Jelly Bellies

Box jellyfish (*Chironex fleckeri*), *Chiropsalmus quadrigatus*, and tiny irukandji (*Carukia barnesi*) are more deadly than sharks on this coast. Box jellies start as little polyps on rocks near estuaries where the eggs were laid. They grow into tiny jellyfish (non-toxic moon jelly juvenile below) with eyes on the bell. When they migrate down rivers in spring, they cause havoc for swimmers because of their invisibility and toxicity of their 50 tentacles. Use vinegar to neutralize the venom and remove the stingers with tweezers, but only if there is a positive ID. Another dangerous jelly's stingers, the Portuguese man o'war (*Physalia* sp.), is activated by vinegar. There are three Physalia jellies found in these waters: small local bluebottles, Portuguese man o'war, and Pacific man o'war. The local species has a single tentacle as opposed to two in the Man o'wars, but otherwise all look similar. Small stinging bluebottle jellies cluster along the coast and get through swim nets: swim instead on the outer reef to avoid them.

these reefs are impenetrable or challenging to navigate. In fact, Torres Strait diving is not for the fainthearted or even the regular ecotraveller: this is extreme wilderness travel.

The outer barrier reefs in this region are crammed with more life than you can find in the southern reef. Closer to shore are a series of inner shelf reefs, coral cays, and high islands that are ready for exploration without any damage from agricultural runoff seen in other areas.

Raine Island is located on the distant outer reef 200 km/120mi southeast of the tip of Cape York Peninsula. The island has the largest green turtle rookery in the world and is a major nesting site for many seabirds. Access is restricted by the Raine Island Corporation.

Next to Raine Island is the extensive Great Detached Reef, which lies at the edge of the shelf and is a fascinating dive destination visited by several dive companies.

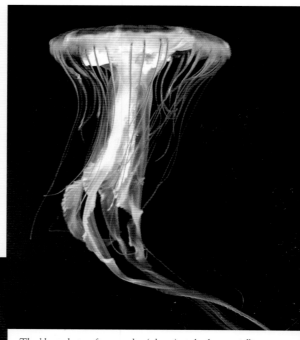

The blunt shape of sea nettles (above) and other sea jellies are not designed to move through the water. Their pulsating movement has recently been found to be a way of circulating currents into the bell's tentacles to capture more food.

Mr. Walker's Caves in Tijou Reef, discovered in 1995, is an incredible dive site, though large numbers of aggressive breeding sharks can occur at Tijou in late November. Tijou Reef is about half way between Lizard Island and the tip of Cape York Peninsula.

Australia has 166 species of sharks, divided into bottom-dwelling sharks and mid-water sharks. Bull sharks and bronze whalers are the most dangerous to humans, as they swim far upriver. Chemical repellents have been tested and so far have not worked, but there are promising developments. The sea cucumber (*Actinopyga agassizi*) releases holothurin, which interferes with shark's scent receptors and can even kill a shark at a very weak concentration.

Sharks have an intense sense of smell. Grouper flesh diluted to 10 parts per billion can be detected by a blacktip reef shark (*Carcharhinus melanopterus*), the most common shark seen around the reef. This is equivalent to telling the difference between an Olympic-sized swimming-pool before and after adding a grain of salt. This reef shark, though not usually dangerous, gets into a feeding frenzy near prey, making it at times unpredictably aggressive toward divers, particularly when spearfish. This shark also snaps at paddlers' legs near beaches. After sharks follow the scent and move close to their prey, they use their sense of electric potential to detect what is going on. Smooth dogfish can sense 5-billionths of a volt over a centimeter, and it has been thought that swimmers' electronic heart pulses and metal boats' electromagnetic frequencies may attract sharks. Sharks also use this sense to navigate using the earth's electromagnetic frequencies. Without them, sharks are directionless. Pregnant female sharks counteract their carnivorous behavior at birth by stopping feeding altogether to protect their young. In the reef, most species give birth to live pups between November and January. Blacktip reef shark females migrate to coastal seagrass areas

Mollusks Who Steal

Thieves or recyclers? The sighting of a nudibranch and its rippling flesh, or cerata, can be fascinatingly beautiful, but most people are not aware that these are incredible thieves. Nudibranchs steal the stinging nematocysts from the sea anemones and corals that they eat, recycling them intact in a state of suspended animation. They move these to their finger-like cerata through gullies connected to their digestive system. Cells in the cerata re-orient the nematocyst ready to be released at a predator, and fire them when threatened. Reef nudibranchs include Spanish dancer and Angas' sea hare. They can be seen all over the reef.

Beautiful cowries, volutes, cones, mitres, strombs, and *Murex* mollusks can be found on the reef, particularly at night. There are 4,000 reef mollusk species, many of which feed off zooplankton including the larvae of coral, crab, shellfish, and fish. Others harpoon fish and mollusks with poison darts capable of blasting a hold in a periwinkle shell. These harpooning species can be lethal to humans.

Sponge Bioprospecting

Sponges are making headlines despite their lack of glamor. Sponges are not colonies of single cells, but multicelled animals made of two cellular layers that sandwich a gel. They have no tissues or organs. Many soft sponge cells contain symbiotic cyanobacteria and a few contain red algae. Being sedentary, one way they get to survive is by exuding toxins to keep their neighbors at bay. These are getting pharmaceutical companies excited. The Queensland Pharmaceutical Research Institute launched a major bioprospecting effort targeting reef sponges and rainforest plants. Johnson & Johnson, Novartis, and Aventis are drug companies funding similar research. Estimates of the number of sponge species that live in Australian waters has been tripled during the last ten years to at least 5,000. Australian sponge families may total up to one third of the world's total of 15,000.

See squirts (above) look like sponges but are primitive relatives of vertebrates.

Coral Bleaching and the Toxic Genome

Coral bleaching is associated in many divers' minds with global warming. From that conclusion, the recent bleaching of the coral on the outer Great Barrier Reef seems to be the hair-trigger indicator telling us that global warming is seriously out of hand. But new research into global warming and into coral bleaching has not confirmed the connection. Instead, the situation is both more complicated and less extreme than news headlines may suggest. Coral on the outer reef is pristine and healthy. Official reports to date indicate that the greatest threats to the reef are not warm water temperatures, but pollution, cyclones, and fertilization from agricultural nutrients and run-off. "Summertime bleaching of corals is a regular occurrence on the reef," said Dr. Terry Done, Australian Institute of Marine Science's Principle Research Scientist, "but does not usually kill too many corals." This is because coral normally lives close to the temperature at which bleaching starts to occur. This is also the temperature at which it grows fastest, 77–84°F/25–29°C. Red Sea corals have adapted to higher summer temperatures than on the reef. Global warming is not currently listed as one of the major threats to the reef by the authorities.

To look a little closer at coral bleaching, take a dive into the world of coral symbionts. We take it for granted, especially with the news of discoveries of the human genome, that there is only one source of DNA in each organism. But coral has five genomes at work in its cells. We have two: one in our cell nucleus from both parents, another in our energy-releasing mitochondria, inherited from our mothers. It is by tuning up these mitochondria that we can develop into good athletes. Each of a cell's added genomes come from genetic hitchhikers that successfully collaborated to create a new organism. In coral, these hitchhikers float around the coral animal polyp's cells in the form of photosynthetic zooxanthellae plant occupants. One of these species found in the Reef is *Symbiodinium microadriaticum*. Coral makes sure the algae does not keep their food to themselves by releasing an enzyme that makes the algae ooze nutrients. When coral is surrounded by hotter-than-average water, the source of one of these genomes, the zooxanthellae, becomes toxic. This happens when one stage of photosynthesis in the algae is blocked by temperatures above 30°C, building up destructive types of oxygen compounds. Under these conditions, the zooxanthellae genome leaves or is expelled from the coral, taking its color with it. This results in coral bleaching, when the coral's white bone skeleton can be seen through its transparent body tissue. Bleached coral is not necessarily dead, but waits out the warm conditions, semi-shut-down. Bleached coral can still capture prey using miniature harpoons and live like other animals do on protein food rather than on sunlight. When waters cool again, the few remaining zooxanthellae re-colonize the surviving coral. Symbiosis, growth, and color resume.

In 1988 and 1998, water temperatures increased 2–3°C/3.6–5.4°F above normal sea surface temperatures during December-February, causing a severe bleaching event in much of the reef. The cycle corresponded to the expected decadal weather pattern affecting the reef, caused by the El Nino Southerly Oscillation (ENSO). This severe coral bleaching occurred worldwide.

Within a year of the 1998 bleaching, the majority of reefs here had rapidly regained coral and associated fish species, with the outer reefs bouncing back with up to 75 percent hard coral coverage, well above average for a healthy reef. Reefs in other areas of the world were not so resilient, with the effects of warmer waters possibly compounded by pollution and other destructive factors. The most affected Reef areas were the inner reefs around Cairns and Townsville, which showed ongoing declines a year after the bleaching. Inner reefs were inundated by cyclonic and estuarine floodwaters, lowering the salinity levels and stressing the corals, predisposing them to bleaching during warmer conditions. High UV-levels are directly associated with coral bleaching, and are found in shallower coastal reefs. Most discriminating divers avoid these inner reefs.

Slashers

You can find palette surgeonfish (*Paracanthurus hepatus*) (below) in schools in areas with a lot of plankton and strong currents. Surgeonfish are a major reef fish. They defend themselves by slashing with a short scythe-like spine that flips out at right angles from the base of their tail. This spine's location is usually highlighted with color, in this case, just inside the yellow apex of the palette surgeonfish's triangle. Nocturnal fish, including red squirrelfish (*Adioryx ruber*), soldierfish, and deep water predators such as coral trout, are often red with very large eyes. You can find striped soldierfish dozing under overhangs and in caves during day. Red wavelengths are absorbed by water below a couple of meters and by low light, and so become merely an absence of color in deep or dark waters—an excellent camouflage.

Coral Spawning

When there is a full moon in November or early December, the entire reef spawns at once, taking a few days from start to finish. This synchronized event is one example of the hidden connection between all living systems on earth. In this case, the linkage spans over 1,000 miles of scattered reefs. The primary unifying factor is the condition of light (full moon), when tides are highest and temperatures are beginning to warm up. Several other factors act as initiatory windows. Once initiated, the ocean glows with a soup of billions of red and yellow rapidly-fertilized eggs, too many for any predator to swallow. These eggs turn into transparent polyps within a couple of days, looking like microscopic jellyfish. The polyps generally move with the current before anchoring once and for all on their next reef home.

*Orange cup coral (*Tubastrea faulkneri*) is common in caves, on flat walls, and under overhangs.*

and away from predators. Whitetip reef shark females select shallow coral lagoons as nurseries. As soon as they give birth, they mate again, forming rarely seen, but huge aggregations of tens of thousands of sharks, with the male sharks biting females aggressively.

From Cairns

Cairns is within the tropics and is a back-packing gateway city to the rainforest and close-by reef.

Beaver Cay

Beaver Cay is accessible from Cairns and Dunk Island and has a marine biologist on site as a guide.

Dunk Island

Dunk Island is a rainforest-cloaked tropical island with a resort and a national park. The main focus is not on the reef but on the terrestrial forest.

Some island beaches on the reef witness a bizarre ritual when ragworms breed. Thousands of these marine worms collect unpredictably at low tide on still nights, glowing with luminescence and dancing in courtship. Then, the males release a hormone. This triggers the explosion of all the bodies of the entire population, releasing millions of eggs and sperm at the cost of mass suicide.

Flynn Reef

Flynn Reef Coral Gardens offer wonderful coral dives, with Gordon's Mooring and Tracy's Bommy being excellent sites for novices.

Green Island

Green Island has a huge number of day visitors that come from Cairns for the varied coral life. There is also a significant resort on this coral cay, and it has a national park. The island offers a huge new underwater observatory. When the day-visitors are gone, it can be fascinatingly peaceful, with the reef right there at the beach.

This is, though, an inner reef resort, and the level of hard coral coverage, mostly staghorn-type *Acropora*, has fluctuated between 1–10 percent. This still means that there are bommies with compact, fascinating coral gardens to be seen, but not much in between. In fact, the northeastern flank between 1993–2000 has shown the lowest level of hard coral among any sites surveyed on the reef. Most of the coral here is soft coral. Green algae cover is about 75 percent. The reef has been significantly affected by bleaching events, mainland runoff, and from an ongoing crown-of-thorns outbreak.

Fitzroy Island

This is a family holiday island, and there are many low-cost wilderness activities to participate in, rather than focusing on diving. Hard coral cover on the island has been hurt by bleaching, as this is close to the mainland, which has lower salinity from estuarine runoff, and higher UV levels due to shallower reef waters. These factors increase coral bleaching during peaks in warm summer temperatures.

Michaelmas Cay

The crescent of Michaelmas Cay is a major bird nesting site accessible from Green Island and Cairns by catamaran. Sooty and crested terns nest here. Small sharks and fish at the shore edge have adapted their behavior to humans by lunging after the crustaceans stirred up in the shallows by paddlers. Burrowing and giant clams, sea cucumbers, nudibranchs, and schools of fish can be seen.

When these giant clams spawn, they puff sperm into the water, followed in about a half hour by eggs if conditions are right, 500 million eggs at a time. Chances are good that a group of clams will fertilize one another's eggs, as they synchronize within the close colony.

Look for varieties of intensely colorful damselfish (*Chromis* sp.), butterflyfish, clownfish,

Seaweeds and Grazing Rights

The major food providers on reefs are algae, not corals. In fact, non-zooxanthellae algae have the highest reef biomass of the reef. There are over 500 algae species on the reef. Over time, a mutual dependence between grazers and algae has resulted, with the herbivorous sea urchins and fishes keeping the algae clean and supple in exchange for limited "grazing rights." Other more invasive and generalized herbivorous species are kept away from the seaweed by the weeds' toxic defenses, which the intruders are not specialized enough to withstand. Co-evolved herbivores are able to digest these toxins as they have developed digestive systems to cope. But they don't eat too much. In exchange for appetite discipline, they get to stay.

Six stripe wrasse (Pseudocheilinus hexataemia) (above) is common but hides in the reef. It probably eats mollusks and crustaceans.

and lionfish, along with tame Maori wrasses. Soft, tabular, and staghorn corals can be found here. The level of hard coral coverage, though, fluctuates at relatively low levels (14–27 percent), harmed by some moderately low but significant activity with crown-of-thorns. Soft coral cover is about 30 percent. Breaking Patches Reef is filled with plate and fan corals in the shallows, and soft and hard corals mid-reef with a steep drop-off.

From Townsville

Reef Headquarters Aquarium in Townsville on the mainland has a live coral reef that approximates the ocean ecosystem in terms of species, rocks, and wave movement. Artificial

Boring the Bommy

Coral relationships to look for when diving include the holes of the tube worms (*Spirobranchus giganteus*) (pointed out above) that penetrate into stony coral (*Acropora sarmentosa*) for protection.

In some corals the female marsupial crab (coral home shown below) will be imprisoned where she has locked herself into growing coral by controlling coral growth, leaving a narrow entrance open to let in males, food, and oxygen. The female crab becomes degenerate and flat.

Calcium carbonate from coral of the genus goniopora is so similar to human bone that it is being considered for bone grafts.

algae screens are used to scrub the water of wastes, and aerate it with oxygen. The marine collection provides a good place for orientation before a reef dive.

John Brewer Reef

John Brewer Reef suffered from severe crown-of-thorns starfish infestations in the 1980s which damaged a lot of coral. Fortunately, it is recovering. Check for local starfish conditions before setting out to dive anywhere on the Reef. Recovery on John Brewer may be complete by the time you want to dive.

Palm Group

The Palm Group includes several island Aboriginal Reserves closed to visitors, plus some that are open. Orpheus Island National Park and resort, Great Palm Island (with Aboriginal dancing), and Falcon Island are accessible through multi-day cruises. The best fringing reefs found here are off Pelorus Island. Night diving, snorkeling, and swimming with the tame fish are part of the experience. Monocle bream, sergeant majors, and harlequin tuskfish are common in the rich mud-floored area. All types of coral can be seen. Check visibility before departing for a dive trip.

Yongala

Yongala is a world-class wreck dive for advanced adventure divers.

Helix Reef

Helix Reef offers great diving for giant clams, bommies, gullies, and swim-through caves. An excellent array of fish and corals is found here out in the open or hiding under the overhangs.

Magnetic Island

Magnetic Island has several resorts and is a national park. It is close to the mainland which

Pelagics That Walked and Now Swim

Pelagics are fish that live in the open seas. They are found in schools swimming around the bommies in sheltered eddies and vortexes. Common reef pelagics include mackerel, barracuda, blue travelly, and tuna. Many of these are "countershaded" with dark topsides and silvery undersides to blend in. The Cetaceans' 30 species of pelagic whales and dolphins seen in the Great Barrier Reef include the humpback whale (*Megaptera novaenglicae*), which is often seen by whale watching trips in warm waters away from the Antarctic winter. Their destination: up past Fraser Island to calving and mating areas between the coast and the outer Great Barrier Reef. Their population has been recovering since whaling ceased in the 1950s. A dwarf form of minke whale 6–8m/20–26ft long may be seen migrating from Antarctica, between the Swain Reefs and Torres Strait, particularly during June and July. Minke whale photographs are being collected by the Museum of Tropical Queensland in Townsville. Bryde's Whale, similar to a humpback whale, is seen year-round. Bottlenose and spinner dolphins commonly accompany dive boats, spinning along the bow waves. Irrawaddy dolphins are seen inshore.

reduces visibility, but there are some good fringing reefs on the eastern side. There is a Geoffrey Bay reef walking trail.

Hinchinbrook Island

This is one of the places to find dugongs, which have declined 97 percent since the 1960s along the coast of the reef from Cairns to Hervey Bay. They can be seen in the "A" protection sites including Hinchinbrook, Cleveland Bay, Upstart Bay, Ince Bay, Shoalwater Bay, and Hervey Bay. A Hervey Bay area cyclone has silted a major seagrass bed. Lost fishing nets and anti-shark netting have drowned hundreds, with illegal fish netting and boat strikes injuring and killing many. Changes to anti-shark netting in 1992, major restrictions since 1997 on fishing and boating, and agreements with Aboriginal communities are all contributing to turning this decline around.

Dugongs love companionship and are good-natured. They probably evolved from a terrestrial ancestor, since they need to come up frequently for air. The young of these affectionate animals are carried at first under the mother's flipper and later follow the mother's every move as they swim close by her side.

From Airlie Beach and Shute Harbour: Central Reef

Whitsunday Group

The Whitsunday Island Group are high islands that used to be part of the main continent. Despite being near the mainland, the reefs surrounding the Whitsundays have been found to contain the highest species diversity and visual variety of benthic, or sea-bottom, oceanic life of the entire Great Barrier Reef. This is due to the orchestra of submerged habitats that the rocky islands have created. In addition to island reef activities, the island resorts offer divers a way to get to the outer reef and the chance to drift across fringing reefs and deep channels just two hours away from the islands by fast catamaran. When visiting the Whitsundays, go to outer barrier reef dives rather than focusing only on the immediate islands: the inner-coastal island waters are rather turbid.

Access is from Airlie Beach resort town and nearby Shute Harbour. These are near the city of Proserpine, 123km/74mi north of Mackay. Proserpine and Mackay are serviced by air from Brisbane, and Airlie Beach is 4 hours by road from Townsville. Reef Air, Helijet, and Seair Whitsunday offer air services from Cairns or Mackay to the Whitsundays and some reefs including Lindeman, Hayman, South Molle, Daydream Islands, and Bait Reef, or you can take a catamaran from Shute Harbour.

Hayman Island

Hayman Island Resort here and other major resorts on the Whitsundays emphasize multifaceted vacation activities rather than ecologically sustainable practices. There are a variety of camp sites, with Conway National Park being booked up well in advance. Strong currents carry a high level of land sediments, particularly in spring, and turn the waters turquoise. This reduces the visibility of these waters compared with more pristine sites in the north, and the waters can be windy and choppy. On the other hand, strong currents tend to clear excessive sediments quickly, too. A large number of beautiful damselfish can be seen flitting around, including *Amblygly phidodoncuracao*, *Pomacentrus* sp., and *Neopomacentrus* sp., and there are many other fish species, including fusiliers and snappers.

The coral variety is excellent, possibly "forced" by the somewhat lower light conditions, though the amount of hard coral coverage is fluctuating at relatively low levels of around 10–20 percent. *Montipora*, related to *Acropora*, is

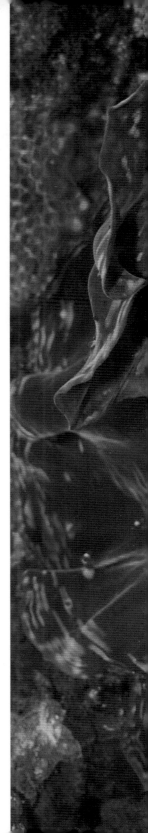

Is Our Air From the Milky Way?

On an earth-dark night, the Milky Way has holes in it that are so black they almost hurt. The Milky Way is our galaxy seen from within and these black spaces that blot out the stars behind them are clouds of dust and gas that are far from dead. They are critical life-givers: the dust shields the diffuse molecules from the interstellar radiation field so that molecular clouds can form. In these clouds, rapid chemical evolution is enriching our galaxy with a soup of newly-formed molecules that combine elements. Cosmogenesis, where elements themselves are built, happens within stars, but combining these elements into molecules of life occurs in these stellar gas clouds. Molecules combining nitrogen, hydrogen, and carbon of up to 13 atoms long have been detected. Hydrogen is the most abundant gas in these clouds, but combinations including cyanide, water, ethanol (a common alcohol and one of the first energy carriers before glucose), carbon monoxide, and many carbon-based molecules critical to life, are popping into existence. Some of these clouds condense into new stars, and this might explain how life evolved relatively rapidly once the earth cooled: it was already seeded with molecules ready for life. Some of the air you are breathing may have been formed in one of these star-light smudges. Research into molecules of the interstellar medium is a major field of excitement, so take a second look at the Milky Way when you are out in the wilderness.

Looking Toward our Galaxy's Central Black Holes

One of the blackest patches on the edge of the brightest, fattest part of the Milky Way has another secret: it is the location of the black holes at the center of the galaxy in which we live. You can spot this central region with the naked eye, behind one of the stars that form Sagittarius, or the Archer.

Sagittarius is easiest to see from the Southern Hemisphere because more of the bright central bulge of the Milky Way in which it appears to reside can be seen from there than in the north. And it is in this central swath that the black holes are located, obscured by a black dust cloud that makes it look as if it is at the edge of the bulge. It is, however, in the center. From Australia, you'll easily notice that these central bulge stars have a greater intensity and hue than Milky Way stars from the Northern Hemisphere. Bulge stars have an orange-yellow glow and much higher density due to their 15-billion year-old ancestry, probably being born with other galaxies at about the same time soon after the Big Bang. Smudges of ionized hydrogen also decorate the interstellar medium. The other type of Milky Way stars, Galaxy arm stars, dominate the Milky Way in the Northern Hemisphere sky and are much paler and more scattered. This is because they are still forming from clumping dust and gas, with even the older arm stars being only a few million years old. It is these younger stars that spiral out from the center. Our solar system is located at the edge of one of these arms. Our sun has been born, consumed, and born again a total of four or five times during its relatively short life.

When looking for the center of our galactic universe, you will be astounded at the intensity of stars that light the sky from horizon to horizon. Two-thirds of residents of the United States cannot see the Milky Way because of the electric-light pollution from sprawling cities. NASA satellite images show that Australia provides one of the rare places on earth where the night sky is not blotted out in this way. Australia is the "darkest" continent of all at night, which makes the night sky brighter. You can literally see more stars here than anywhere else.

Above: Sagittarius, the Swan, on the Milky Way's brilliantly glowing central bulge, seen from the Southern Hemisphere. Naked eye camera image, photo © David Malin Images

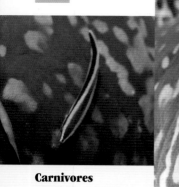

Carnivores

Snappers are a major group of reef fish species that you will see at 15–200m/49–654ft, often in schools. Two-spot red snapper (*Lutjanus bohar*) is a nocturnal predator. It is illegal to sell this and some other reef fish species for food because of the danger of ciguatera poisoning. This potentially fatal condition is caused by toxins from the dino-flagellate (*Gambierdiscus toxicus*) that build up through the food chain when snappers eat herbivorous surgeonfishes and parrotfishes. There is no way to test fish for these toxins. The fish carriers are immune to the poison. Trumpetfish including the yellow *Aulostomus chinensis* are related to seahorses, and are as thin as their name implies. Several trumpetfish species stalk small fish before sucking them in through their elastic snouts using a sideways vacuum action. Look for them hiding on one side of a large grazing fish, such as a parrotfish, waiting for this browser to stir up prey among the algae.

The predatory Queensland grouper (Epinephelus lanceolatus) *(above) grows to 400 kg, the largest fish you'll see unless you spot a whale shark. A cleaner wrasse (left) does its work.*

the dominant coral. Soft corals, including *Sinularia* and *Sarcophytum* sp., and algae are prolific. You can also find stinging coral (*Millepora* sp.) here, so watch out. Some coral bleaching occurs occasionally, mainly because of the freshwater runoff from the mainland, which increases coral sensitivity to high water temperature damage. The agricultural runoff from Proserpine River may also have had a negative effect on the islands' reef health.

Hook Island

Hook Island Underwater Observatory, in the Whitsundays, is an alternative way to see the reef. Easily reached from the mainland and Whitsunday resorts, Hook Island was home to Aboriginal peoples for 8,000 years. Their rock art can be found around Nara Inlet. Manta Ray Bay, the Pinnacles, and Butterfly Bay are popular among Australians and can get a lot of dive boat traffic. There is a private (commercial) camping site on Hook Island. The general turbidity of the water can be high and the coral can be damaged and less varied, since the island is close to the mainland and its river waters.

Bait Reef

Bait Reef Stepping Stones, northeast of Hayman Island, are made of several large bommies and the associated Bait Reef. In addition to a wide variety of fish and the usual staghorn coral, you can see mushroom, whip, and soft corals.

Hardy Reef

Hardy Reef is the center for much of the local reef ecotourist activity, accessed from Shute Harbour. Hardy Reef is northeast of Hayman Island and is accessed from several pontoons studded with marine life, overseen by lifeguards. There are glass-bottom boats, coral-viewing "submarines," and other options to see the underworld without getting wet. A suspended lagoon plus a deep channel provide great diving and snorkeling. All types of anemones and coral are found on the bommies: rare black corals plus soft, encrusting, staghorn, and boulder corals, and exquisite Gorgonian fans. This is the place to go for nudibranchs and mollusks. The reef itself is very resilient, having recovered several times from a major crown-of-thorns outbreak in 1986–9, a minor outbreak in 1992, and the effects of Cyclone Justin in 1997, all of which temporarily killed a lot of coral. Normal coral levels are very high.

Capricorn and Bunker Groups: South Reef

The Capricorn Group and Bunker Group reefs consist of a string of coral cays and platform reefs surrounded by deep waters, separated from the coast by the Curtis Channel. These can be reached from the Gladstone area, 116km/70mi south of Rockhampton. This is the southern-most region of the Reef and offers interesting reef walking, many turtle rookeries, and well defined diving opportunities. There are several research stations in the southern reef, which is also nearest a larger Australian population base.

Planktivorous Fish

Blue damsels and sargeant majors are very abundant reef fish that feed mostly on zooplankton and algae. Eggs are laid in nests that are stuck to seaweed, guarded by the male fish. Other planktiviorous fish include surgeonfish that defensively slice other fish with a side-swipe of their caudal spines. A hint of this behavior, and other fish withdraw. Most cardinalfish are red and eat zooplankton at night while hiding in crevices during the day. Red is a color that appears an invisible black a few meters below the surface. The coral cardinalfish (*sphmaeramia nematoptera*) (above) is an exception, with large eyes for nocturnal living. Nearly all reef fish have a couple of distinct development stages that are found in completely different habitats. Early on, the fish larva are found dispersing to new locations in a planktonic refuge form. At this stage, planktivorous fish are predators, but the value of fish larvae staying small and numerous is the multiple exploration potential of finding new habitats for the species. Larger juveniles develop from these larvae and are recruited to settle in a new coral home, far from their parents.

photo © Tim Hellier/
imagequest3d.com

Finding Turtle Rookeries

Green turtles nest in the Capricorn-Bunker Group and at Raine Island. Loggerhead turtle rookeries can be found in the Capricorn-Bunker Group, around Bundaberg, and on Swain Reef cays.

Hawksbill turtles nest on Torres Strait and northern reef islands.

The vulnerable flatback turtle breeds only in Australia, with rookeries found between Bundaberg and the Torres Strait.

The olive Ridley turtle (above) makes scattered nests all along the Gulf Coast. Leatherback turtle nests are found near Bundaberg.

Turtles are protected, so stay inland and do not interfere with their nesting. Contact the Queensland Parks and Wildlife services for more information.

photo © Roger Steene/imagequest3d.c

As a result, the Capricorn and Bunker Groups are the most well-studied reefs of the reef, even if the diversity of coral types is low compared with other areas of the reef. This is probably because these cays offer a set of very similar habitats. If you want eye-popping variety to last for more than a few days, go further north.

Green turtles have major nesting rookeries in this group of islands, mating from October to November, the other concentration within the Reef being at Raine Island in the north. Green turtles eat seagrasses and algae, loggerhead turtles have heavy jaws to crunch mollusks and crustaceans, hawksbill turtles use their beak-shaped mouths to pry away sponges and other sedentary animals, and white-spotted leatherback turtles search for jellyfish. Turtles do not reach maturity in the wild until they are 30–50 years old. Female turtles nest only every few years because of the energy drain of egg-laying and the associated three months of starvation from migrating to the nesting area until she returns to her home feeding grounds.

Lady Elliot Island

The only outer-shelf-reef coral cay resorts are found on Lady Elliot Island (in the south) and Heron Island (parallel with Gladstone) under the Tropic of Capricorn. The only other coral cay resort in the entire reef is Green Island near Cairns. Other resorts are on rocky islands. Although prices at these resorts can be steep, the advantage is that the coral starts practically at the edge of the sandy beach. Lady Elliot Island is best reached from the sugar city of Bundaberg.

There are a series of reefs between Lady Elliot and Heron Islands that can be reached by dive boats from the resorts, once you tire of dipping straight into the reef from the beach. These include Fairfax Islands, Hoskyn Islands, Keppel Islands Outer Rocks, Lady Elliot Island Blow Hole, Heron Island Bommie, and Gorgonia Hole.

Lady Elliot Island has several bommies on the west and east side that are worth beach or boat dives including Lighthouse Bommies, Anchor Bommie, the shallow Coral Gardens, Maori Wrasse Bommie, Shark Pool, Blowhole, and Hiro's Cave. You can walk far out on the reef itself and fossick, or feed the fish at Fish Pool. If you have the chance, take a reef walk at night. Most coral polyps shut during the day, pulling in their vibrant color from view. At night, the stunningly beautiful tentacles come out in starry bursts of color as the carnivores search the currents for prey. Keep an eye out for octopus, moray eels, brittle, and sea stars. Beware of the toxic cone shells, blue-ringed octopus, and stinging corals that tend to come

Crown-of-Thorns

Massive outbreaks of crown-of-thorns starfish (bottom) are killing acres of coral reefs. These boom cycles are caused when a series of complex ecological barriers and controlling agents are removed. One of these may be associated with tourist incursions, but a definite set of causes is yet to be identified despite intensive research. Fossil evidence indicates these starfish have had occasional swarming peaks for thousands of years.

Below: Crown-of-thorns starfish eating coral

photo © Peter Parks/ imagequest3d.com

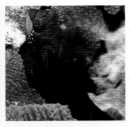

Bottom Oddities

What looks like tangled string is in fact from a spaghetti worm (*Loimia medusa*), which extends its thin white tentacles up to 60cm/24in from its central burrow. Cilia-lined grooves move food along the tentacles to the mouth. Gobies are often overlooked because of their small size, linear shape, and place on the substrate level, yet there are 60 more-easily-found species on the reef and 1,900 species worldwide. Like many goby species, the Steinitz's prawn goby (*Amblyeleotris steinitzi*) makes its den home with a commensal shrimp. In return for being a watch-dog for both of them, the carnivorous goby is given a bolt-hole maintained by the shrimp. Titan Triggerfish retreat to a favorite hole in the reef at night or when threatened, into which they wedge themselves with their dorsal spine. They eat a wide variety of invertebrates, algae, and sponges with their powerful teeth and jaws. They should be avoided if nesting in the sand. Yellowfin goatfish stir up the sand with their barbles. Mandarin fish (*Synchiropus splendidus*) (above) have no scales and are found on muddy floors.

out after dark. There are 80 species of cone shells in Australian waters, feeding off fish, mollusks, and worms. The harpoon that they release has the power to crack through a periwinkle shell, and carries a venomous toxin that is rapidly lethal to humans. Wear hiking boots for night walking, not open-toed sandals, and wash the salt water off later.

The island has seabird breeding and is a major sea turtle rookerie for green and loggerhead turtles, which are around between November and February. The bungalows of the resort are built on stilts to let turtles crawl where they want, underneath.

Lady Musgrave Island

The island can be reached from nearby resorts or the mainland, and is fascinating because it attracts species from the Coral Sea as well as the inner reef. The Entrance Bommie and coral cay of this island are excellent dive sites. Fish are much more abundant than many other sites, particularly at the back of the reef. So look for parrotfish, damselfish (including pomacentrids), and colorful surgeonfish. The hard coral coverage here is very high and there are wonderful plate and branching corals to be seen. Coral bleaching and crown-of-thorns starfish were not seen in a 2001 survey. Not far away, Broomfield Reef also offers diving with high densities of coral and prolific fish.

Heron Island

Heron Island is closest to Gladstone for mainland access. The Heron Island Bommie is one of the world's most filmed dive sites and has a collection of tame fish, including Moray eels. You can see a cleaner wrasse station at work, with sweetlip, manta rays, hussars, trevally, and a tremendous variety of other fish. Boulder, staghorn, and turret corals can be seen, browsed by parrotfish. For soft corals, visit the Gorgonia Hole, an excellent spot for photography, with its fan corals, sea fans, and feather stars with

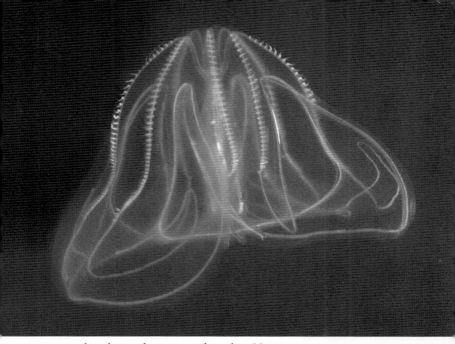

commensal gobies, shrimp, and crabs. Heron Island has a research field station run by the University of Queensland.

On Heron Island, several terrestrial species stabilize the sand to form a vegetated coral island. Pisonia (*Pisonia brunoniana*) forests grow 40 feet high with flesh-colored trunks. Seeds are covered with glue, which adheres to nesting bird plumage for distribution. There are a lot of seed distributors here: white-capped noddy tern (*Anous minutus*) and mutton birds, or wedge-tailed shearwaters, (*Puffinus pacificus*) nest all around these trees. The noddy terns nest in the trees and the mutton birds in burrows below. The mutton birds stay out at sea during the day, and may blunder into humans on return at night. *Pandanus tectorius* grows in sandy areas in association with *Tournefortia argentea*, both with buttressed roots and heavy fruit. *Tournefortia fruits* can withstand saltwater for months and then sprout when they run ashore. Beach oak casuarina equisetifolia is found in a line along the edge of the strand. Seeds are wind-distributed. Cardwell cabbage (*Scaevola koenigii*) is a flowering shrub that stabilizes sand strand and conserves water in large yellow-green leaves. Goat's foot

Scintillating

Watch for the must-see daylight-glowing comb jellies (above) in reef waters. Small plates along the combs diffract sunlight into colored twinkling lights. Very little is known about these delicate creatures, which exist without a brain. They are found from the ocean surface to deep sea trenches. Unlike many other jellyfish, they do not sting humans but trap prey in their bells. The frolima is a shrimp-like animal that steals a comb jelly bell to use as a home and a nest for its eggs.

Swimming Relationships and the Daily Grind

Parrotfish produce more sand in the tropics than any other among reef's 1,500 fish species. They do this by grinding algae, coral, and rocks in their pharyngeal mill and sucking nutrients from these before spewing out the sand sediment. These herbivores have fused teeth with incredible power, creating bite grooves in the chalky surfaces. Listen for them chomping when you are diving among corals. Parrotfish hide in mucus cocoons at night like some of the wrasses from which they evolved.

The 25 reef parrotfish species change sex and color from a drab female or hermaphrodite, to a male that is usually brightly colored blue or green. These parrotfish look very variable, because they share 120 color patterns for different occasions. Some lone parrotfish have an unpatterned color that changes to a striped "school uniform" when they join a group. They do this by controlling chromatophore pigment cells that adjust the appearance of white, yellow, orange, red and black dots, somewhat similar to an HDTV screen.

(*Convolvulus ipomaea*) pescapre is an early establisher on sand and *Thurea sarmentosa* is a grass that binds sand.

A green turtle that nested on Heron Island in 1990 was fitted with a transmitter and tracked for 3,300km/1,980mi to the ocean north of Darwin, taking 234 days. She returned to Heron Island eight years later. Turtles are best seen on Heron Island and the northwest islands of the Capricorn Group, or on the mainland at Mon Repos near Bundaberg. Do not use a flashlight as this disturbs the turtles and draws hatchlings to run away from the ocean, usually the brightest object for them at night. Follow the female turtle tracks, walking quietly on the landward side of the turtle, and sit still until one stops digging in the sand and starts laying. At that point, observers can take a closer look.

On One Tree Island (dedicated to a University of Sydney field station), the white-breasted sea eagle nests on the peak of the island, a nest still used 160 years after the first observed breeding season. This is one of the 242 species of reef birds, of which 24 breed on the islands. One Tree Island's reef is closed to recreational ecotravel.

Swain Reefs

The Swain Reefs and Pompey Complex are found within the southern section but are scattered the farthest away from the coast than any other series of reefs here. These can be reached from Gladstone. There are a couple of islands that are promising for ecotravellers here: Gannet Cay is closed in summer during bird nesting but is worth visiting the rest of the time, as is East Cay. Both are excellent photography sites and the night diving reveals fantastic mollusks.

The Swain Reefs form a huge complex of 270 reefs and 25 cays that are relatively unresearched and unexplored. They form an S-pointing "V" shape that offers a large variety of exposed outer and protected inner reef habitats. This has increased the diversity of coral here compared with the Capricorn Bunker Groups, and there appears to be little or no bleaching. Crown-of-thorns have been very active, though, and several areas are recovering from an early-1990s outbreak, making hard coral coverage lower than usual (at 10–30 percent in some places), though it is growing back slowly in some areas, including Snake Reef. Horseshoe Reef was undergoing an active outbreak in 2001/2. Depending on the crown-of-thorns status, good shallow diving may be experienced at both these reefs plus other areas on the Swains. Look for beautiful mollusks, gorgonians, and feather stars. Divers are likely to see coral trout, cod, sweetlip, fusiliers, baitfish, angelfish, butterflyfish, and surgeonfish. Look for outer edge species including whales, leatherback turtles, whitetip reef sharks, and plankton-eating whale-sharks.

The Swain Reefs are an important breeding site for olive sea snakes. Sea snakes are air breathers and have adapted physiologically to avoid getting the bends. They eat fish eggs, eels, and fish. Sea snake venom is more toxic than the most dangerous land snake venom, but they rarely bite. They have a habit of wrapping themselves around divers' legs: do not provoke them under these circumstances. They are probably experimenting with what they think is a snake of the opposite sex and should leave without harm.

Wrass Heartthrobs

Watch for hump-headed Maori wrasse (*Cheilinus undulatus*) and green moon wrasse (*Thalassoma lunare*). All young wrasses are females and change sex (and sometimes color) later. When the alpha male green moon wrasse dies, the next largest harem fish replaces it. If female, she takes ten days to develop into a male. The green moon wrasse has a throbbing sex life. About every hour at low tide the brighter-colored alpha male turns from green to blue and attacks dull-colored fish in his male and female harem. This keeps lesser males in check so he can corral the females. During spawning season and just before high tide, this male segues from his aggressive behavior to a mating display in full blue regalia. He and his female harem members participate in a spawning rush. But he doesn't get his way all the time. Some dull males have special large testes and gang up to release their sperm alongside the alpha male. This only occurs in reefs where groups of wrasses congregate. Then the fish returns to normal coloration and calm behavior.

White-banded or Picasso triggerfish can wedge themselves in holes by locking dorsal spines.

Small Dive Boats

For a more peaceful dive, check out the smaller dive boats, which leave on single or multiple-day expeditions.

Heron Island Resort
diveboat, Gladstone (day)
Kelly Dive, Airlie Beach
(3-day)
Oceania Dive, Airlie
Beach (3-day)
Reef Dive, Airlie Beach
(3-day)
Salty's, Bundaberg (day)
Dive Bell, Townsville
(2-5-day)
**Lady Elliot Island
Holidays**, Torquay (day)
**Mike Ball Dive
Expeditions**, Townsville
and Cairns (3-day)
Dive 7 Seas, Cairns (day)
Great Diving Adventures,
Cairns (day)
Ocean Free: schooner
(day)
Quintessential Diving,
Cairns (day)
**Santa Maria Yacht
Cruises**, Cairns (3-day)
**Taka II Dive
Adventures,** Cairns (5-day)
TUSA Dive Charters,
Cairns (day)
**Poseidon Outer Reef
Cruises**, Port Douglas
(day)
Undersea Explorer,
Port Douglas (6-day)

*Windowpane butterfly
and stick insect are
among the fauna above
sea level on the reef's
islands (above).*

The Pompey Complex is a difficult-to-reach series of deltaic reefs: a series of immense outer reef barriers called the "hard line" that channels strong tidal currents like reverse river deltas from the open ocean. The current then flows into the sandbars and lagoons of the enormously fascinating but highly dangerous reef complex. Many sponges grow in these lagoons. Sponges are prime subjects for a new type of anti-inflammatory drug that is in the early stages of testing. One of these, from nearby Papua New Guinea waters, is being chemically synthesized as IPL576092. This is no minor drug. It could work much better than inhaled or orally administered steroids in the treatment of inflammatory diseases and infections including asthma. Related sponge-drugs that function as this new type of leukocyte-suppressing anti-inflammatory drug, LSAID, are being assessed for the treatment of multiple sclerosis and rheumatoid arthritis. The primary limitation in this research is the availability of the natural sources until enough is known about the drugs to synthesize or "farm" them in the laboratory by adjusting microbial DNA to culture them within other organisms.

Stradbroke Island

Humpback whales go north outside the reef, past this island from Antarctic waters in June and July, then south in mid-August to mid-October, mating and calving between-times in the warmer reef area. The mothers return last with their calves and swim south more slowly back to their Antarctic feeding grounds, where they gorge on 2 tons of krill crustaceans in 24 hours. These whales come on schedule: a male was timed at Stradbroke Island 30 minutes from the time that it swam by the previous year. You can also catch sight of them in Hervey Bay by Fraser Island, off Cairns, and on many whale boat trips. Look for them breaching above the water, or putting their heads up to "periscope" and look around. They spend about 2 minutes at the surface and 20 minutes below. They leave a patch of smooth water at the surface, called a footprint, a tell-tale sign that a whale is around. Each whale can be recognized by its fluke (tail) shape and bite notches. A male white humpback whale was spotted in 1992 off Queensland. It returns each year and started singing in 1998.

Male humpback whales can be heard singing continuously for up to twenty minutes. They hang immobile in the water, head down, and sing these mating songs that they have carefully developed into a characteristic pattern of tones and squeals unique to each animal. Humpback whales have been found to swim in genetically isolated pods with surprisingly little sexual exchange between neighboring groups. Yet an Australian study shows that their song dialects are shared, taking about a year for a popular song to appear in another group. This means that there is some contact, either because the sound-waves

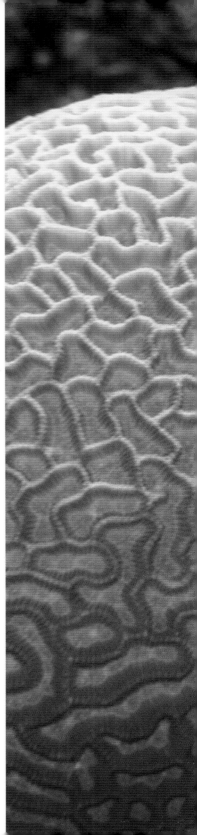

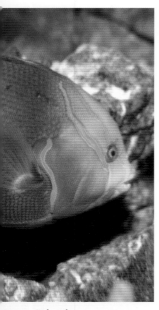

*Male rockmover wrasse
(Novaculichthys taeniourus),
terminal color phase.*

of these songs carry for several miles, or because there are encounters between groups that, so far, have not been observed.

Occasionally, black and white killer whales can be seen far offshore. These have the capability of killing a humpback whale calf by chasing it with the mother to exhaustion, then flipping on top of it until it drowns. They are under a quarter of its size, yet their strategy can work. The mother fights back with lethal tail swipes and moves under the calf to keep it at the surface. Humpback whales and dolphins instinctively push struggling calves and even drowning humans to the surface to give them air. A dolphin saved a swimmer from drowning in Italian waters during the last decade using this protective sense.

Stunning new research by two separate US researchers working in northern Pakistan, the region where whales originated, has revealed that whales were living on land as wolf-like carnivores 50 million years ago. These Cetacea had already split off from hippopotamus, pig, and camel relatives, and specialized in hunting for food in shallow river areas. Within 8 million years they had transformed themselves into sea creatures via the intermediate *Ambulocetus natans*, a crocodile-like swimmer.

Coral Sea

To the east of the reef lies the deep ocean of the Coral Sea, but this is sprinkled with a few reefs that are remnant tops of volcanic islands. The Coral Sea reefs are not part of the reef in geographic or management terms, but these can be superb sites for diving.

Far North Coral Sea

Just over the northern boundary of the Reef Marine Park Authority and outside the Yule entrance to the reef are places for extreme wilderness adventure: atoll-like Ashmore Reef, distinctive Portlock Reefs, and Boot Reefs. And

Female scalefin anthias

farther east, on its own isolated pinnacle, lie the Eastern Fields.

These reefs are wonderful for experienced divers. They have species that are thought to be exchanged with the nearby reefs of Papua New Guinea. Yet, research in Australia and the Caribbean has recently shown that fish and shrimp larvae move surprisingly little from their original home. Although these minute planktonic organisms are not strong enough to resist the movement of strong currents, they move vertically to pick currents going in the direction they prefer. This allows them to drift but also to navigate home, perhaps using the sense of smell as Pacific salmon may do. This unexpected finding has been confirmed by research in Indonesia by Stephen R. Palumbi who has discovered that the genetic signatures of *Haptosquilla pulchella* shrimp are remarkably similar in the same geographic location, yet very distinctive for the same species living in close-by Indonesian reefs served by similar currents. This indicates that some efforts to repopulate Indonesia's damaged reefs with juveniles from other areas may fail. Only 6.5 percent of Indonesian reefs are healthy, in stark contrast to the Great Barrier Reef, which is largely undamaged.

Bougainville Reef

The stellar Bougainville Reef lies northeast of Cairns and bursts out of deep ocean in the

Anthias

The red male scalefin anthias (*Pseudanthias squamipinnus*) (above), also called the lyretail anthias, has a harem of beautiful orange females (left page) with purple eyestripe. This is the most common anthias on the reef. Anthias species are among the most exquisitely glowing reef fish to look out for among the corals.

A marine biologist identifies the wealth of coral at Agincourt Reef.

Central Coral Sea. This is accessed from Port Douglas. Several intense dive sites offer intermediate-skill drift and boat-diving opportunities, including the Zoo, which has a line to a bommie and swim-through-studded gully. Sea fans, soft corals, vibrant-colored basslets, gray reef sharks, and green turtles abound.

Gray reef sharks are such instinctive carnivores that they start in the womb. Embryos duke it out before they are born, the most developed and strongest consuming its fetus-mates until only one remains. When it is born, the mother goes into an instinctive starvation period to avoid eating her own pup. If you encounter a gray reef shark in a swim-through, keep your distance and act calmly. Be ready to leave the water without panic if necessary, an unusual event. A gray reef shark signals if it is getting riled up by wagging its head and tail: become fully alert if you see this. If its challenge continues, the shark moves into a threat posture with back arched, nose up, and pectoral fins down. In the final stages, the shark swims in tight figure-eights before it bears down to chase whatever is bothering it. Your divemaster will advise you of local conditions for safe diving.

Flinders Reefs

Northeast of Townsville a series of isolated reefs extends beyond the limits of the Great Barrier Reef. Of these, the closest and most explored is Flinders, which is served by several dive companies. Other reefs clustered to the south in the Coral Sea are Marion, Kenn, Frederick, Cato, and Wreck.

6
Red Center

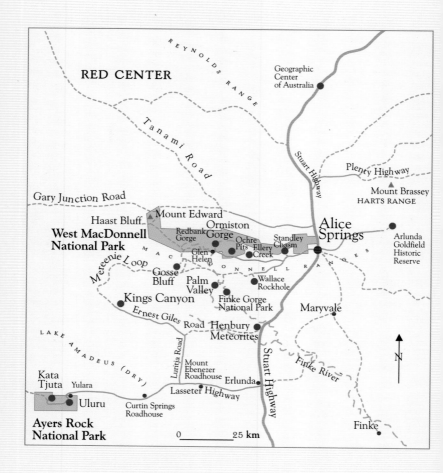

Red Center

Uluru (above) surrounded by mulga.

Many of those who travel to the Red Center to see Ayer's Rock, now named Uluru, do not realize that it is a true icon of Gondwana. When India, South America, Africa, Australia and Antarctica slammed together and formed Gondwana, stress-lines snapped and the Petermann Mountain Range popped up in central Australia. Uluru's intense rust color comes from these red mountains, which were subsequently leveled by snowmelt from alpine streams and washed into a shallow inland sea, forming Uluru's sedimentary strata. The new sediments later buckled again, upturning Uluru's layers into vertical strata and drying out about 5 million years ago. Eroding sand storms marooned Uluru's slab and created the largest single piece of rock, or monolith, in the world. Nearby stand the Olgas, now named Kata Tjuta, formed of larger pebbles strewn from the Petermanns by the same alpine streams. These are part of a World Heritage Site of outstanding importance.

Don't Miss
❖ Uluru/Ayer's Rock
❖ Gosse Bluff from a helicopter
❖ Mereenie Loop
❖ King's Canyon
❖ Palm Canyon
❖ Bush tucker guided walk

Access

Uluru and vicinity can be fascinating, but the main access vehicle routes are across uninteresting plains. A much more compelling

Uluru's Oasis

At the base of Uluru there is a permanent water-hole (page 149 and this page). Not surprisingly, 3 frog species are frequently found around Uluru: trilling frog (*Neobratrachus centralis*) tadpoles are common in these pools in winter. You can also find shoemaker frog tadpoles (*Neobatrachus sutor*). And there are Main's or burrowing frogs (*Cyclorana maini*) estivating in the sand around Uluru, waiting until the rains come. If you are there after a severe rainstorm, you are likely to see lots of these burrowing frogs emerge to breed, bleating like sheep.

route is to drive to Uluru from Alice Springs via the West MacDonnell Ranges along a back road route that includes the 4WD Mereenie Loop and takes travelers through most of Australia's main arid and semi-arid habitats. This takes 3.5 days minimum round trip from Alice Springs, from which you can combine walks along sections of the new Larapinta Trail. Another alternative is to fly direct to the outpost Connellan airport by Uluru and Ayer's Rock Resort, which is set up for holiday jets. Otherwise, Alice Springs is the transportation hub of Australia's center for planes, trains, and cars. The new Ghan train departs once or twice a week from Adelaide, reaching Alice Springs overnight.

Other 4WD trails from Alice Springs include the Tanami Track all the way to the Kimberleys in West Australia; the Plenty Highway, which first passes through Gemtree and the eastern MacDonnells near Alice where fossicking can easily reveal gem-quality stones; Sandover Highway for 547km/339mi east along the Sandover River; and, of course, the hard-top Stuart Highway, which cuts across the entire Red Center from north to south through Alice, the old telegraph station. Close to Alice are the eastern MacDonnell Ranges, which can be reached via Trephina Gorge, and Ruby Gap, 85 km/52.7mi away.

Desert flowers: Sturt's desert pea (Swainsona formosa) is widespread (top left), lantern bush (Abutilon leucopetalum) (top center) is a member of the hibiscus family. Several eucalyptus sp. are common and have gorgeous flower puffs (top right). Peas, very important nitrogen recyclers, include twining glycine (Glycine clandestina), a twiner found from deserts to mountaintops (bottom left). Potato relatives also are common: Thargomindah nightshade (Solanum sturtianum) is widespread (botttom center), and in arid mulga-scattered areas you will see cattle bush (Trichodesma zeylanicum) (bottom right). Desert raisin (Solanum centrale) and bush tomato (Solanum chippendalei) were important Aboriginal foods high in vitamin C.

Uluru

Uluru is truly a stunning sight. Uluru is made of arkose, a kind of sandstone with a high level of feldspar that originated from granite. The red color that glows in the lenses of so many cameras at sunset and sunrise is made of rust— pure and simple iron oxide—that has stained the rock. Arkose is silver-grey before being stained by the rust, giving Uluru a dappled color gradation up close.

The microclimate produced by Uluru's steep sides slightly increases the rainfall and allows many varied living communities to thrive, from frog ponds on one side to ephemeral shrimp puddles on top, encircled by flowers, melons, and butterflies. These are hints of the fascinating ecology that is hidden for careful visitors to discover, concentrated especially in the spinifex. (Spinifex appears to be tussock grass but is in fact made of a few species of non-grasses that roll their leaves to conserve moisture, have tips as sharp as cactus

Mistletoebird

A tiny red-breasted mistletoebird delights in the 65 species of mistletoe berries found in Australia. It wipes the sticky berries from its behind onto the twigs (box, top). *Amyema maidenii* mistletoe (second from top) is found on mulga and witchetty bush. Harlequin mistletoe (*Lysiana exocarpi*) (below) is found as a stem parasite on mulga and other shrubs. Some mistletoe have leaves that mimic the host.

Thorny Devil Aqueducts

The thorny devil (*Moloch horrodus*) (right) is a strange lizard. Its spiked surface is covered by a microscopic network of open capillaries that spread across its rough skin surface. This network wicks moisture from its feet to its gaping mouth. In a land where the only moisture may be ground-level dew vapor for months or years on end, this is a handy little adaptation. The phenomenon was discovered when biologists dabbed a spot of dye on its skin, and the color spread to a broad fuzz over the body. The moisture worked its way over the animal's surface toward the corners of the lizard's gaping mouth. There, the water layer was swallowed into its stomach where the dye was retrieved. No dye was absorbed directly through the skin or feet. Thorny devils are common lizards that are found on roads in the afternoon, lapping up the heat of the sun. They stay put and do not run away, so watch out for them as you drive. Their gait is rather cryptic: they move more like a leaf blowing across the ground than a purposeful animal. If you are fortunate enough to see one walking rather than just sunning itself, watch it putter around and you'll see a lizard's version of break-dancing in action.

spines, and produce large amounts of nutritious seeds.) Uluru's immediate surroundings are the center of the highest reptile diversity in the entire arid and semi-arid Red Center.

Beyond the flowers and shrubs immediately around Uluru is mulga scrubland, which is relatively limited in species variety. Mulga is a habitat dominated by the mulga tree (*Acacia aneura*), with linear gray-green phyllodes and yellow bottle-brush flowers. Phyllodes are flattened stems that resemble leaves and are more drought-resistant. You will probably see the crested spinifex pigeon sitting under a mulga tree in the shade. The mulga unfolds into spinifex, which looks more barren but is in fact teeming with life, relatively speaking.

It is worth looking for surprises around Uluru: right behind the Uluru sunset viewing station (in the opposite direction from the one everyone normally faces), is a good place to spot the rare marsupial mole (*Notoryctes typhlops*) as it emerges from its swim beneath in the sand dunes. Look for the wavy tracks left by its tail and claws as it moves from one self-enveloping burrow to another. These sand dunes formed 2 million years ago, and the marsupial mole soon learned how to swim through them. Deaf and blind, with huge claws and a backward-facing pouch to keep her young grit-free, this honey-colored sleek creature is unrelated to the identical-looking golden burrowing mole of South Africa. Both have similar claws, color, size, near-blindness, fur, and underground sand-swimming habits. These moles are examples of convergent

Yellow-faced whipsnake (Demansia psammophis) *(top left) has large eyes to hunt skinks and lizard eggs by day. Its venom is a mild neurotoxin. Whipsnakes are very active and are adapted to do well in temperatures several degrees higher than snakes that burrow or hunt at night. Centralian bluetongue* (Tiliqua multifasciata) *(bottom left) eats plants and is as big as a brick. Dingoes (bottom right) eat anything they can catch, including reptiles. Termite mounds (top right) are nature's recycle bin, and they support the majority of reptiles in the Red Center.*

Desert Reptiles

There are 70 species of reptiles found around Uluru, plus 13 snake species and 4 frog species. The abundant skink lizard species found in spinifex feed on spiders and termites (top right), with each species specializing on a different type of termite. The Western bearded dragon has been observed by Aboriginal people to lay eggs in a deep hole with a hidden entrance. The female leaves, then returns at hatching time to let the young out. Aboriginals from the area have many insights into wilderness behavior that surprise and help scientists. Much of Australian wildlife has not been researched in depth scientifically. Scientists are beginning to chronicle Aboriginal observations and incorporate them into their understanding. Aboriginals observe that the mother and father muluny-mulunypa (*Menetia greyii*), a smooth-skinned lizard, carries the young in their mouths while they are being raised. The rare woma python (*Aspidites ramsayi*) hatches its eggs by coiling around them and contracting its muscles to release incubating heat during cold desert nights.

evolution from different ancestors to fill similar ecological niches. Australia has many such examples that confused the Europeans settlers. The marsupial mole offers another surprise: it did not move underground as an adaptation to escape the increasingly searing sun, as ecologists thought until recently. It became mole-like in the cooler Gondwanan rainforests and swam into the desert from there, as shown by an ancestral 15-million-year-old mole fossil found recently among rainforest fossil flora in Riversleigh, Queensland.

At the sunset viewing station, you may also spot the mulgara, (*Dasycercus cristicauda*), a small vulnerable marsupial predator from the quoll family with a taste for insects and spiders. This is one of six quolls, or dasyurids, found in

Soil Crusts

The spinifex grassland around Uluru and the western McDonnell range has a delicate, felt-like soil surface. In fact, it is a crust of active algae organisms. The algae and fungi in this crust create thread-like networks of hyphae and mucilaginous sheaths that form air pockets that are then cemented together in a spongy structure. This is essential to maximize the hydrology of these soils. Fire, cattle, sheep, and people walking over the surface break this cryptogamic cover down. It takes about seven years to repair. Mary White, author and expert on plant evolution, feels that the too-frequent burning around Uluru is destroying this essential aspect of soil health, causing slow degradation.

West MacDonnell Range (this page) threaded by one of the oldest rivers in the world, the Finke River.

the spinifex around Uluru. Members of the quoll family are predatory mammals with pouches and they range in size from rats to cats. A few decades ago there were many more mammal species, but local extinctions have been occurring among the 46 mammal species previously found here. This mirrors much of Australia's small native mammal decline. The causes include competition by feral cats and foxes, reduction of the mosaic of related habitats, and collapse of Aboriginal fire stick farming practices that created the essential mosaic pattern of varied foods. Recent knowledge has integrated fire management using a combination of traditional Aboriginal practices and science-based approaches, and several captive breeding programs are rescuing scarce species from immediate peril. Marsupials appeared acutely adapted to survive in this terrain of harsh decadal weather patterns, far better than mammals that require higher overall nutrient levels and more consistent seasons year in and year out. This is because marsupial young are born much earlier than mammals, so that under starvation conditions, the young die but the female is left stronger than a mammal that has brought a larger fetus to term. Marsupials have other reproductive advantages over mammals in lean years. But these delicately adapted marsupials show signs of stress everywhere when their fragile food system is damaged.

Getting the balance of factors right for the restoration of these arid land species is an art being developed at several sites, including the Alice Springs Desert Park run by the Northern Territory Parks and Wildlife Commission, a must-see in Alice Springs. Captive breeding programs are in place at the park for the adorable bilby (*Macrotis lagotis*), the large Australian marsupial version of the long-eared, burrowing Easter bunny. This is a member of its own bilby family. Until a few years ago, bilbies were found around Uluru and across arid Australia but, after a precipitous decline, are now found mostly in the Tanami Desert and southwestern Queensland. You can take the Tanami Track from Alice Springs if you are interested in exploring more bilby territory.

Other predatory quolls found around the spinifex at Uluru include the locally common wingai ningaui (*Nignaui ridei*), which is found sheltering in hollow logs; the rare hairy-footed dunnart (*Sminthopsis hirtipes*), with hairs on its

Emus are considerate parents: they gently remove any dung from the nest where eggs and young are incubating, and pitch it far away. Predators are therefore not alerted to a new brood. When frightened, emus can run 80kmph/50mph.

Plague Preventers

Some ecologists have observed that boom-bust insects and diseases are primary symptoms of ecological problems. They propose that these issues won't be remedied until the ecological relationships, not just the individual species' problems, are addressed. In Australia, the annoying population of black flies (*Austrosimulium pestilens*) is the result of an ecological imbalance. People not only caused it, but compounded it. Until corrective measures kick in, a net over one's hat with loose one-inch holes or fine gauze may be effective in keeping the flies away from mouth and eyes, as these flies avoid confined spaces. Black flies cannot bite and carry few pathogens, but their mouthparts can rasp the skin and cause bleeding. Their over-abundance was caused by the lack of dung beetles after European cattle and sheep were introduced. The flies breed in the dung. In arid climates, dung beetles are essential recyclers of wet herbivorous waste and are being reintroduced. Composting microbes need a damp environment in which to thrive, but the waste dries out so fast in arid conditions that the nitrogen just sits there. Australia had its own dung beetle once, but it became extinct after most of Australia's large browsing marsupials disappeared when man appeared on the island.

Kangaroos: Socialites with Boundless Energy

Y ou may see some big kangaroos driving to or from Uluru, and these are likely to be red kangaroos (*Macropus rufus*). Yet thousands of years ago, there were many more kangaroo species browsing these plains. Why did the red kangaroo survive when all other large browsing marsupials became extinct in Australia when man entered the scene? The answer lies in their limbs. Kangaroo limbs store much more bounding energy in their elastic tendons and muscles than human and quadruped structures. This is based on their physical and physiological design. Once kangaroos speed up to a comfortable hopping rhythm, they can hop along or even speed up for long distances without increasing their energy expenditure. Marsupial muscles are also built differently and are able to sustain a high aerobic capacity. As a result, even when going 50kmph/31mph, kangaroos do not need muscle glycogen stores like we do. Because of these factors, kangaroo oxygen consumption does not increase proportionally to speed, unlike in human athletes, but plateaus into a major, lasting "second wind." The kangaroo's elastic batteries that store mechanical energy in their tendons, plus their aerobic muscle capacity, help give them an escape advantage, particularly from man. Man runs out of sprint energy before the red kangaroo, and the hunter of the past let this quarry go. Red kangaroos survived because they had this swift, sustained physiological advantage. Some marsupials of 60,000 years ago, when men came to Australia, were the size of rhinos but couldn't sustain a sprint because they were quadrupeds without the essential bipedal battery design. They had to adapt to man quickly, and their breeding rates didn't allow it. They soon became extinct. Other large marsupials were bipedal kangaroos that could hop away but not fast enough. A more tubby kind of tree-grazing kangaroo, the Macropodine, needed a larger digestive system than red kangaroos to cope with the tougher low quality fibers and this made it too big and slow to escape the spears and boomerangs. They, too, kicked the bucket, leaving only the red kangaroo to leap to freedom. Red kangaroos prefer extensive grass plains with mulga and patches of snakewood (*Acacia xiphophylla*), and do not like spinifex areas. They are not nomadic. You are most likely to see them at dusk. The euro or common wallaroo (*M. robustus erubscens*) (left) is found in rougher rocky areas around Kata Tjuta and throughout Australia. Due to the secretiveness of this smaller kangaroo species, its population is larger than it appears.

Kanga-treads

The value of kangaroos to Australia is in their feet. Yes: their feet are not cloven-hoofed. As a result, their soft paws do not tear up the already-ancient and leached ground. This is a major benefit for the long-term health of kangaroo habitat, as Australian land is much more delicate than any other continent. It is so old that the few remaining plant-food minerals need to be carefully husbanded, or entire tracts of land will degenerate. Introduced cattle and sheep have created major problems of erosion, reduced land fertility, and species imbalance. Some people feel that replacement of farm animals by kangaroos is one way to go.

Bush Tucker

Desert bloodwood (*Eucalyptus opaca*) has bumpy fruits on its stems that are called "bush coconuts" (top left). These are made when a female Coccid insect lays her egg in the twig. The developing grub changes the DNA switches in the tree, causing a gall to form around it, complete with delicate white coconut-like flesh. The grub and white flesh can be eaten like an apple.

Aboriginal peoples enjoyed several types of seed from acacia species (below right) which appear in bean-like pods for mulga types and in fluted shapes for the earpod wattle types. Mulga seeds have a high protein and oil content similar to peanut butter, but also contain bitter juices that can be roasted away.

Black gidgee (*Acacia pruinocarpa*) exudes gum from wounds in its limbs. The gum is a prized edible resource. Juicy mistletoe berries of the *Amyema* and *Lysiana* genuses are enjoyed by children, although the seed itself is inedible. Pencil yam roots (*Vigna lanceolata*) were roasted for a highly nutritional starchy meal and formed an important part of Aboriginal economy.

Feathery groundsel (Seneco anethifolius, opposite page, top), foxtail (Psilotus sp.,bottom left), blunt-leaved senna (Senna artemiosioides, bottom right) are common in arid areas inland.

feet that act like snow shoes over the sand; and the sparse fat-tailed antechinus (*Pseudant-echinus macdonnellensis*), which lives in termite mounds and rocky hills, and stores energy in its bulbous, fatty tail. This antechinus is concentrated around the rocks of both monoliths.

Australia has its own species of native rodents that came over from Asia when land bridges were established. The desert mouse (*Pseudomys desertor*) is found in spinifex communities and in kangaroo grass at the base of Uluru, though not after dry times or after burning. Rain can increase Uluru's density of mice up to 24 times in a couple of years. The desert mouse eats shoots, rhizomes, seeds, and flowers and can gain weight on a diet of dry seeds without water.

Around the mulga and spinifex of Uluru, look for crimson chats, which eat insects and drink nectar but not water; pied honeyeaters and striated grasswrens, which are often found near the flowering shrubs around sunset

viewing parking lot; dusky grasswrens; painted fire-tails; western bowerbirds; and chiming wedgebills. Brightly colored companions include mulga parrot, budgerigar, cockatiel, mistletoe birds, little woodswallows, and little button-quail. Also found here are common wallaroo kangaroos and the thorny devil lizard. During the day it is difficult to see some of the desert adapters, but they are there. At night there is much more activity. Desert adapters include the desert scorpion (*Urodachus* sp.), sand monitor or Gould's goanna (*Varanus gouldii*), and the loud barking spider (*Seleno-cosmia stirlingi*).

Intensely colored fairy wrens and crimson chats breed here. Fairy wrens are fantastic cooperative breeders that have entered into a socialized system of giving behavior that ensures the survival of the species by sacrificing the breeding success of younger individuals.

Shield shrimp (*Triops australiensis*) and fairy shrimp (*Imnadopsis* sp.) are found in areas

Cooperative Birds

About one-third of Australia's landbirds are cooperative breeders, which is unusually high and is probably linked to the decadal El Niño weather pattern. In the case of the gorgeous blue variegated fairy wren that is found around the Kata Tjuta Monolith, mature young adult males of about a year old are non-breeding helpers. The breeding female builds the nest and incubates the eggs, but one or more non-breeding sons cooperate with their father to help feed the young. Older males are adorned in bright blue plumage earlier in the spring than younger male fairy wrens. Younger males scope surrounding territories. One significant advantage of group living is that it increases awareness of predators and provides an army of defenders. Watch for the "rodent run" display that distracts potential predators away from the nest.

Fairy-wren cooperation has prompted scientists to explore clues about whether man's capacity for virtue has evolved as a biological instinct. New research in math and science, demonstrated in the movie *A Beautiful Mind*, has confirmed our hope that the competitive world-view is false. Instead, the selfishness inherent in genetic selection does not mutually weed out selfless actions, but in fact often selects for selflessness.

Cosmic Impact

Gosse Bluff shows rocks in the act of bouncing back after being plasticized by a comet impact. The upper crater has eroded completely away. This stunning sight, a moment of cosmic force frozen in time, is worth taking the Mereenie Loop to see.

surrounding Uluru and Kata Tjuta, and respond to rain by multiplying several generations in seasonal waterholes when they get wet and before they dry up. They leave their eggs embedded in mud to be desiccated. If you climb to the top of Uluru after rain, you can see them swimming in the puddles there, a fantastic reminder of the ocean that used to cover this rock.

Uluru is a rock that the local Anangu Aboriginal people recommend not to climb. They regard the site as both sacred and dangerous. It is a difficult scramble and falls do occur, especially on the way down under circumstances of dehydration and heat exhaustion. The surrounding Base Walk is fascinating enough, and gives you an up-close view of the rock's varied facets. You can also take a guided walk near the base to learn about bush tucker, juicy Aboriginal desert food.

Meditative waterholes nestle at the base of Uluru and support a large number of species directly and indirectly. Budgerigar, zebra finch, mulga parrot, crested bellbird, and rufous songlark are some of the seed-eating birds found nearer water sources as they are less arid-adapted and need water many times a day. Waterhole birds attract brown goshawks and collared sparrowhawks.

Anangu art in the form of rock paintings can be seen long the Mala and Mutitjulu Walks. These were created for ceremonial and story-telling purposes and have much meaning for the Anangu today. Sand painting is now the method of expression used.

Ayers Rock Resort is the only place to stay within commuting distance of the rock. This is newly developed with all levels of budget in mind, like a mall of accommodation choices.

Desert Soaks

The crested pigeon (above) can be told apart from the spinifex pigeon by its black crest. The spinifex pigeon has a chestnut crest and bronze coloring on its body. It has two races, one around Alice Springs and central Australia, the other in the northwest. Look at water soaks for the commonest finch around, but nevertheless a very handsome one: the zebra finch. It has zebra markings on its rump and tail, black tear drop cheeks, and the male has orange cheeks. It flocks in groups of 10–100. Crimson chats are also striking birds, collecting in nomadic flocks around water sources.

Kata Tjuta

Kata Tjuta is made of conglomerate rock containing pebbles that are coarser than Uluru but from the same origins. Listen for the descending 4–6 note chime of chiming wedgebills among the Victoria wattles on the Kata Tjuta foothills. Victoria and colony wattles are acacia trees that announce springtime with cream and yellow flowers. Colony wattle seeds are eaten raw by Anangu people, after being ground into a paste.

Crimson chats, pink cockatoos, several fairy wrens, little eagles, woodswallows, and singing honeyeaters are associated with the open grasslands and dunes around Kata Tjuta. Birds associated with the spinifex of Kata Tjuta's rocky slopes include the beautifully spotted painted fire-tails and dusky grasswrens, a larger shy bird that can be seen running over boulders. Take the Valley of the Winds walk and look for the very rare gray falcon, unique to Australia and one of the world's six at-risk falcons. The western bowerbird may be found in dense thickets.

Larapinta Trail

The Larapinta Trail is a newly-opened series of stunning walking track sections covering 250km/150mi along western MacDonnell Ranges habitats, including sheltered gorges, stunning ridgelines, and dry river valleys. The trail runs more-or-less parallel to the road from Alice Springs to Glen Helen on the way to the Mereenie Loop. So you can combine some great

Spinifex Fauna

The nocturnal spinifex hopping mouse (*Notomys alexis*) (right) creates huge burrow complexes with plugged entrances and exits. The burrow is shifted as food supplies move. The mice have deep humid burrows lined with vegetation. Mating is wild, with a lot of violent fighting, and the male locks into the female with an adapted penis that has special spines. Males and females care for the young and they live with multiple families in one burrow. But they come out at night, so go spotlighting if you want to find them. During drought, but not before, this medium-sized animal stores spinifex and other seeds, quick action which probably accounts for its widespread success. Look for large round quondong (*Eucarya acuminata*) seeds that have been drilled with a small hole on one side by this mouse in its efforts to get a meal. These mice get all the water they need from their food. There are several species of hopping mice in other countries, but each one developed the ability to hop individually and not from a common ancestor.

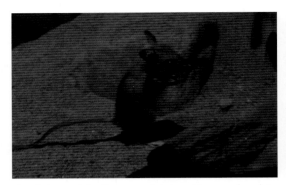

day hikes with distance driving if you take this back road to Uluru. The Larapinta Trail is particularly interesting walking as some sections are so wild that you may encounter extremely rare marsupials and Gondwanan plants. The central rock rat, a species thought extinct, was found recently on the Larapinta Trail. This is another species that has become part of a captive breeding program to restore it back to nature at Alice Springs Desert Park.

Although the focus is on long-distance walking from Alice Springs to Mount Sonder, the trail is set up as a series of very achievable 1–3 day hikes that can be entered or left at different stages by hikers of varying ability. Not all sections are open, but the full trail will take about two weeks. You can go on your own or with a wilderness guide such as with Trek Larapinta (www.treklarapinta.com.au) which runs tours from April to October during the somewhat cooler, drier months. Camping is permitted. The CATIA visitor information center in Alice Springs has an information brochure for $1; check to make sure your chosen section is opened before departure.

Walking sections for ecotravellers can be accessed by road, which takes you directly to the section. Part of Section 10 at Ormiston Gorge is one of the best walks of the area, rated highly for the brilliant cliff colors in the morning (3 hours loop). Section 2 follows rocky outcrops from Simpsons Gap west to Jay Creek through the locally now-rare brushtail possum colony (23km/14.2mi overnight), and unfolds onto

Tussock Communes

Spinifex tussock communities (left, around crimson turkeybush, *Eremophila latrobei*, in flower, widespread on sand plains) are worth exploring even though they may look dried up. You can tell if you are in spinifex if you seem to be surrounded by rolling grassland, but the leaf tips are as sharp as glass shards when you touch them. Spinifex tussocks are of several species including *Trioda* sp. and *Ptectrachne* sp., and provide essential microclimates that harbor birds, lizards, snakes, mice, and marsupials. More species are found around spinifex than any other habitat experienced across the Red Center. Spinifex's huge root systems stabilize the dunes so well that the dunes are 20,000 years old here. Only the crests move. Spinifex is not related to grass, which came to Australia much later.

Section 3, Jay Creek to Standley Chasm (14km/8.6mi). Section 3 has steep ups-and-downs; it's a challenging wilderness hike among rare plants and wildlife. Section 8 from Serpentine Gorge to Ochre Pits is good for even novice backpackers (19km/11.7mi overnight, or two day-long walks without camping). In this section you can see stunning views from the top of the quartzite ridgeline across to Haasts Bluff, Mount Zeil, at 1,531m/5,006ft, the highest mountain in the Northern Territory, plus nearby Mount Sonder and distant Gosse Bluff, formed by the comet impact that occurred just before flowers first bloomed on the earth.

Glen Helen

To reach the 4WD Mereenie Loop going south to Uluru, you need to go deep into the western side of the MacDonnell Ranges, and the best first place to stay is at quiet Glen Helen, with its one motel and no houses. Take Larapinta Drive west from Alice Springs and at 52km/32.2mi turn west onto Namatjira Drive to Glen Helen 85km/52.7mi farther on, taking about four hours by car. This is a picturesque drive on a sealed

Melons and More

Native cucumber (*Cucumis melo*) is a small melon eaten by Aboriginal peoples as bush tucker. Unlike cattle, emus disperse the seed of this cucumber without destroying the seeds in digestion. Colocynth melon (*Citrullus colocynthis*, above and top left) is an introduced species that grows among native melons. The hibiscus family is abundant, including the desert rose (*Gossypium australe*) which has short hairs on its stems and furry leaves (center right) and similar-looking flowers to Sturt's desert rose (*G. sturtianum*, below right), the floral emblem of the Northern Territory. Sturt's rose is differentiated by its hairless stems. Gibson's desert fuchsia (*Eremophila gibsonii*) has hooked leaf ends, and similar desert fuchsia (*E. gilesii*, bottom left) has straight-pointed leaves. Native bluebells (*Wahlengerbia radgelii*) nod in the breeze (bottom right). The bush is colored by large shrubs of striking slender fuchsia (*Eremophila decipiens*), magenta emubush (*Eremophia alternifolia*), which has whorled leaves with hooked leaf ends, and similar crimson turkeybush (*E. latrobei*), which has grayer leaves that curl under at the margins (right, second from top). Yellow butterfly bush (*Petalostylis labicheoides*) is a shrub found on rocky sites in central Australia near water (center left).

road along a shrub-decorated valley parallel to the red spines of the West MacDonnell Ranges. Don't expect mountains: erosion has reduced these once-mighty Alps to an average of a few hundred feet, but they are still hypnotically attractive and have a geological history to match. On the way are several interesting turn-offs that reach the Larapinta Trail and make good side-trips. You can see the normally extremely shy rock wallabies being fed at Standley Chasm if you arrive by 9:30 AM from Alice Springs. The chasm is a narrow gap in the 80-m/266-ft MacDonnell Ranges. Here and at Ellery Creek, Big Hole, Serpentine Gorge, and Ochre Pits you can access the Larapinta Trail. But just before Glen Helen is the north turnoff to a particularly well-loved ecotraveller site: Ormiston Gorge.

Glen Helen Resort, is recommended for its quietness, the cliff-face view out of the riverside cabins, its quirky Australian charm, and its priceless back-roads atmosphere. Do not expect resort-level accommodation, however, but warm minimalism. A campsite is situated by the lodge. The helicopter tour of Gosse Bluff and surroundings is a must, though be prepared to get into a flying bubble the size of a bath tub. You can also dip into the peaceful Finke River and Glen Helen Gorge on an inflated inner tube. The Finke River is one of the oldest rivers in the world, if rivers have any age at all. You can pick this river up again at Palm Valley to the south where you can celebrate the river's 100 million years of crafting a prehistoric habitat.

You can get a pass to traverse the next leg of the trip, the Mereenie Loop itself, from Glen Helen lodge or from Kings Canyon if you are going in the opposite direction. These outlets also offer Tnorala Conservation Reserve access permits that are needed if you wish to explore Gosse Bluff, which you may want to do once you see it. Glen Helen is the last stop for gas going south, and Kings Canyon going north. Side trips can get you to three gas stations along

A juvenile brown falcon (above) waits to flush prey from around its roadside perch. These falcons pursue mammals, birds, insects and reptiles. Black-breasted buzzards (below) are widespread across the Red Center.

She-Oaks

You will spot many narrow trees with gray needle-like leaves. These are the casuarinas and she-oaks and include desert oak, (*Allocasuarina decaisneana*). These only grow on deep sand. Desert oak is not killed by brush-fire. Its branches are used as fire sticks by Aboriginal people. The apparent leaves are in fact stems, the leaves being reduced to scales that form minute rosettes. Male and female flowers are found on one tree, males at the tips of the lower branches and female red flowers are found higher up its branches, forming cones later. Port Lincoln ringnecks eat the cone seeds. Major Mitchell's cockatoos are associated with desert oaks in dune country near Uluru. She-oaks probably evolved from the earliest flowering plant types, the catkin bearers.

Bush Candy and Mulga Tools

Honeypot ants (*Melophorus bagoti*) store an abundant but short-lived nectar harvest in ant repletes, or ants that swell up to live as honeypots. These live storage workers disgorge enough nectar to last them through lean times. Aboriginal peoples dig deep under mulga trees to collect the honey delicacy. Mulga seeds were husked, roasted, and then ground into a peanut-flavored paste for food. This was one of the main food sources for Aboriginal peoples.

Lerp scale insects cover mulga leaves. The chunky red semi-spherical insects exude honeydew that can be sucked off the leaves or used to make a sweet drink with water.

Aboriginal people used polishable mulga wood for many tools, including boomerangs. Mulga is an Aboriginal name for a narrow shield made of mulga wood.

Larapinta Drive after Gosse Bluff, if essential, at Tjuwanpa, Hermannsburg, and Wallace Rockhole where there are also basic accommodation facilities plus Aboriginal tours. Overnight camping is not allowed once you reach the Mereenie Loop Road permit area, but there are camp sites and accommodation facilities before and after this Aboriginal land.

Gosse Bluff, Tnorala

The 4WD unsealed road starts immediately west of Glen Helen across a ford. This can become impassable during the wet season, when the road can wash away, as Glen Helen itself did a few years ago. The road continues along the side of the attractive western MacDonnell Range until Tylers Pass, when it turns south. Many colorful parrots, birds of prey, and honeyeaters can be seen close-up as few people drive this route and the daytime wildlife is relatively tame. There are abundant flowering shrubs. After Tylers Pass is a panoramic viewing station at about 56km/34.7mi from Glen Helen on the top of a hill that looks across rolling spinifex toward Gosse Bluff.

Gosse Bluff is what remains of a huge comet impact. Just before flowering plants evolved 120 million years ago, a large comet's impact vaporized rocks miles below the earth's surface at Gosse Bluff. The kick-back punched slabs of debris and dust 20km/12.4mi into the upper atmosphere and released energy equal to hundreds of thousands of nuclear bombs. The crater and layers of land surface have eroded completely away, leaving what lies beneath: the up-welling cone of rocks frozen in the act of vertical decompression, just after vaporization. This explains why the "crater" floats "up" above the horizon. The comet impact associated with the demise of dinosaurs was much larger, but Gosse Bluff may have had a major ecological effect at the time it hit. Perhaps it aided the evolution of flowering plants in some way.

Palm Valley

At Tylers Pass the road enters Aboriginal land. After the Gosse Bluff viewing station, you can either turn south along the new road around Gosse Bluff to Kings Canyon, or take an extra day's detour and visit fascinating Palm Valley. To reach Palm Valley, from Gosse Bluff turn east on Larapinta Drive to Hermannsburg and the Ntaria Aboriginal Community, which is located 50km/31mi from Tylers Pass, and then turn south to Finke Gorge National Park. You will need a good 4WD vehicle for this part, not any old 4WD, plus a wading passenger to go ahead of the car and guide it if the river is deep during summertime. Be aware of cloud formations that may signal flash floods, particularly during the wet season, when access may be closed.

Palm Valley is a destination visited by 4WD vans from Alice Springs via Larapinta Road because it is a remote Finke River site in the middle of arid land with relict plant species from dinosaur times. These include the red cabbage palm (*Livistonia mariae*), from which the valley gets its name. There are 333 plant species in this valley, some very rare, with lineages dating back 12 million years. The George Gill Range not far away has 600 of these types of Gondwanan and other plants, but this region is not easily accessible to ecotravellers.

Mulga

Dense groves of mulga (*Acacia aneura*) (left page) alternate with casuarinas, grass trees, and spinifex.

Mulga is a nitrogen-fixer, converting atmospheric nitrogen into amino acids in its roots. It also associates with mycorrhizal fungi that act as a nutrient and water source. As a result, its leaves are high in protein. But high tannin levels in the leaves tend to make the protein indigestible, though it is used as fodder.

Mulga grows as a bushy shrub with silvery-green vegetation and delicate yellow bottlebrush flowers. It is highly variable in all physical aspects, having 15–20 variations in "morphotype," or appearance, in a single population. Mature leaves are usually elongated flattened green stems, or phyllodes. These are arranged to funnel water into a central root system, like an inverted umbrella. An enormous tap root extends under the tree. Saplings of 10cm/4in high have been found to have tap roots 3m/10ft long. Fire is part of its lifecycle: although the tree cannot survive fire, intense heat cracks the seeds, which then germinate well. In sheltered, arid conditions, wizened forms of mulga have been found to be 150–240 years old. Current land use has shown that removal of mulga in favor of grass depletes the land of nitrogen.

ENSO

It does rain in Australia's Red Center, usually in January through March, coinciding with the monsoon in the tropical north. Every decade or so, it pours 200mm/8in in a single month. This is tied to the decadal El Niño Southerly Oscillation (ENSO) on which the weather of all Australia depends. As a result, species have to survive sparse years of aridity, interspersed with flash floods followed by food aplenty. In between underground water systems contain water aged from this year to 7,000 years ago, and this bubbles up into rock pools and rivulets. After rainy years, the resulting habitat of the Red Center is a brilliant mix of red and green filled with brightly colored parrots, fat hawks, iridescent reptiles, and emerging mushrooms.

Mereenie Loop

Mereenie Loop Road going southwest starts as you take the new road from Gosse Bluff and merge with the far west end of Larapinta Drive. A restricted-access turnoff to the Areyonga community is located at Katapata Pass. If you wish to visit this closed Aboriginal community you must join an organized tour booked in advance. The CATIA office in Alice Springs can provide information. Otherwise, no stopping is allowed on the Mereenie Loop except at the scheduled rest area at the Kings Canyon end, which has panoramic views back across Gosse Bluff and mulga from the south. The road is relatively untraveled and so is a welcome immersion into the true wilderness of the Red Center.

Kings Canyon

Kings Canyon is now on the map as a major tourist stop. The red canyon walls rise above the horizon and can be seen for miles around. This is an example of a rare gorge 270m/883ft deep where the microclimate has allowed a few handfuls of non-arid land species, including palms and cycads, to cling on since

Gondwanan times, surrounded by intensely colored rocks. From the entrance parking lot you can take the 3-hour Canyon Walk through the Garden of Eden. Add a day to your trip to allow ample time to experience it. A shorter 1-hour Kings Creek Walk takes you to the waterfall.

Accommodation at Kings Canyon Resort, as at Ayer's Rock Resort, is well-organized for large numbers of tourists in pleasant, newly built high-quality surroundings. Options at the resorts include camping, budget lodge, and hotel accommodation. There are no additional choices at either Resort.

A pair of parrots rest at sunset in an acacia tree (top). There are 930 species of acacia or wattle in Australia, 93% being endemic. 70 are newly identified species. The best way to differentiate between the many acacia species is to look at the flowers. Mulga flowers (middle) are on single stems with several pom-poms on a strand. Mulga apples (bottom) are formed by wasp larvae that create edible galls tasting like apples. Watch for zebra finch at desert soaks (left).

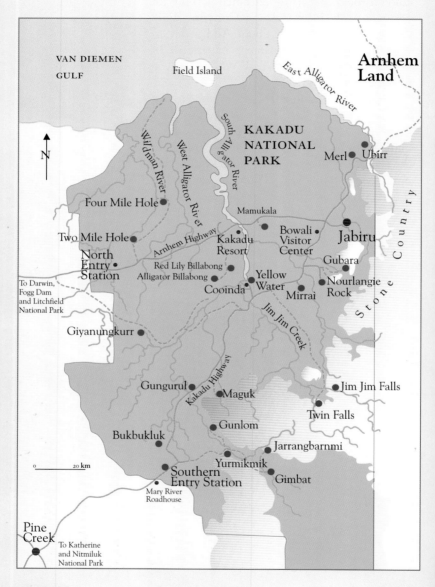

Don't Miss

❖ Nourlangie Rock with rock art
galleries, a billabong, and Barrk
Walk

❖ Ubirr with rock art, sandstone
walk, and crocodiles in the river

❖ Fog Dam filled with waterbirds,
crocodiles, and nightlife

7

Top End & Kakadu

Territorial Spat

Intermediate egrets (previous page and above) are the commonest egret around the Northern Territory, with about 90,000 birds breeding in Top End mangroves. These two individuals played "chicken" over territories. The right-hand bird maintained his territory with a vertical flight at the edge of his claim, and the left-hand bird flinched and lost the spat. Great egrets are similar-looking but are solitary and their gape extends behind the eyes. Denise Lawungkurr Goodfellow, a respected Kakadu guide and author, notes that the plumes of egrets ("aigrette" is old French for plumed), with birds of paradise and grebes, were collected and sold to decorate hats in Europe. This caused near-extinction of many species until the Importation of Plumage Prohibition Act of 1921 outlawed the practice.

Top End & Kakadu

When Paul Hogan and Linda Koslowski took the plunge in the movie *Crocodile Dundee*, they kicked off into the green waters surrounded by the two billion-year-old escarpment of Gunlom Falls. This is in Kakadu National Park, a unique World Heritage Area of tropical savanna that holds more species and habitats than any of Australia's other savannas. And it represents the best of the Top End, the tropical region of the Northern Territory. Nitmiluk National Park, near Katherine, and Litchfield National Park, are also significant destinations.

Kakadu is a vast floodplain encompassing the entire river system of the South Alligator River. It is made even more interesting by being bordered on the eastern side by an ancient sandstone escarpment marking the edge of Arnhem Land stone country and filled with ancient species. In summer months the floodwaters recede, leaving dancing brolga cranes and other waterbirds congregating around the flood plains and the slimming waterholes. This life is surveyed by 117 species of reptiles, including a high snake density and the largest population base of "salties" or estuarine crocodiles (*Crocodylus porosus*) in the world. In the folds of the rocky outcrops are many microhabitats with plunging waterfalls, cooling rainforest slivers, and expressive Aboriginal rock shelters. Spectacular Aboriginal rock art dating from 30–20,000 years ago can be seen at several sites, most easily at the base of Nourlangie Rock and Ubirr. If you climb onto the sandstone outliers above, you can see the enormity of the floodplain and hear birdsong of locally common endemics echoing around of one of the most ancient habitats in the world.

Erosion has turned the gnarled plateau sandstone into quirky statues. But you won't

Paperbark trees (Melaleuca sp., above) must dry out completely after flooding to re-charge their styrofoam-like bark and aerial roots with air. Nymphaea waterlilies flower from February to July. The tubers can be cooked for a nourishing meal popular with Aboriginal people.

find any visible fossils: a microscopic fossil found in the nearby Gulf of Carpentaria indicates that the sandstone is a monument to the time when the first nucleated cells evolved in the ocean, long before life on land. So, these particular rocks have witnessed earth's evolution from when unicellular organisms started to mark time with the first cellular death. Until then, organisms did not die until they were destroyed by something else.

The Arnhem Land plateau was also there when the first plants moved onto land, when the first lungfish followed them, when the last dinosaurs were overtaken by mammals, and when people first arrived in this area about 50,000 years ago. Some of the ensuing changes are chronicled in the Rock Art series, which depicts game like the marsupial tapir

Northern Territory Camping

The camp sites around Kakadu and Katherine offer the best chance for close encounters with wallabies and bird life.

• Check that you have good netting on the tent and that the tent is in good repair.

• Carry effective insect repellent and sunscreen. Take an extra tarp for shade.

• Camp more than 15m/49ft from the water's edge to avoid crocodiles.

• Carry water in your vehicle for the trip, plus a metal water bottle for day trips. Some camping sites have reticulated water.

• Take extra plastic bags and observe low-impact bush camping practices.

• Use antiseptic tea tree oil instead of detergent for washing cooking implements.

• Take some recreational diversions: binoculars, a camera, some cards, a notebook, an ankle ball.

• Be prepared for monsoonal rain during the wet season, and pitch the tent on high ground.

• Bring waterproofing spray.

Gather information and check for campsite access during the wet season by contacting the Bowali Visitor Centre, Kakadu National Park, Box 71, Jabiru NT 0886.

When to go

There are six major seasons in Kakadu. The best time to go is June–September when the Wet dries out and birds mass at waterholes. Yegge in April and May is the beginning of the Dry, with waterlilies starting to flower as the drying winds kick in. Darwin woolybutt and *Acacia oncinocarpa* flowers signal the start of the Dry. Easter bush flowers profusely. The flowering of flood plain plants occurs between March and September, most finishing flowering by August. Flying foxes and colorful birds crowd noisily into nectaries. Fern-leafed grevillea (*Grevillea Pteridifolia*) has nectar-laden flower puffs that attract many birds including silver-crowned and little friarbirds when flowering May–September. Controlled brush fires are started to clear grass and trigger fire-adapted growth.

Wurrgeng in June and July is cooler. Waterbirds huddle in profusion at diminishing watering holes. July–August is the peak visitor season. Gurrung around August to September is the time when the swamps dry to cracked mud. Freshwater crocodiles start digging their nests in the sandbanks. Wallabies are very social and you'll see them congregating near water conducting boxing matches to assign rank.

Gunumeleng from October to December is the "buildup" of very humid and uncomfortable weather, with thunderstorms threatening increasingly but with little rain at first. Hotter fires occur after lightning strikes hit dry brush. Ranger-led walks are suspended until June. The red lily blooms the longest of the water lilies, finishing around November. The floodplain starts to green and fish migrate. Watch for frill-necked lizards coming down from the trees at end of the Dry to battle for breeding rights on the savanna.

Gudjewg in January and February is the Wet proper, with violent, heavy rains, usually in the afternoons. Waterbirds spread out and the area is verdant, lush, and dramatic. Kakadu has more thunderstorms than anywhere else on earth, deluging about 5 feet of rain a year with eighty lightning strikes a day. Estuarine crocodiles, magpie geese and brolgas nest. Some trees are crowded with refugees, and millions of fish move through the flooded areas only to be eaten by the piscivorous bird species. Half of the estuarine crocodile nests are washed away, and, of those that remain under their mother's watch, an average of 6 eggs survive. Only one in a hundred live to be 5–8 years old. Many of the roads are closed but helicopters fly over the cascading waterfalls. Ubirr is accessed by boat.

Banggerreng continues the Wet in March with chicks hatching everywhere despite "knock-em-down" storms flattening the tall speargrass. Female crocodiles stay with their babies for 2 months. As they grow older, the baby crocs fight and leave the safety of the creche. Half of these wide-eyed explorers are swallowed up by predators, including barramundi that eventually grow 6 feet long and can be seen wallowing under bridges.

and huge megafauna, now extinct, signs of the dramatic effect people have had on this continent over time.

Pre-Estuarine Rock Art

Kakadu rock art is grouped into four broad artistic and ecological phases, which may sometimes be seen in the same gallery. The early symbolic art can be spotted in hand outlines (right) and stick figures noted from Pre-estuarine rock art date from 25,000–8,000 years ago. These show red-ochre animals before and after the extinction event caused by the introduction of more frequent fires set by humans, the effect of the dingoes they brought with them, and direct hunting. During this time, 98 percent of Australia's large mammals were wiped out, a much higher figure than in other countries where extinctions were also caused by new hunting techniques.

Estuarine Rock Art

Over time, the huge and fertile hunting plain on the Gulf of Carpentaria east of Kakadu was inundated by the rising ocean, taking Asian island connections with it and flooding Kakadu with seawater. About 16,000 years ago, mangroves silted up Kakadu and stabilized ocean levels, creating huge saltwater swamps, which leveled out about 6,500 years ago. The Yam Style images plus simple people and the legendary Rainbow Serpent of Ubirr are typical of this period of Estuarine rock art, which dates 8,000–2,000 years ago.

Freshwater Rock Art

The environment we now see in Kakadu was formed about 2,000 years ago when floodplains finally reclaimed themselves after natural levees formed. The enormous freshwater refuge was critical for bird species adjusting to a more arid inland. This time of abundance led to the famous X-ray art style that shows internal structures of animals. At Anbangbang shelter

Early Symbolic Communications

Some of the earliest cave art in Kakadu is symbolic, a form of abstract coded communication. An example of symbolic art is the hand in the center of this picture, with two fingers held together. These images were created by blowing wet ochre held in the mouth onto hands that were used as stencils. These art figures are from the Pre-estuarine period of rock art which range from 8,000 to 25,000 years bp. European cave art tends to range from 12,000 to 19,000 years old. The oldest dated cave art in the world was dated recently at 27,100 years, in Cosquer Cave near Marseilles, France, which was discovered in 1991.
The oldest petroglyphs dated in the world are in Wharton Hill, South Australia; they are at least 42,700 years old.

50,000 Years of Aboriginal life

Aboriginal peoples entered Australia around 10,000 years after all non-African races first left Africa and spread across the world, about 80,000 years ago. This exodus has been traced through genetic mapping. New thermo-luminescent dating of sands studded with Aboriginal artefacts show that Kakadu was occupied 50,000 years ago. The Aboriginal way of life continues. East Alligator River cruises are lead by Aboriginal guides who will show you the implements in current use by local clans. These include serrated spears once legally used to stab and punish offenders of Aboriginal laws, and Iron-wood spear heads (above) used in hunting.

X-ray art style fish (below)

Two sisters at Ubirr (top right), Macassan ship (opposite page), and Lightning Man at Nourlangie Rock.

the Namarrgon, or Lightning Man (opposite page, image to right of main figure), is depicted in this style with stone axes emerging from his knees, elbows, and head. These knock together to form thunder and lightning, which also forms an arc over his head. The X-ray style started during the end of the Pre-estuarine rock art period and developed more fully during the Freshwater rock art period. When you look at the art sites, you'll notice that these images crowd with abundance, and this is probably a reflection of the desires of the artists for large hunting yields. Fish, goannas, bats, yams, snakes, kangaroos, turtles, extinct animals, and mythical figures are all interwoven with images of people.

Contact Rock Art

The beche-de-mer sea cucumber trade with Macassan seafarers may account for the reason that these Aboriginal people appear to have had better negotiating skills than others before Europeans became established within Australia. Tim Flannery has argued that this enabled them to negotiate for a larger area (Arnhem Land) than other clans to call their own.

Of the accessible rock art in Kakadu, the site with a good range in art ages and styles is at the Nanguluwur Gallery, away from the crowds. A Contact Period painting of a 200-year-old picture of a Macassan ship is found near excellent X-ray style fish paintings. There are also some grotesque sorcery figures and symbolic hand paintings. Nanguluwur is found by taking the Nourlangie turnoff and then turning north just before arriving at the more-visited year-old Anbangbang Galleries that are on the opposite, south side of Nourlangie Rock. Drive toward Gubara, then turn southeast to Nanguluwur for 2 km/1.2mi. Then walk up to the rock face. Visit both galleries if you can.

Dating Rock Art

Until recently, rock art has been difficult to date. Major ways of dating art include grouping similar styles of images, cross-referencing with fossils of animals depicted in the art, dating beeswax figures, and carbon-dating associated cave artifacts. Rare traces of human blood in the saliva of pigments have allowed accurate dating of some of the oldest layers and images. New dating of human blood has placed one Australian rock shelter image at 10,730 years old and another at 20,320 years old. In Queensland, human blood dated Sandy Creek art at 24,600 years old.

Some of the oldest art appears bright and fresh. Underneath are the oldest layers, stretching back through time.

In the case of ancient petroglyphs chiseled into the rock, a new dating technique has come from analyzing the organic material trapped beneath the layer of varnish deposited naturally on the petroglyph over time.

Fogg Dam

Fogg Dam coexisters (above): pied herons, royal spoonbills, little black cormorants, intermediate egrets, and little egrets. Each waterbird has developed distinctive foraging styles that help them coexist without starving their neighbor. The common royal spoonbill sweeps its bill with several zig-zags per sweep and catches more fish and plants than the uncommon yellow-billed spoonbill. The yellow-billed is slower and stabs at the aquatic vegetation after sweeping its bill like a pendulum, turning up a few more crustaceans and water insects than the royal. Black bitterns forage for fish mostly at night under cover of dense reeds. Great-billed herons wait for large prey during the day, immobile.

Top End Wetlands

The extensive wetlands are one of the major attractions of the Top End. Kakadu's wetlands are relatively young, and are vibrant in comparison with their ancient sandstone escarpment. Paperbark trees dominate Kakadu's floodplain swamp vegetation, fringed by pandanus palms. Holding from a half-to-one million waterbirds during the wet season, these floodplains desiccate to cracked mud during the dry, stirring up willi-willi vortexes of dust. This environment accounts for some evolutionary quirks such as the tiny predatory marsupial, the planigale, which has a thin, flattened head designed to wedge between mud cracks in search of insects. Avoid walking close to the water's edge due to the danger of crocodiles.

Fogg Dam

The manmade but excellent Fogg Dam wildlife wetland is on the way to Kakadu 70km/43.4mi southeast of Darwin on the Arnhem Highway. This is outside Kakadu National Park. The dam was established to grow rice. During the 1960s, the rice-growers supported the change of use to a nature preserve as a way of attracting magpie geese away from other agricultural properties. The area is now a wonderful haven for wildlife. Driving or walking the raised causeway and looking to the east is an ideal way to see the waterbirds, red waterlilies, and

dragonflies on the floodplains or surrounding monsoon and paperbark woodland. There is a good chance you'll see a white-browed crake in the open, plus brolga, jabiru, and jacana. Depending on the season, you may see tawny grassbird, clamorous reed-Warbler, and golden-headed cisticola. Look for the stunning crimson finch, chestnut-breasted manikin, and double-barred finch in the reeds and sedges. At night look for bush stone-curlews, owls, and nightjars. Water python and keelback snakes may also show themselves. And in the Rainforest Walking Trail from the parking lot you may see rainbow pitta and broad-billed flycatcher. Check out the nearby visitor center on the Arnhem Highway for an orientation before exploring the dam.

Kakadu National Park
South Alligator River Wetlands

From Darwin, the northern park entrance is 133km/82.4mi along Arnhem Highway. As you enter, you pass through rolling eucalypt savanna and a smattering of wildflowers in the early dry season. Then the southern alligator floodplains open up with low sedges and variable water levels from one horizon to the other. The floodplain birds include 68 species that use the area as primary habitat, plus 18 migratory species. Huge numbers of magpie geese, wandering whistling-duck, intermediate

Fire Sticks

Kakadu's only banksia, swamp banksia (*Banksia dentate*, below) is found around the swampland. The dense seed heads were used as ember-carriers to take fire from camp to camp. Over thousands of years, the use of these fire sticks selectively favored fire-adapted plants and animals. The cessation of these practices in Arnhem Land is now threatening existing species. But overzealous "managed" burning in other Top End areas is wiping out another set of fragile species. One third of the Top End is burned every year—too frequently and too much.

Yellow Water Cruises

This boat trip is really popular during the dry season when many waterbirds and crocodiles are likely to be seen. At peak times, cruises may be fully booked a year ahead. Nearly all commercial Kakadu tours include Yellow Water in their itinerary. During the wet season the cruise may not be very exciting, but it may be one of the few activities open due to flooding. Yellow Water is neither yellow, nor are there many yellow waterlilies (you can find those at Magela Creek floodplain during Yegge). Some say the floodwaters here used to be called Dirty Water from the buffalo-churned sediment, and perhaps public relations adjusted the sentiment. Reserve cruises through Gagudju Lodge Cooinda, near where the cruises depart. The lodge was the first wilderness tourism site in Kakadu, established when crocodile hunting was in vogue. (800-835-7742 from the US and Canada, 1-800-500-401 from Australia, 0-800-801-111 from New Zealand, 0345-40-4040 from Britain, or 08-8979-0145. Fax 08-8979-0148). Cruises are 90 minutes during the wet season and 2 hours in the dry season, departing from 6:45AM in the dry and 7AM in the wet. The best birding cruises are at sunrise.

Paperbark (Melaleuca sp.) at Yellow Water (above).

egret and glossy ibis are found here. The first two are highly mobile in order to find enough food to keep their flocks going. The intense concentrations of magpie geese rely on large wetlands from several catchment areas in order to support themselves through the wet and dry seasons. Southern and eastern alligator river areas are key food sources for magpie geese in the dry, and they move to breeding sedgelands in the wet, especially in the Mary River area outside Kakadu.

Most Kakadu waterbird species are fish-eaters, but Kakadu's largest populations are tuber-eaters. The tubers of bulkuru sedge, found in coastal freshwater marshes, are the starchy dry season staple eaten by the brolga, supplemented by insects, crustaceans, frogs, mollusks, and other small animals. Look for brolgas soaring at high altitudes when they cool themselves during the middle of the day, or dancing by their nest sites and feeding grounds. These cranes have opportunistically adapted to Australia's diverse climates and agricultural cropland. There are many legends about brolgas, and their dance is woven into those performed by Aboriginal people.

Yellow Water Billabong

Yellow Water is the only place in Kakadu where you can take a scheduled boat cruise on the floodplain itself. In terms of what you will see, the cruise can be a hit-or-miss affair depending on the time of day and season. Outside peak dry season or on later than the first excursion of the day it may be a limited excursion, but you will still get a feel for what it is like to survive predators on a tropical floodplain. During the dry you may see large numbers of magpie geese, and a few brolga, jabiru, plumed whistling ducks, and estuarine crocodiles. You may catch a glimpse of little kingfisher, rainbow pitta, common nankeen night heron, rarer black bittern, barking owl, tawny frogmouth, great-billed heron, white-browed crake, and rufous owl. Common water birds include green pygmy goose (a duck related closely to the wood duck found in the United States), various egrets, royal spoonbill, white-headed shelduck, pratincole, and whiskered tern. Waterlilies flower from April and paperbark trees decorate the edge of the billabong, their styrofoam-like bark and adventitious roots helping them seek and retain oxygen during immersion in the wet season.

On the way to the Yellow Water boat ramp you may see tawny grassbirds, cuckoos, and golden-headed cisticola, also known as the tailor bird. The insignificant brown male tailor bird takes about five days to make a nest by drilling holes in leaves and pulling them

Goose Camp

Magpie geese root for bulkuru sedge tubers, foraging in reedy wetlands and open water. During the dry season, they congregate around the South Alligator River in an area known as "Goose Camp" (below). They do not breed there, though, but move to scattered lagoons and marshes in Kakadu to nest when the wet season begins. These primitive geese have semi-webbed toes, a compromise that assists them when they perch in trees. They also use their feet to scratch out the reeds that they collect for nesting material. They nest in a foot or two of water on platforms built over a foundation of living rushes. More than one female shares each nest in a version of cooperative breeding, and the birds are polygamous. The chicks have downy cinnamon-red heads and gray-and-white bodies. Despite the huge local numbers that give the illusion of permanency, magpie geese are under threat from severe changes to their habitats. One of these is the introduction of non-native plants that choke water systems and cost millions of dollars to control the degradation they cause.

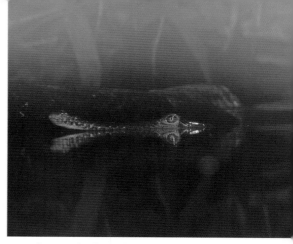

Crocodiles

Freshwater crocs (right) are less dangerous to humans than estuarine crocs, but they still can bite. They have tapering fish-adapted snouts. They nest in holes built in embankments during the dry season between July and September. Freshwater crocs "pulse" the nesting of a population of females within a three-week period. They sometimes nest close together in groups when they may destroy one another's eggs. Freshwater crocodiles have been hunted less than estuarine crocs because the hide is lower in value. The more dangerous estuarine crocodile or "saltie" was hunted commercially until 1972. Since then its numbers have grown. It is pushing out the freshwater crocodile that had encroached on the old "saltie" territories left open by hunting. Croc hatchlings are protected by vigilant maternal behavior, with estuarine mothers guarding their nest and enclosed eggs laid between November and March. Mothers of both species gently pick up their young in their jaws to take their babies to their first swim meet where the hungry, cheeping juveniles chomp on crabs and other invertebrates. The sex of both types of croc is determined by egg temperature, not a sex chromosome.

together with threads of spider web. Its barrel-shaped leaf nest is lined with soft leaves and attached to reeds above the marshland. You are likely to see the white-breasted sea eagle, which rears its young in the vicinity before the rains come.

Yellow Water is found 50km/31mi south of Jabiru on the Kakadu Highway, and 7.5km/4.5 mi along a signposted turnoff. There is a 0.8km/0.5mi Yellow Water Walk during the dry season over boardwalks and paths to Home Billabong. Outside Kakadu there are more boating options including Wildman and Mary River cruises.

Brolga

The Northern population of brolga found in Kakadu (above) has distinct differences in behavior and breeding season from the Southern population found in Queensland and New South Wales. This may indicate the early evolutionary stage separating into two future species. The breeding season of Kakadu brolgas starts in the pre-wet of November/December in select nest sites. Brolgas nest in freshwater swamps or brackish water and are the only cranes with salt glands in their eyes that can excrete brine. They protect their nests from January flooding by making their grassy mounds up to four feet in diameter.

East Alligator River and Crocodiles

The Guluyambi Aboriginal Culture Cruise on the East Alligator River (1-800-089-113 from Australia only or 08-8979-2411) starts near the Border Store and gives an Aboriginal perspective of estuarine crocodiles, wildlife, hunting, and bush lore around this tidal river. Estuarine crocodiles may move to the saltier waters here from preferred freshwater breeding territories, sometimes going as far as the ocean where they have been known to ride waves and surf.

To glimpse a crocodile's power on the way to Kakadu, you can witness the Famous Jumping Crocodiles cruise at Beatrice Hill and the Adelaide River on the Arnhem Highway 64.5km/40mi from Darwin (08-8988-8144).

Estuarine and freshwater crocodiles are dangerous to humans, so swimming and even camping within a few feet of crocodile waters should be avoided. Freshwater crocs only bite if harassed, but estuarine crocs will eat you without provocation. Wallowing water buffaloes used to be a major threat to nesting crocodiles. After they were introduced, they destroyed much habitat, so recently a government program virtually eradicated them. Some sites may be free of dangerous estuarine crocodiles, but there are freshwater crocodiles around. The best place to swim is in the hotel pool.

Mamukala Wetlands

Mamukala is located 7km/4.3mi east of the South Alligator River, south of the Arnhem Highway. An observation building and walk overlooks the grassy Mamukala wetlands where thousands of magpie geese, egrets, herons, cormorants, little curlew, Australian pratincole, and oriental pratincole can be seen in the late dry season.

West Alligator River

Look for Nankeen night heron, black bittern, and azure and little kingfishers after you stop your car to walk by the West Alligator River.

Nasty Neighbors

Sundews (*Drosera* sp.) (top three) are common on the floodplain areas that dry out into savanna. There are 70 species in Australia and they trap insects on their glandular hairs to obtain nitrogen and phosphorus. Dodder (bottom) is a parasite that sucks sap from other plants on which it sprawls.

Extreme Wetland Survivors

You'd think that wetland fauna would eat aquatic food. But here, a reliance on terrestrial food is the way that this swampland fauna has learned to survive the extreme seasonality from Wet to Dry. Archer fish *Toxotes chatareus* (top left) dislodge terrestrial prey by squirting them with their water gun. Black bream and sharp-nosed grunter fish eat land-based food washed into the wetlands. Rainbowfish (bottom right) eat food blown onto the water surface from terrestrial areas, and their beauty has earned them a place in aquariums all over the world.

Other fish are aquatic feeders. Purple-spotted gudgeon (bottom left) in Jim Jim Falls even swim up to the top of the plateau for food. They are carnivorous, and the males guard the female's eggs until they hatch. The eel-tailed catfish (top right) probes the sludge with its highly scent-sensitive barbels. Silver barramundi *Lates calcarifer* (below) compete with equally huge gulf saratoga *Scleropages jardini*. The Saratoga broods eggs and fry in the female's mouth for protection, and eats terrestrial insects and fish. When looking at fish, do not park or slow down on bridges, due to rear-ending danger. Park off the road by clear creeks.

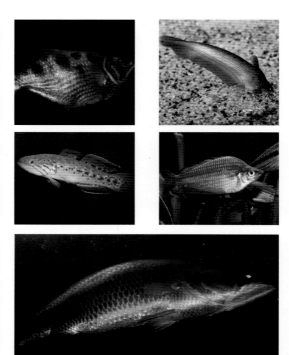

This river has several branches crossed between the Northern Entrance Station and Kakadu Resort. Kingfishers have eyes adapted to see above and below water. When plunging underwater, they look through the side of the specially-curved lens. This gives them accurate vision despite the sudden decrease in apparent distance caused by water's magnifying capacity increasing by one third.

Gungarre Rainforest & Anggardabal Billabong

The 3.6km/2mi Gungarre Monsoon Rainforest Walk is a good way to see both rainforest birds and water birds, starting at the fig tree just to the east of Kakadu Resort on the Arnhem Highway and going beside the excellent Anggardabal Billabong. In the rainforest look for rainbow pittas, Torrey Strait pigeon, little shrike-thrush, varied triller, orioles, green-backed gerigone, and rose-crowned fruit-dove.

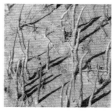
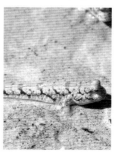

Fiddler crabs preen the mangroves (male: top, female: below). Mangrove (Soneratia caseolaris) on the banks of the South Alligator River (above, with snorkel type pneumatophores: top right). Mud skippers (right) are the primary food of young crocodiles.

Muirella Park and Sandy Billabong

Sandy Billabong is the place to go if you want fantastic waterbird variety. This water hole is found 6km/3.7mi down a 4WD track from Muirella Park, a campground 30km/19mi south of Jabiru along the Kakadu Highway, 7km/4.3mi south of the Nourlangie Rock turning. When at Muirella Park it is worth also taking the 5km/3mi Bubba Wetlands Walk. From the highway nearby, experience the 360-degree vista of central Kakadu from the Mirrai Lookout, a strenuous climb.

Red Lily Billabong & Alligator Billabong

These billabongs provide excellent destinations in which to see a wide variety of waterbirds without encountering bus-loads of visitors.

Iligadjarr Wetlands

16km/10mi south of Jabiru are the campgrounds of Burdulba and Malabangbandju. Here you can take the 3.8km/2.2mi Iligadjarr Wetlands Walk between the two

The brahminy kite is seen around coastal floodplains and mangroves. Look at the phone booth at Kakadu Holiday Village where you may see one. This one is a resident at the Darwin Wildlife Park (uncaged, trained) from where it flies free and back again.

Dino Eyes

Crocodiles, like birds, see in color. Not only that, but they have four types of cones, so their color vision is better than ours. Crocodiles and birds may have inherited these four cone types from dinosaurs, which probably had colored hides and color vision. Or they may have evolved them independently, as happens frequently in nature. On a crocodile cruise or farm tour, look at the crocodile hide for the darker pits near the center of each scale. These are integumentary sense organs that play a prominent role in enabling crocodiles to pick up signs of dimly seen prey. After all, water is 1,000 times less transparent than air, and crocodiles, adapted to pinpointing their target with their eyes pricking through the water surface, can't see very well underwater. These sense organs cover the head and some of the body to form a network of pressure- and possibly salt-sensitive receptors that together act as a sensor array to map the underwater eddies produced by swimming life. This explains how crocodiles distinguish between a submerged pebble and prey, even in turbid floodwaters.

billabongs. Displays show how Aboriginal people have used local plants and animals.

South Alligator River Mangroves

From the Arnhem Highway you can see the mangroves lining the South Alligator River. There is a marked turn-off leading to the popular boat ramp where you can get a closer look. This is the only place where you can see saltwater mangroves in Kakadu without taking a boat trip. Mangroves flower between August and March and although they have one name, are made up of many different species that have evolved worldwide to the point where they have adapted to thrive in salty or brackish water. Lorikeets and other nectar-eaters flock to these flowers. Mangroves look similar to the uninitiated eye. Look for the otherwise-rare mangrove (*Soneratia caseolaris*) common to this location—it has large white pom-pom brush flowers and long thin leaves. Look too for the pneumatophores, airborne root structures that oxygenate the waterlogged mangrove roots. You may also see salt-tolerant cottonwood (*Hibiscus tiliaceus*) here as well. This has large yellow flowers with chocolate centers.

The fishy smell of crocodile burp could be picked up in this paperbark swamp.

Look for the rufous owl around the South Alligator River roosting on exposed, low branches. It likes to sit on a bare branch away from the tree trunk under dense foliage. Look for pellets and fur under its roost, which can be approached closely. It catches bats and large insects at night in flight, and snatches mammals and birds (including the northern rosella) from tree branches. It makes a "woo-hoo" call. It likes rainforest and *Melaleuca* paperbark trees around rivers, plus eucalypts when close to rainforest.

Northern Territory mangroves can extend up to 12.4km/20mi inland along estuary banks but other than at the South Alligator River, they are difficult to see in Kakadu due to limited access. Near lowland freshwater streams, the freshwater mangrove (*Barringtonia acutangular*) can be found flowering at night (Aug-Feb). This species came from Asia after the last ice age, 14 million years ago. It is also called barringtonia, or itchy tree. It attracts a collection of grubs with stinging hairs that sit under the leaves during the dry season. The bark and leaves were used as a fish poison by Aboriginal people. It shares a distant, common ancestor with the eucalypts, and its mangrove relatives originated in Australia and spread worldwide. Other mangroves are more salt-tolerant and grow at specific salt levels in the estuarine habitat. Some pump salt out of their stems until they are covered by a rime of salt crystals.

Kakadu's Stone Country

The sandstone of this region predates the coming together of the southern landmasses of Gondwana, was present during the formation of Pangea when all the world's continents were connected, twice floated on rocks of hardening "plastic" to the south and north pole, and is four times older than any life on land.

As a result, it is Kakadu's stone country, and not the fertile floodplain, that offers the most important refuge for endemic biota in

The Water Buffalo Contribution

Water buffalo have been brought under control by a feral eradication program, and this initially allowed exquisite red lotuses (*Nelumbo nucifera*) and wetland flowers to regenerate in the permanent swamps. The buffalo eradication program ceased in 1997, after it had removed most buffalo and controlled the transfer of disease to domestic stock, the goal of the hunting effort. The control program was welcomed by conserva-tionists at first, but in the end may have created more ecological problems than it solved. Feral Asian water buffalo got a bad name in Kakadu because they broke levee banks and perma-nently drained some freshwater wetlands. They wallowed in billabongs, destroying red lilies and delicate crocodile breeding habitats. But the buffalo were removed so quickly that an ecological vacuum occurred, favoring invasive native species, including flammable grasses that burn much hotter than before, destroying the ecological system.

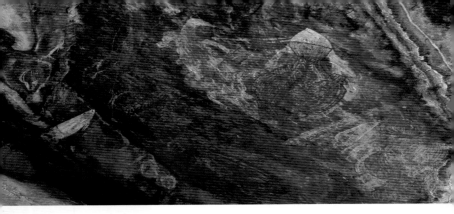

Ubirr rock art overhang

Ubirr Water Bus
Rangers go to pick up school children along the road leading to Ubirr and Arnhem Land. The road is under several meters of water during the wet season, so the rangers take a boat. You can follow this water route during the wet season on a cruise to the Ubirr rock art site. During the dry, Ubirr is accessible by road.

the entire Northern Territory. Their two billion years have collected a diversity of remnant species from the entire scope of land-based biology. The floodplain has the highest biomass. The lowland area forest has the highest diversity. The "high land composed of horizontal strata of sandstone, seem[s] to be literally hashed, leaving the remaining blocks in fantastic figures of every shape," observed Ludwig Leichhardt in 1845, after whom the bright-colored Leichhardt grasshopper (*Petasida ephippigera*) is named. This gaudy purple and crimson grasshopper hatches underground and can be found on the fragrant leaf spikes of *Pityrodia jamesii*. Mammals and birds found nowhere else include the shy black wallaroo (*Macropus bernardus*), a rock kangaroo with black male and paler female; the recently-discovered Oenpelli python (*Morelia oenpelliensis*); and the sandstone strike-thrush, which looks heavenwards as it lets loose its haunting melodic call from the top of an outcrop. It searches for insects close to the rocks. Arnhem Land passes take up to a year to obtain from the Northern Land Council Office, Jabiru, (08-8979-2410), but you can explore stone country escarpment and rainforest without needing one, in the following areas.

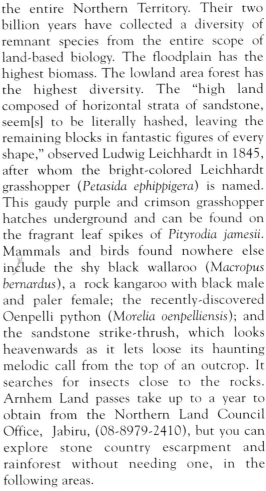

Ubirr

Ubirr is a sandstone outlier by the eastern Alligator River, close to Arnhem Land. A 30.6-m/100-ft climb up Ubirr Rock where an array of X-ray style and earlier Aboriginal art is found depicting fish and land animals from the Pre-estuarine and Freshwater Periods may be found 2.4km/1.5mi north of the Border Store. The galleries are at the base of Ubirr and half way up. The stepped rock climb to the top of Ubirr should be easy for most visitors and gives a breathtaking sunset view of the Nardab floodplain, where you can witness panoramic lightning strikes. Hidden in the woodland to the south is the Jabiluka uranium mine, which was recently put on hold. Ubirr Rock is opened from 2PM to sunset in the wet season, and from 8:30AM in the dry. The access road gets flooded during the wet, and a boat must be used to reach the rock. Ubirr is one of the busiest tourist destinations in Kakadu, but if you look very carefully, you are still likely to see a tail or two of the short-eared rock wallabies hiding in the crevices.

Around the campsite at Ubirr, the Merl woodlands may unfold great bowerbirds, partridge pigeons, northern rosella, varied lorikeets, and black-tailed treecreepers. The great bowerbird props sticks into two sheaves to form a tunnel, and the entrance to the tunnel is highlighted by a path of bright shells and other attractions enticing to the female. Bowerbirds are the only animals other than humans to use inanimate gifts as a major part of their romance ritual. Partridge pigeons used to be common across the Top End but are now only common in Kakadu between the Merl campground and the East Alligator River in the eucalypt woodland. Look for the "platelets" that signal the work of a rare chestnut-backed buttonquail, which can also be spotted at night. Once you see a fresh set of platelets, or six-inch scrapes in the leaf litter made as they search for food, listen. Once

Predator's Menu

The barn owl (above) has dispersed worldwide with a menu of a variety of local small mammals.

In Kakadu, 42% of the food of the rarer rufous owl comes from arboreal mammals (including northern brushtail possum, sugar glider, northern brown bandicoot, and fawn Antechinus), 10% from climbing mammals, 29% from terrestrial mammals, 15% from fruit bats, 3% from birds, and 1% from large insects. The nest fills with food scraps, which are then cleaned by a crew of resident maggots and ants, according to Denise Lawungkurr Longfellow, a guide to the area and author of several informative books on Kakadu wildlife.

The locally common barking owl (opposite page) is declining to a rare status in many formerly common areas. Male and female owls bark duets to indicate that their territory is occupied. They scream when dingo or goannas approach and will attack human intruders if threatened.

Ranalian Flowers

The red lotus and blue lily (right) look particularly Ranalian. That is, they are simpler, earlier forms of flower that evolved from a different branch of Glossopterid than other flowers. Glossopterids are extinct precursors to flowers that existed in several bizarre forms. Five varieties of Glossopterid may have given rise to angiosperms, pandanus palms, cycads, and other plants. The Glossopterid that may have unfolded into ranalian flowers had a whorl of modified leaves with colored tips encircling a reproductive seedpod. Both lotuses and ranalian plants have a delicate whorl of unfolding color that takes us back to simple basics: resting serene over still waters, they symbolize peace and tranquility.

The water lilies bloom at the end of the wet season. Comb-crested Jacana tiptoe across the water lily pads. The tubers of blue lilies (*Nymphaea violacea*) (right) were used as a dry season food by Aboriginal people.

The delicate petal fringes of minute snowflake lilies (*Nymphoides indica*) are delightful when massed flowering occurs—indeed, they look over the flooded plains. The yellow snowflake lily (*Nimphoides hydrocharoides*) flowers on paperbark swamps.

located by their rustle, use stalking techniques to see the bird. Hardly anyone sees them.

This loop links up with a longer 6.4-km/4-mi route to the pillars and caves of the Rock Holes Walk, passing by the river. If you are early, you may catch sight of a short-eared rock-wallaby.

Don't overlook the Manngarre Rainforest Walk, a 1-mile stroll by the East Alligator River, north of the Arnhem Highway, 2.4km/1.5mi southeast of Merle campsite. This goes through a monsoonal rainforest niche where mammals and birds can be spotted around fruiting tropical trees. Two species of black and little red flying foxes roost right alongside the walk, and beautiful rainbow pitta turn over the ground leaf litter. You can hear the pitta's call best in October and November. Look too for orange-footed scrubfowl and emerald doves. Listen for the cicadabird attempting to catch its prey through imitation of the male cicada's call to attract females.

The floodplain to the north of Ubirr is a high-intensity lightning-strike zone that can produce dramatic light shows. To the left, outside the image, is the site of the closed Jabiluka uranium mine. One point of controversy was the proximity to unpredictable floodwaters.

Nourlangie Rock

Visiting this major sandstone site 30km/18.6mi south of Jabiru combines an experience of all the habitats in Kakadu with excellent rock art. You can take a gradual climb to the Gunwarddehwarde Lookout to get good views of the honeycolored Nourlangie Rock and its rainforest shroud. The challenging full-day 13-km/8-mi Barrk Walk across the top of the Rock is recommended. This is one of only six half-to-full-day marked trails in Kakadu. There is also a short 1-mile walk around the quiet Anbang-bang Billabong.

Several local endemic birds are sought-after by birdwatchers (although to the international traveler there are many fascinating birds to fall in love with). Look for the white-lined honeyeater, often seen around Nourlangie. You may also be able to find the sandstone shrike-thrush with its characteristic call, the endemic banded fruit-dove, and chestnut-quilled rock pigeon. The endemic chestnut-quilled rock pigeon eats seeds of acacia, herbs, and grasses, and it forages in pairs or small groups around rocks where it is highly camouflaged. It is active in the early morning or late in the afternoon and claps its wings loudly if flushed. It flies to higher ground to hide or flies a short distance away and spreads its wings

Uranium Mines

Mining from the tropical savannas of the Northern Territory generates most of the region's $13.5 billion/year income. Bauxite is mined for aluminum cans, and lead, zinc, nickel, silver, tin, gold, manganese, magnesium, and uranium are also dug out of ancient rock strata. Two uranium mines are on land owned by the Mirrar clan within Kakadu and leased and managed by the Energy Resources of Australia for the government. The Ranger uranium mine's open-cut system is in stark contrast to the wildlife reserve. Tours of the Ranger uranium mine run May–October, and can be booked through Kakadu Tours (08-8979-2411 or in Australia by calling 1-800-089-113). Near Ubirr, the Jabiluka uranium mine was opened recently and then closed again after Aboriginal protests reached UNESCO and uranium prices declined worldwide.

Barrk Walk

I had climbed up into the honeycomb of the Nourlangie sandstone escarpment framing the vast green floodplain below. After three months' visiting Australia's natural sites, I recognized that this would become my most cherished spot. Here I was among sandstone formed at the very moment when life first differentiated into nucleated cells 1.6 billion years ago, before life crawled onto land. "That's when the trouble began," grinned Ian, a guide at the Sydney Museum of Natural History when a few days later we looked for the fossil "tetrad" that was discovered in the Carpentaria Bay ocean bottom east of where I walked. I wanted to glimpse this fossil, the first sign of nucleated cells on earth, as it pinpointed the start of biological time-clocks. The tetrad was fossilized in mid-division after it had made four cells, a unique formation only found in nucleated cells. Adding a nucleus eclipsed the prior approach to reproduction, the cloning of replacement parts. The advantage of these individualized organisms with definite life spans was that each new generation could boost the speed of evolutionary change, each with its unique set of genes and slightly different capabilities for surviving in diversifying environments, instead of being exact clones of the parent generation. Soon after this, sexual reproduction evolved, and genes were mixed along the parental male and female chromosome, to create even more individual offspring. As I looked at the wizened 20-foot rock pillars around me, they seemed to lean toward me like a crowd of inquiring citizens from another time. Somehow I did not feel like a stranger among them.

The excellent 8-hour, one-way counterclockwise Barrk Walk is best started at first light, to avoid climbing in the tropical heat and humidity that can cling itself like saran-wrap to the body. You can enter the Anbangbang Galleries at the start of the walk, so take some time to admire Aboriginal rock paintings under a rock slab sheltering space the size of a three-story house. There are several galleries of art accessed by the path here. Then walk east to the end of the Anbangbang Trail toward the lookout. Here the Barrk Walk trail branches left up the canyon at an unnamed signpost. You can pick up maps there from a box at the trailhead. The path winds up through steep woodland onto a patch of rainforest and a small waterfall. A short climb up the rocks takes you to superb views of Nourlangie. The bright red berries of the *Alyxia ruscifolia* bush greet you as you reach the rock slabs on the plateau, berries that are the delight of the banded fruit dove.

On top, sightings of several endemic species are sought-after by wildlife visitors. Small but powerful Arnhem Land rock kangaroos called Barrk, or black wallaroos hide, rarely seen in the cool shadow of rock crevices, and the beautiful plaintive song of the endemic white-lined honeyeater echoes from the rocks either side. Apricot and scarlet-colored Dryander's grevillea flower spikes drip nectar over perfectly arrayed cushions of spinifex grass, heavily laden with grain. These flowers are a foodbank guarded noisily on scree slopes by sandstone friarbirds, which are easy to distinguish if you notice their bald casques on top of their beaks. Another delightful sight that you may find is the lavender-flanked wren. In rock pools you can spot large black and gold endemic tadpoles and the whorls of native water plants. The sandstone grasshopper is black and yellow, clearly distinguished among the other grasshoppers. The trail then passes through two huge boulders to start the undulating descent through a patch of *Callitris* pines, fire-sensitive trees that used to be more dominant in the area before man came to Australia. Then there is a steep descent to the valley floor. At this point you are about half-way around the trail.

Older and more varied art dating from 2,000 to 20,000 years ago is found as you walk through the flat woodland around the base of Nourlangie rock to Nanguluwur Gallery. This gallery offers some of the best art in the entire park, away from crowds. (You can also access this gallery without going on the Barrk Walk from Nourlangie road.) The walk continues around the Rock through flat sandstone and woodland areas, over a rocky ridge, and through some sharp spinifex. The trail ends back where you started at the Anbangbang Galleries.

Walking tips

Wear hiking boots rather than sneakers, as boots provide a much better grip on the rocks. Carry 4-6 liters per person of water for a full day trip plus high-energy trail food. Walk at a comfortable pace and rest frequently to avoid burning out muscles on climbs, and do the same on the way down. Use the whole surface of your foot for the steep parts rather than springing on your toes. On Nourlangie Rock and other marked trails, follow the orange triangular markers. On Nourlangie these are only designed to be seen one way, anticlockwise. You should not hike alone, but if you do, let others know when you are due back and the route you plan to take. Pack a whistle in your day pack in case of emergency. Beware of the large webs of golden orb weavers in the rainforest across some tracks. The spider's venom should not harm you, but the strong webs are covered in gold slime and disentanglement can distract you from good footwork. Take sunscreen for open areas and use mosquito repellent. Although malaria is not endemic to Australia, Ross river virus and dengue fever are carried by a few of the mosquitoes in isolated areas of the Top End and tropical regions. Local bulletins will keep you informed if there is an outbreak. It is best to avoid being bitten at all.

A sandstone fig (above) and slender sandstone palm (below) grace the rocky outliers and Arnhem Land. Orioles, bowerbirds, and rock wallabies love the palm fruit.

Comb-crested jacana tiptoes across lily-pads.

out to lie still in a camouflaged blend of rock and feathers. It drinks at dusk and during the day, when it jostles for a place, calling excitedly. It can be seen at the escarpment base on plains next to the plateau by rocky outcrops, often in open eucalypt woodland or in spinifex, especially during its feeding time either side of the extreme heat of the day. A bowing display is used when fighting, when males will chase other males away.

During the evening, the red-cheeked dunnart (*Sminthopsis rufigenis*) might be spotted. This mouse-sized marsupial is actually an aggressive carnivore that hisses like a cat and shows its teeth when cornered. Its diet of insects can extend to small birds and lizards.

As you explore Stone Country, look for smoothed surfaces on rocks, cave floors, and sandstone crannies made by thousands of years of rock-wallaby foot-traffic. The grey short-eared rock-wallaby (*Petrogale brachyotis*) and reddish Narbalek rock-wallaby (*Petrogale concinna*) are found in colonies across the Top End. Their scat is elongated, not round as that of other wallabies. Highly adapted to rock living, the pads of their feet are encompassed by stiff hairs and are as granular as tire treads for gripping. Their dark-tipped, long, furry, cylindrical tails are sturdy enough to act as counter-balancers. They carefully select the deep caves and rock shadows as their way to adjust the climate, usually keeping their surroundings within a range of 80–90°F, even though the rest of the environment fluctuates to the extreme 65–115° range. They live in colonies and, although they are difficult to spot, you may flush one from its hiding place. Try to catch sight of these delightful, agile creatures sunning themselves during the day or when they feed during the late afternoon or evening. They are often accompanied by their single young. Also found here is the nocturnal rock ringtail possum (*Petropseudes dahlii*), which likes the fruit of the rock fig to add to its leafy diet.

Cave Dwellers

A giant cave gecko (left), the Kakadu gehrya (*Gehrya pamela*) hides under a rock overhang silhouetting a termite tunnel. Its bite can be severe, so keep your hands away. The short-eared rock wallaby (*Petrogale bra chyotis*) (above) looks similar to the Narbalek rock wallaby, (*P. concinna*) which is smaller and frequents the sandstone areas. Both are secretive, yet you can spot them during the day if you peer carefully for movement in the rocky shadows. The Narbalek's teeth never stop growing, compensating for its gritty diet. You can look for their caves by spotting where the rocks have been worn smooth by thousands of years of pattering rock-wallaby feet. The leaves of sandstone plants may have signs of gnawing, perhaps by the Woodward's rock rat (*Zyzomys woodwardi*), which is fairly widespread in the Northern Territory's rocky outcrops.

The local endemic Arnhem Land rock-rat (*Zyzomys maini*) is found here, along with long-tailed giant lizards called rock monitors (*Varanus glebopalma* and *V. glauerti*). You may even come across the unusual carpenter frog (*Megistolotis lignarius*), which makes wood-tapping sounds. At the base of the rock is the three-story house-sized Anbangbang Shelter, used by Aboriginal people beginning 20,000 years ago. Nearby is the Anbangbang Gallery, which has art works that were repainted according to traditional practice by Nayombolmi, also known as Barramundi Charlie, in 1964.

Gunlom

One of the very best places to see all three Kakadu and Arnhem Land endemic birds is at Gunlom Lookout. Look for these three: the handsome banded fruit-dove on the walk up the escarpment through the evergreen *Allosyncarpia ternata* trees above the campsite, white-throated grasswren in the needle-sharp spinifex at the top of stone country (best looked for at dawn and harder to find in the first half of the year), and chestnut-quilled rock pigeon at the escarpment base and plateau after the climb at the top.

*Central and axial leaves of basket fern (from top), carpenter tadpole (*Megistolotis lignarius*), striped endemic masked rock frog (*Litoria personata*), and endemic water pincushion decorate 2-billion-year-old rock pools (top right).*

The banded fruit-dove likes to forage in a canopy of ficus trees and is mainly frugivorous, feeding singly or in pairs and sometimes small groups. It will hang upside down. Its food sources are the rainforest fruit trees *Eleocarpus arnhemicus, Ficus leucotricha, F. platypoda, Myristica insipida, Solanum mauritianum,* and *Polyanthia nitidissima.*

The white-throated grasswren is a striking Arnhem Land endemic that forages in spinifex gullies between the escarpment face and ensuing stone country plateau woodland behind that. Listen for its loud, melodic, trilling call. Grasswrens are arid-land specialists who prefer spinifex and have poor flight strength. This flight weakness has increased its isolation, thereby accelerating the local adaptation over time. Dark sandstone gorge species are dark brown, and spinifex sandhill species are paler and striped. Thicker-billed species consume seeds, and the thin-billed majority (including the white-throated grasswren) forage for insects.

A more common and bizarre-looking honeyeater seen among the grevillea flowering trees here is the large silver-crowned friarbird. Listen for the sandstone shrike-thrush, in the rocky areas where you can also find variegated fairy-wren, helmeted friarbird, and white-lined honeyeater.

The bright day-flying moth (Cyphrabrassolis major, above left) under a corkwood tree leaf with which it is associated. Hawk moths (right) are major pollinators. Mosses and ferns (below) extract essential minerals from leached sandstone.

The scrubland vegetation that survives on the soil-less Stone Country tops appears sparse until you look carefully. Growth is restricted, but because the area is so old, there are many more species than you would expect, and flowers can be found all year round. Commonest trees include multi-stemmed, flaky-yellow-barked scarlet gum (*Eucalyptus phoenicea*), interspersed with wild peach (*Terminalia carpentariae*), and variable-barked bloodwood (*E. dichromophloia*). You may find the rare *Ilex arnhemensis*, the Australian holly that appeared with the first flowering species in the continent's pollen record. This is the only remaining relict from the Aquifolieaceae family, which was once fairly dominant among flowering trees about 100 million years ago. The first flowers of all evolved 20 to 30 million years before that, in Africa or North America.

Koongarra Saddle

This is another great sandstone outlier to go to for solitude. In the future, access may be

Clock Watch

One of the first nucleated organisms was frozen in mid-division 1.6 billion years ago, the time when the sandstone ripples of Jim Jim Falls were forming. This was found as a fossil of four dividing cells in the Gulf of Carpentaria, which borders Arnhem Land. The development of the nucleated cell was one of only a handful of major transitions in the story of life, and moved living organisms out of the reign of bacteria into the world of time. Nucleus-free bacteria have no time-limit set on their individual lives and so never die, unless physically torn apart or killed with antibiotics. Individual bacteria mutate constantly and share clever tricks genetically within their single lifetime, including drug resistance. Nucleated cells know death: time is built in. Nucleated calls retain the same DNA for a finite lifetime, the offspring having change built-in at the start of each life. The contrast is stark: a 250-million-year-old bacterium was found alive in the year 2000, floating in a brine droplet trapped in salt crystals in New Mexico. By comparison, aging and death is a paradoxically positive step that enabled nucleated organisms to keep more in sync with the pace of change set by environments. After this transition to nucleated cells, the step to multicellular organisms happened rapidly.

Stone Country Grevilleas

Dryander's grevillea (*Grevillea dryandri*) (right and opposite page top) forms hummocks of striking red or peach flowers. Ants harvest the sticky resin from the young seed pods February to May. *G. heliosperma* is found in gorges and has edible seeds. Look for its divided leaves and unmistakable flowers (Jun–Sep). Flame grevillea (*G. pungens*) has sharp, holly-shaped leaves and is a common shrub (Sep–Nov). *Grevillea* sp. "Mount Brockman" (opposite page, below) is a prostrate rambler with needle-like leaves that is common on high rock platforms (Dec–May). Holly leaf, of the same species, has spikes of yellow flower clusters and grows by stony creeks (Apr–Jul). Many grevillea and other stone-country shrubs here have holly-shaped leaves with sharp thorns. Holly-shaped leaves are common adaptations in arid habitats the world over, with prickles probably offering a critical defense against herbivores. Here, drought tolerant adaptations result in plants being so slow-growing that they simply cannot afford to replace many munched leaves without making a severe impact on their chances of survival. So prickles are an advantage.

The white-line honeyeater can be found squabbling with other honeyeaters around flowering Darwin woolly-butt and other flowering eucalypts and paperbarks. Its main habitats are the escarpment gullies and it is occasionally found in the nearby rainforest. White-lined honeyeaters glean insects by probing bark, and are less dependent on the nectar for energy. This enables them to coexist noisily with other honeyeaters that are more reliant on nectar from the same trees. In fact, although foraging a wide range of nectar-producing flowers, each honeyeater is selective about the type of habitat that it prefers and the way in which it gathers food. Look for the large honeyeaters, the silver-crowned friarbird, aggressively defending its territory where enough nectar-dripping grevilleas (above) are included for its daily nectar needs. Smaller little friar-birds are squeezed out and adapt their behavior to favor less energy-rich flowers. But they can do this because they are unaggressive and therefore more energy-efficient in their activities. They also avoid local hawks better by playing a lower profile than the more active, large honeyeaters. Honeyeaters and lorikeets increase in density and diversity after moderate fires, living on the new growth that is often infested with lerp of psyllid scale bugs, who are coated with a sugar crust of lerp, a carbohydrate. Doves, pigeons, and quail also increase after mild fires due to the easy availability of seeds.

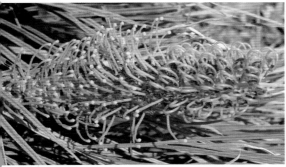

Nectar Hierarchies

In Australia, the bigger the honeyeater (below left), the more it will defend the best nectar source. The length of bill determines the nectar hierarchy. Long-beaked honeyeaters (New Holland honeyeaters, spinebills, and wattlebirds) favor nectar over lerp, honeydew, and manna. These last three are important alternative carbohydrates. Lerp is a sugar crust that coats the psyllid scale bugs that infest eucalypt leaves. Up to 50 pounds a day of lerp have been harvested by Aboriginal peoples for food. Honeydew is exuded by aphids. Manna is a sugary substance that seeps from the bark of eucalypt and wattle wounds created by sap-seeking sugar gliders. Short-beaked Australian honeyeaters (Meliphaga, Melithreptus and Lichen-ostomus honeyeaters, and the miners) avoid compe-tition with long-beaked species by taking more insects along with a bit of lerp, honeydew, and manna. Honeyeaters have differently-shaped nectaries to eat from. Grevilleas have gullet-shaped flowers rather than the brush-like inflorescences of banksia and eucalyptus. But Australian honeyeaters remain broad-based in their flower selection, unlike Darwin's finches, whose bill shapes co-evolved with associated nectaries. This is probably because Australia's weather and flower availability is less predictable.

restricted by traditional owners to foot traffic only. In common with Nourlangie and Ubirr Stone Country scrubland, many sandstone scrubland plants look similar to one another as a result of convergent drought adaptations. Small scale-like leaves are common: look for these on resurrection grass (*Micraira* sp.), whose desiccated leaves and stems swell into verdant cushions during the wet season. Spinifex (*Pectrachne* and *Triodia*) form hummocks of micro-communities around boulders.

Pandanus fruit must be baked before eating.

Foods of the future

Australia offers world markets the foods of the future that can thrive in arid, poor soils. One supplier exporting from Australia to gourmet chefs is Vic Cherikoff. You will probably have a chance to learn about "bush tucker" while you are in Kakadu. Bush tucker being flagged for commercial attention from other areas in Australia include lemon aspen *Acronychia acidula*, aniseed myrtle *Backhousia anisata*, lemon myrtle *Backhousia citriodora*, Davidson's plum *Davidsonia pruriens*, desert lime *Eremocitrus glauca*, rosella *Hibiscus heterophyllus* and *H. sabdariffa*, muntries *Kunzea pomifera*, native lime *Microcitrus* spp., Illawarra plum *Podacarpus elatus*, Kerguelen cabbage *Pringlea antiscorbutica*, native mint *Prostanthera* spp., wuandong *Santalum acuminatum*, bush tomato *Solanum centrale*, and native pepper *Tasmannia* spp.

Kakadu's Rainforest

Deep gorges cut the cliffs and outer areas of the sandstone plateau, producing breathtaking waterfalls that plunge hundreds of feet down the escarpment. Here, monsoon rainforest micro-habitats are fed by sandstone springs that have kept many Gondwanan species in a time warp.

Jim Jim and Twin Falls

The distance from Cooinda to Jim Jim Falls is 70km/43mi, but allow over two hours by 4WD because most of it is over a rough one-way track. A nearly meter-deep ford is a big obstacle for all but large 4WD vehicles. Jim Jim Falls has

Spinifex community

a 200-m/700-ft drop from top to bottom, with a clear fall of 160m/500 ft. At the base of Jim Jim Falls are ripples in sandstone made by shallow water 1.5 billion years ago. You will also find an inviting plunge pool.

Look for the huge incubating mounds built by scrub fowl from composting leaf litter. The trees are dominated by *Allosyncarpia ternata*. Most of these rainforest trees look similar to mango trees with deep green broad leaves and luxuriant tropical fruits that ripen during the wet season after the inconspicuous flowers are over. Then flying-foxes, fruit-eating pigeons, orioles, cuckoos, and figbirds come to rainforest patches from the open savanna to eat this concentration of fruit. Birds, bats, and water disperse the fruit without damaging the seed. Unlike seed-eating birds that have grit in their tough-walled crops to grind seeds, frugivorous birds in these rainforests have delicate digestive systems with no grit, so they leave the seeds intact. Birds disperse many seeds immediately around the fruiting rainforest tree and also far away after the smaller seeds exit their gut. Some bats, competing among one another for a favorite fruit tree, will "steal" fruit in their claws, dispersing large seeds over great distances even though their mouths are too small to consume anything other than the fleshy fruit juices.

Rufous fantails glean flies, beetles, and hymenoptera in the dense understory. Agile, they dart out in a zig-zag and can spin 180 degrees as they hop along branches. They fan their tails and flash their wings to flush insects from hiding. They are so active that they capture 2.5 prey items a minute, twice as many as the larger willie wagtail, but they do this at greater effort, changing perches four times as much. Grey whistler and green-backed gerygone are also insectivores that you will find in the rainforest.

Native bees (*Trigona* sp.) make their nests in termite-hollowed *Allosyncarpia* limbs and produce the "sugar bag" honey prized by

Brainy Jumpers

The fun and colorful jumping spiders of the Salticidae family are very aware of their surroundings. They see in color using simple eyes like our own, and their central eyes are on long tubes that turn to gaze at what's moving around them, including human observers. They are very curious and will jump onto cameras and fingers to explore new sights, but they are not harmful. *Portia fimbrata* is found in tropical jungles of Australia, and is unusual in that it hunts other spiders. It can jump 20 times its length using its last two pairs of legs. It even stalks prey evasively and tricks its intended victims into dropping their defenses by moving out of sight (just as cats do) before pouncing. When it jumps, it anchors itself with a dragline. It can use this silk rope to dangle into the web of another spider without touching, kidnapping the victim and hauling it back up. For spider-size brains, they are very clever.

Spider silk has many uses. The tailor bird uses spider webs to sew their nest together. The willie wagtail lines its nest with silk and the rock warbler hangs its nest from a web rope. Spider silk has enormous strength, and is also a great shock absorber. Bio-engineered spider silk is being synthesized and researched by the US defense department in order to improve on the Kevlar used in bulletproof vests.

Pied imperial pigeons (above) are one of the most important seed dispersers for fruiting rainforest trees. Waterfalls sometimes last year-round (right, at Barrk Walk base).

Sandstone Trigger Plant

Under the shelter of sandstone, at the base of the escarpment and on top, you will see tiny pink flowers of the trigger plant. Look carefully and you'll see the white anvil that smashes down on pollinators when touched (before and after, below), distributing pollen.

Aboriginal people. There are few understory plants other than one or two vines. *Smilax australis* trails its sharp spines with it across low shrubs, laying out a bushwalker's razor wire. The tips of supplejack leaves (*Flagellaria indica*) coil and help secure this liana's ascent toward the light. In canopy breaks along the streams are shrubs with large attractive flowers including *Osbeckia australiana*, flowering from February to August near water soaks; lassiandra (*Melastoma polyanthum*), common in sandy gorges all year with edible fruit; and the spine-tipped leaves of the shrubs *Alyzia fuscifolia* and *Lavichea nitida* which have widespread flowers (Dec–May) on the shade side of cliff ledges and damp gorges. A member of the ginger family is the striking turmeric relative, *Curcuma australasica* (above), a tuber whose bright flower spears carpet the slopes of shady canyons (Nov–Apr).

Farther along the dirt road is Twin Falls (10km/6.2mi). Access is via swimming to the

The rose-crowned fruit-dove (above) is a rainforest frugivore. On the forest floor, the flower of a turmeric relative: curmuca lily (Curcuma australasia, left).

falls or by climbing steadily from the parking lot. Beware of the freshwater crocodiles.

In the wet season and well into the dry, Jim Jim and Twin Falls are closed, but spectacular scenic flights by Kakadu Air from Cooinda Airstrip or Jabiru Airport make up for their inaccessibility (about A$100). Jim Jim can also dry up. The best time to visit is at the beginning of the dry season when the road is open but there is still a lot of water cascading over the escarpment.

Gubara Pools

The walk to the pools takes about 3 hours round trip across sandy savanna and then a thin sliver of rainforest around dancing river pools at the base of the escarpment scree. As you arrive, look for the darker green of the lofty Anbinik evergreen tree (*Allosyncarpia ternata*), which can live longer than most others here. Be sure to go to the very end of the path by crossing the wooden bridge and turning left to follow the river path to the boulders. Gubara Pools are away from the crowds and provide a very cool place to go on a hot day. You are likely to see a good cross-section of rainforest birds among the native nutmeg trees and native ginger

Rainforest ICU

Room-sized rainforest patches have come and gone in Kakadu since Jurassic times, surrounded by savanna. These rainforests are helped by visitors from the savanna that move the rainforest edges as the environment changes. The survival of this kind of miniature rainforest gives hope for growing diverse rainforest patches (and valuable medicines) in Australia and elsewhere, in cases where surrounding rainforests have recently been removed by man. A trigger for rainforest regeneration here is the adaptable rainforest milkwood tree (*Alstonia actinophilla*), which can establish itself on damp savanna. This dense tree fosters the birds and bats that then drop their rainforest fruit seeds. The tree becomes what is called a "nurse tree," as it shelters saplings from extreme sunburn and heat and helps them grow. If a small area gets wetter than usual, a single pioneer milkwood tree can replace savanna plants with an entire patch of rainforest.

The matchstick grasshopper (top) is native to Australia. Molting caterpillars (above) provide cast-off nutrients for ants, termites, and fungi. Centipedes (center) can reach many inches long. This one has powerful jaws that can eat frogs, mice, and geckos. Predatory antechinuses, however, can win a pitched battle. Centipedes use venom fangs that cause severe pain, but are not lethal to humans. They wave their longer tail projections to distract from their head. Female phasmids or stick insects have stunted wings (bottom right).

wildflowers. Water-squirting primitive archerfish flit in the pools with escarpment long-necked turtles.

As you walk, you may see Halloween-like webs spun by tropical dome spiders (*Cyrtophora moluccensis*). Dome spiders are social spiders that build webs together under an equal caste system. The domed sheet at the center of each web is connected with vertical threads that can stretch 3m/10ft. Baby spiders build their webs inside the protection of their mother's web, and adult spiders defend each individual web. The web smells yeasty and sweet as a result of the biochemical action of this spider's venom, which prevents proteins from rotting and encourages yeast growth, an aroma that attracts more flies. In Mexico and South America, these spiders are encouraged in some houses to get rid of flies.

Northern short-necked turtle eats mussels.

Kakadu's Tropical Savanna

Savanna woodlands cover three quarters of what you will drive through to get "there" in Kakadu, but otherwise they are often overlooked. The taller savanna forests that surround the Arnhem Highway as you enter the park from the northwestern entrance house many wildflowers. More open woodlands are seen across the hills unfolding along the Kakadu Highway around the southwestern entrance. Other than the raucous screeches of cockatoos, rosellas, and parrots, the savanna hides its diversity carefully. One reason is that many animals, birds, and reptiles hide in limbs of the dominant eucalyptus tree that have been hollowed out by termites. Most of the animals are nocturnal. Many are fed by enormous levels of nectar released by the eucalypts, wattles, and wildflowers in the area, and termites keep the whole nitrogen system going.

Look at eucalypts for signs of other life: blood mistletoe (*Amyema sanguineum*) seeds sprout on their branches after the seed glue-balls are pasted on by the mistletoe bird. The seeds stick to this true fructivore's tail until it wipes them off. And chocolate orchids (*Cymbidium canaliculatum*) grow from hollow eucalypt limbs.

Frogs: Wired for Movement

Unlike in humans, most frog eyes decode for movement in the retina before the signal reaches the brain. If there is no movement, the retina "sees" nothing and the brain can add nothing. These frogs only perceive what moves. In humans, our eyes do less of the decoding, which allows the brain to expand far more on its interpretation of still images.

Dahl's aquatic frog (*Litoria dahlii*, above) can jump around and hunt for food during hot daytime temperatures.

The frogs of the Top End are about to be swept by an ecological wave front: large poisonous cane toads (*Bufo marinus*) are moving westward from tropical North Queensland. Unlike many other frogs, these can decode un-moving food and eat it. Cane toads were introduced to sugarcane fields from Central and South America to control cane beetles, unsuccessfully. The skin on their back is so toxic that they can kill the snakes that eat them. These toads are wiping out frogs and predators in an ecocrisis.

Strangers in Paradise

Weeds are smothering plants that rapidly take over native habitats (unidentified native flower, right). Fifteen major weed species are being battled directly by park managers in Kakadu, from wild cotton to bellyache bush. Since the introduction from tropical America of giant sensitive plant (*Mimosa pigra*) in the 1970s , its dense thatches have irreversibly changed the ecology of 80,000ha/197,680acres of coastal Northern Territory wetlands. A close second threat is that of para grass (*Brachiara mutica*). Adapted to semi-aquatic life, its growth prevents magpie geese and other birds from feeding on open water, chokes nesting habitats, halves water flows, and obliterates native vegetation. Like strangers in paradise, 60 of Australia's 463 exotic forage species introduced between 1947 and 1985 became weeds, and only four were found useful for pasture. One of these, buffel grass (*Canchrus ciliaris*), is both a valuable pasture plant and a weed when it takes hold in the arid areas of Central Australia. Salvinia (*Salvinia molesta*) affects fish populations in Kakadu. Control by the salvinia weevil is used successfully at Magela Creek in Kakadu.

In the open you may see the delightful agile wallaby (*Macropus agilis*) conducting boxing matches. Kangaroos are often more difficult to find during the day, but in the dry season they move nearer water where they can more easily be seen. Look for them at dusk. They have heat-pumps of massed blood vessels that cuff the surface of their forearms, and they lick these to cool themselves by evaporation. Look out for the northern brown bandicoot (*Isodon macrourus*) snuffling around the woodland at night. The brush-tailed possum (*Trichosurus vulpecula*) is happiest in trees, along with the brush-tailed tree-rat (*Conilurus penicillatus*) that flees up a tree when surprised. The black-footed tree-rat (*Mesembriomys gouldii*) makes its stick nest in tree hollows and can chew through high tensile steel.

Two Mile Hole and Four Mile Hole

These are trails to fishing areas that are accessed by 4WD track from near the Northern Entrance section. Two-Mile Hole is 8km/5mi from the Arnhem Highway; the distance between the two is 30km/19mi. These are accessible by 4WD only, and offer strenuous bush walks and 4WD excursions into the savanna. The tracks are impassable during the wet season.

Termite as Eco-Accelerator

Unlike the fertile floodplains, the soil of the surrounding savanna is so leached and poor and the eucalypts are such hoarders of resources that the land should be practically barren. Termites are the central ecological accelerators that spur the tropical savanna's remaining diversity by recycling nutrients, helping to confound the nitrogen statistics that indicate net losses after the annual fires. Nitrogen-rich termite mounds are high-quality nutrient "sinks" that concentrate scarce nutrients and fertilize the soil when the termite waste, stashed to avoid attracting attention, breaks down. This is dependent on a 230-million-year-old symbiotic association between cellulose-digesting micro-organisms and their termite hosts. Termites have to live in a community in order to repopulate the micro-organisms after every molt. Their caste system has lasted twice as long as that of ants, and is probably the oldest animal society in the world. These symbioses enabled a new habitat, the tropical savanna, to become established on this old and nutrient-poor soil where it is now the dominant community.

Termite mounds, two-thirds above ground, can get as dense as 30–40 mounds per acre. Kingfishers, hooded parrots, and tree-creepers

The lemon migrant (Catopsila pomona, top) eats golden raintrees (Cassia fistula) as a caterpillar. This adult is sipping at a Grevillea heliosperma. Black and white tiger butterflies (center) are most common from March to May, with blue tigers (Tirumala namata, below).

Focus on Tropical Savanna Plants

Kakadu's 1,600 plant species include the dominant Darwin stringybark (*Eucalyptus tetrodonta*) and Darwin woolly-butt (*Eucaluptus miniata*). The woolly-butt is one of several species that undergo mass-flowering during the mid-dry season from May to August when the orange flowers are invaded by bar-breasted honeyeaters and varied lorikeets. Occasionally a sand palm (*Livistona humilis*) punctuates the woodland. Palms entered Australia from India among the earliest Gondwanan angiosperms arriving 100 million years ago. They are fire-adapted and provide an important source of fruit and seeds for Kakadu animals. The dominant eucalypts are eaten by the northern brush possum (*Trichosurus arnhemensis*), which lives near water and looks like a slender version of the brush-tailed possum found commonly elsewhere in Australia. The northern brush possum has a bright pink nose, a pink prehensile tail, and large ears. You can also find and eat small wild yams here, although they may have an influence on your hormones. Diosgenin, found in the *Dioscorea sp.* wild yams from Mexico and Guatamala, was used in the development of the contraceptive pill.

Borrea exserta glade (above).

sometimes nest in the mounds, with kingfishers making the first hole in the concrete-like walls with their sharp beaks. Sometimes a kingfisher will kill itself when it flies into the mound to blast a hole in it. Brown falcon, swamp harrier, and whistling eagle use the mounds to dine on prey: look at the base for signs of pellets, scattered feathers, or fur.

Cathedral mounds up to 5.5m/18ft high and 100 years old can be seen as you enter Kakadu. Magnetic mounds are not found in Kakadu but in Litchfield Park south of Darwin. Some mounds house nasute termites (*Nasutitermes triodiae*), named for their soldiers' bulbous "nose." A nasute soldier's head houses a gland that fires noxious chemicals when alarmed by fellow workers. The largest mound may house a 100-year-old queen that may be hundreds of times the size of her workers. Everything in the nest is controlled by pheromones. She is tended by workers, and sometimes scarred by the over-eager workers who lick the fatty substances that constantly exude from her skin. She wastes away as her workers lick and tend her to death.

Live termite "hot spots" feed insect-eating birds, mammals, and reptiles including the versatile echidna and nocturnal fawn antechinus (*Antechinus bellus*). Echidnas have been seen outside termite mounds with their

Eucalyptus Oils: Heaven Scent

Each eucalyptus has a distinct spectrum of aromatic oils. Eucalyptus oil is so close chemically to menthol that it is converted into it for commercial use in toothpaste and medicines. Menthol evolved as an insect neurotoxin, designed to relax insects so much that they fall off the target plant. In humans, menthol acts as a nerve-blocker that numbs the temperature sensors on our tongues, giving us a sense of cool freshness. From eucalyptus leaves and seed buttons, in addition to the familiar eucalyptol component, you may be able to discern touches of musty-smelling valeric acid ester, turpentine-like pinene, lemony citral, and peppermint-like piperitol. The last three are terpenes, an important group of aromatic compounds, some of which have anaesthetic and antiseptic properties to protect the tree from insect and bacterial attack. Complex terpenes have several active roles that highlight the common chemical basis shared by plants, insects, and even humans. In insects, the same terpene, farnesol, that gives lily-of-the-valley its aroma is the terpene hormone that triggers the change from caterpillar to pupa, and again from pupa to moth. In animals, terpenes have another key role: without them, we would see nothing. Retinene, the terpene that is converted in our body from carotene, lines the retina of our eye. When light hits retinene, the molecule snaps from a bent shape to a straight one, opening up the surface of the retinal cell to a flood of nerve-stimulating calcium, which we see as light. The process is so sensitive that if five photons reconfigure five retinene-protein pairs out of the billions that form our retina, a flicker of light is perceived.

*From top: bush everlasting (*Gomphrena* sp.), unidentified fringe-petaled flower,* Sowerbea alliacea, *burr-producing* Borrea exserta, Buchnera *sp.*

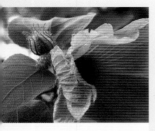

The Savanna Year

Kakadu's savanna has a rolling season of flowering trees and annuals that feeds bird and insect nectar-eaters all year. When the wattle (*Acacia oncinocarpa*) flowers, it signals the onset of the dry season in April. In May, the easily-identified flower spikes of common fern-leafed grevillea (*Grevillea pteridifolia*) come into bloom, decorating this shrubby tree's silvery leaves and thin black tree trunks with its flame-colored blooms. Silver-crowned and little friarbirds noisily attend the blossoms. In the flood plains during the dry season (May to October) you will see the cajaput tree (*Melaleuca cajaputi*) in flower, the only paperbark tree flowering during this time. In June, the bare branches of Darwin's floral emblem, the kurrajong (*Brachychiton paradoxum*), burst with striking orange flowers. Its bark is used to make string for the dilly bags created by Aboriginal women. Silver-leafed paperbark (*Melaleuca argentea*) is found on sandbars of freshwater streams. It has a new flush of silvery leaves in June and sickly-smelling, bird-laden blooms starting in July. The bark was used for Aboriginal roofing material. Other paperbarks flower along river banks until December, and at night fruit-bats flutter among their scented branches. The fragrance of several gardenia, including *Gardenia megasperma*, permeates the woodlands at the end of the dry season from August. Widespread bush currant (*Vitex glabrata*) flowers in September, producing tasty black berries eaten as bush tucker. Chocolate orchid (*Cymbidium canaliculatum*) blooms in October from hollow limbs of its host white-barked eucalyptus trees. The rest of the time its inconspicuous leaves go unnoticed. In the wet season, the annuals bloom, including the looped pink flowers of the common annual *Grevillea goodii*—look for it under sprawling grasses.

Hibiscus

Specialized spiders hide at the center of hibiscus species (above) ready for protein-rich pollen-dusted visitors.
Hibiscus leptocladus *(top)* is found on sandstone outliers, cottonwood (H. tiliacus, *center*) is found among mangroves and has chocolate-centered yellow flowers, with heart-shaped leaves. Hibiscuses are covered in acrid hairs to repel locusts (below) and these hairs can cause allergic reactions in people. Dramatic Astromertus sp. stars attract white-lined honeyeaters (third from top).

Savanna Birds

The 274 bird species found in Kakadu include waterbirds like the huge, stately jabiru (left) and many savanna birds. Look for the red-collared lorikeet, brown honeyeater, silver-crowned friarbird, weebill, white-bellied cuckoo-shrike, red-tailed black-cockatoo, and partridge pigeon. Among the birds you'll see are fructivores, including parrots and fruit-doves, that travel around the savanna to go in and out of the high concentration of fruit produced among the scattered rainforest remnants. The long memory that parrots have, plus their intelligence, ideally prepares them to map and return to distant locations of favorite fruit trees from year to year. They depend on these food hot-spots, and the fruit trees, in their turn, depend on the fructivores for seed distribution and pollination. So, if the scattered Kakadu rainforests disappear, many birds of the open savanna woodlands would also disappear. Insectivorous birds, including the area's little shrike-thrushes, fantails, sittellas, and thornbills, eat about half the insects growing on Kakadu's eucalypts each year and are less dependent on rainforest nearby. The black-tailed treecreeper is found around rough-barked eucalypts and bloodwoods where it probes for prey. Its loud call will help you find it.

Parrots and Termites

The hooded parrot is a near-threatened, very striking bird closely related to the golden-shouldered parrot from Cape York Peninsula, and is only found around Kakadu and Katherine. Look for hooded parrots on telephone wires and around Melaleuca floodplains, spinifex grassland with termite mounds, or around eucalypts near rivers. It nests in termite mounds and there is one nest around every 1–2km² around Katherine. Black-faced woodswallows are often seen with these parrots when near roadsides. The hooded parrot makes chattering calls with "chiwee" and "tchick." It needs annual and perennial grass seeds, and its numbers have been reduced by grazing, changed burning patterns, mining within its territory, plus trapping in the past for the pet trade.

Termite mound (clockwise from top left), termite trail, Nasutermes triodiae *termites, nest-filled trunk.*

tongues outstretched to let termites crawl into their tiny mouths. Their main method is to rip open the nest carton. The antechinus is a small but savage carnivorous marsupial that eats insects and lizards. They are so aggressive in life that male antechinuses usually die of exhaustion after their first mating, despite being only one year old. Termites also boost the bottom of the food chain of predators such as the handsome red goshawk that is only found in the Tropical Savanna and has a precious 200 breeding pairs in the Northern Territory. This powerful raptor primarily eats birds, with mammals and reptiles as its secondary prey.

Another key to the savanna's fertility are the tropics' warmth and humidity. These foster bacteria that release a potent hydroponic soup of nutrients during the wet season, from November through March. This helps spear grass (*Sorghum intrans*) grow 6–9-ft high within a few short weeks, and animal life explodes into a surge of nesting activity. The bacterial life becomes practically dormant during the dry season.

Focus on Parrots

Parrots preen and groom one another constantly, keeping their plumage dazzlingly bright. Parrots have been around for over 40 million years and have adapted to all sorts of habitats, from a rainforest lifestyle in South America to a nomadic existence in the deserts and savannas of Australia. Parakeets and probably other parrots see in color, and can also see UV light. This allows them to see the nectar guides in flowers that glow with UV light to pinpoint the nectar food source, plus the pollination site. The bloom on some fruit surfaces is also designed to reflect UV light. Most parrots, cockatoos, and rosellas search out a variety of seeds and fruit, while lorikeets specialize in nectar and pollen.

To manage their wide-spread food sources, which fluctuate enormously in availability, parrots have developed an intelligence that may rival a two-year-old human being, and can distinguish and count up to six. (By comparison, ravens can understand numbers up to eight.) Parrots have been kept as intelligent, affectionate pets since at least 400 BC in India, Greece, and Rome. They communicate by bowing, bobbing, stretching, preening, and playing. They have a sense of humor and drop sticks on one another and on predators, which they actively mob. Unlike South American parrots, which eat clay, Australian parrots eat charcoal to supplement their diet with trace minerals and to detoxify dietary poisons. They usually drink early in the morning before leaving to feed, then rest at midday, and feed again when it gets cooler in the afternoon.

The characteristically Australian galah is a pink and gray parrot that performs evening aerobatics and eats wattle and other seed from the ground including crops, button grass (*Iseilema membranaceum*), and weeds. Its flocks

Bird Trading

Until the export of wildlife was banned in Australia, up to 6,500 Gouldian finches were caught by licensed trappers between 1968 and 1981. Each year, only a few hundred reached their destination alive. During this time, the wild population of Gouldian finches plummeted, and trapping licenses were first cut back and then prohibited as officials reacted to the crisis. The decline was surprising, as the wild population of other trapped finches fluctuated or even increased. But Gouldian finches were being decimated by not one lethal vector, but two. The first was man; the second was a mite. An endoparasitic mite was infesting their airsacs. The metabolic rate of these finches is so high that infested birds get sick within hours and soon die. Man and mite have virtually wiped out an entire wild population, though aviary populations, treated with insecticides, have recovered. Now, Gouldian finches are extremely rare in Kakadu, though occasionally seen in the southern areas.

Partridge pigeons are very quiet but locally common in the Top End and Kimberley regions.

Mates and Mites

The bright plumage of parrots and finches makes them vulnerable to being snatched by birds of prey. Attractive colors, however, are indicative of a bird's potential to survive a more pesky pest. It has recently been found that individual birds and bird species with more intense colors have fewer ectoparasites. Lice and mites chew feathers and suck blood, making birds anemic and disease-prone. Ectoparasites can even reduce feather weight by up to a quarter, crimping a bird's temperature control. Female birds select mates with the brightest plumage. This is because a more stunning bird is a good indication that it's got its act together behaviorally and genetically. Birds preen one another to reduce mites and lice by a level of 10 to 60 times the ungroomed rate. Or they smear formic acid from ants all over themselves, effectively fumigating a quarter of their stowaways in one go. Dust bathing behavior probably evolved several times among different bird families, as their methods differ so much, but the result is to keep their feathers from matting with oil while stopping themselves from getting lousy. Birds use insecticides from plants, too. Starlings can reduce their nest load of mites 45 times, from an average of half a million mites in a reused nest, when a fresh sprig of wild parsley is placed in their nest and replenished.

charm overseas visitors and are Australians' answer to blond bimbo jokes. In light rain it will perform a rain dance, leaning into the rain or hanging upside down from a dead tree, with wings outspread and plumage fluffed up. This is followed by preening. They also play a lot and fly into willie-willies aerobatically, unlike the varied lorikeet, which doesn't play at all. Galah parents approach the nest indirectly and sit quietly before entering, to avoid attracting predators. These parrots form lifetime pair bonds and congregate in the hundreds, sometimes joined by the noisy sulfur-crested cockatoo that look like a bunch of bananas stuck into a sno-cone. They are found near the coast of northern and eastern Australia, often with corellas. The sulfur-crested cockatoo calls "kai-yah," whistles "scraw-leek," and yells "raaa" in alarm. It eats seeds, sprouting grain, roots, berries, flowers, and larvae. This cockatoo posts a sentinel lookout and will mob raptors. It nests between May and December in tall eucalypts near water or in cliff cavities. They rest in trees during high noon.

The varied lorikeet is endemic to Northern Australia and breeds in Kakadu. Like honeyeaters, it is brush-tongued to eat nectar and pollen from eucalypts and melaleuca. It can be approached closely when feeding, and feeds in small groups or flocks of up to 100. Sometimes it fights banded honeyeaters and silver-crowned friarbirds. It drinks water by clinging to a twig bending over water and then putting its head back and down. It pairs for life and breeds in holes. It bathes by diving into water and then sitting in a tree to preen. It performs various displacement activities on aggressive interactions or on greeting, including vigorously shaking its body and scratching or shaking its head.

The red-collared lorikeet is found in riverine eucalypt woodland and flowering paperbark woodland. It feeds on nectar, fruit, and insects, often accompanying varied

This is one of the eleven species of goannas, or monitors, found in the Top End savanna. It is sniffing the air with its forked tongue to identify the direction of the aroma.

lorikeets. The varied lorikeet is green, distinctive, and has a white eye-ring. Look for it around bloodwoods (*Eucalyptus terminalis*), paperbarks (*Melaleuca leucodendron*), grevilleas, and kapok (*Cochlospermum heteronemum*). It has a cricket-like call and chatters. It nests in tree trunk hollows. Look for noisy flocks hurtling toward a distant feeding area.

The red-tailed black cockatoo can live to be 50 years old, and is an incredibly handsome bird. Males display to females by puffing out chest feathers and erecting his crest. The Northern race found in Kakadu has a larger bill and crest than the four other races of this solely Australian bird. It prefers eucalypts around rivers, especially river red-gums. It feeds in trees on a variety of foods. It nests in winter in tree hollows.

The fairly common red-winged parrot is found in the tropical savanna all across northern and inland northeastern Australia and Papuan New Guinean islands. It is usually in small groups of up to 15 but forms groups of up to 50 after the breeding season. It eats seeds, fruit, flowers, and insects in the savanna and callitris forest. Look for it around the mistletoe (*Loranthus*) in mangroves. It starts nesting in Kakadu in April in deep eucalypt holes. It chirps "chillup" and calls "chit chit."

The northern rosella is found in groups of two to five around woodlands in monsoonal callitris habitat, paperbark (*Melaleuca*), mangroves, and roadsides. The northern rosella is the only rosella in Kakadu. This rosella eats fruits, buds, blossoms, nectar, and seeds of

Savanna Reptiles

The yellow-spotted monitor (*Varanus panpotes*, below) can be differentiated from the similar sand goanna (*V. gouldii*) by the dark stripes on the end of its tail. Both have vertically flattened tails for swimming when things get flooded.
Tree monitors (*Varanus tristis* and *V. scalaris*) can be spotted on the ground. Frill-necked lizards (*Chlamydosaurus kingii*) display their magnificent collars in the savannnas of Kakadu at the end of the dry season.

The Monotreme with a Hundred Fingers

Echidnas are highly mobile and inquisitive creatures so adaptable that many ecological organizations use the echidna as their emblem. Echidnas are found all over Australia and are monotremes like platypuses, laying eggs and producing milk. They have fur and spines. They are as intelligent as cats and rats: they assess a situation and prioritize information before figuring out what to do. They have long memories and can learn to come upon being called. Echidnas have such excellent hearing that they can tune into the sub-sonic sound of dirt moving through an earthworm's digestive system. They use this to find and dig up earthworms, slugs, termites, beetles, eggs, and larvae with their incredibly strong forearms (they could bench-press 80 pounds). They sometimes dig themselves into trouble, ending up in natural underground chasms, but have evolved a clever way to get out. Each spine is equipped with musculature that allows it to be used as an extra finger. They undulate these spine fingers in sub-terranean crevices to climb vertically back home. They have no teeth. Instead, they use their tongues to select their meal, then smoosh their prey with their beak tips into a "smoothie" that they can slurp up through their tiny mouths.

Yellow fungi help recycle nutrients quickly.

acacia, eucalypts, grasses, and paperbark. Although widespread in the Northern Territory, the northern rosella is uncommon. Look for its typically rosella-like undulating flight. It is a hole-nester and some of its flocks are non-breeding, perhaps to maintain a constant level of well-fed birds to put the brakes on the boom-bust populations found in some savanna parrots. At this point, the northern rosella is probably declining. It is seen in pairs or small groups in trees or on the ground. It whistles "pi-pi-pi-pi," "click-a-du," "cuick-quick," and pings and chatters. It nests close to water in a eucalypt hole.

The cockatiel is common across most of Australia in large flocks. It eats acacia and other seeds. Little corella is a cockatoo that is common in large flocks up to 70,000 all over Northern and inland Eastern Australia, Indonesia and Papua New Guinea. It is often found with Galahs. It squeaks "wi-rup" and "wi-ri-rup," and calls an alarm "schaaair." It is found in all types of savanna. After drinking in the

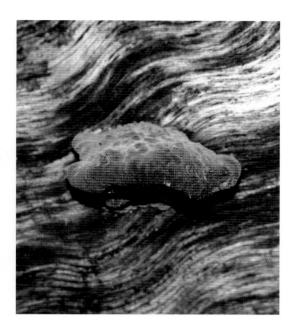

The Bizarre

Instead of just glancing at what's around you, take another look, and you will find more going on than you think. The red spongy fungus (left) is helping to hollow out a nest space inside a living eucalyptus tree. These fungi may be found on trunks on the leeward side of fire where hotter flametips have licked holes in the bark. This white flower spider (*Thomisus spectabilis*, center left) is camouflaged to match the flower and catch the European honey bee. Each flower spider species selects flowers similar to their own species color, and can adjust color slightly. This spider can bite painfully, but it is not toxic to humans. This huge golden orb weaver (*Nephila* sp., center right) is being visited by an *Argyrodes* spider. Some of these *Argyrodes* have long orange bodies like this one, others have silvery drop-shape bodies. The little spider is about to steal the orb-weaver's dinner by sipping it under her gaze. The rainforest robberfly (*Colepia lanata*, bottom left) can catch native bees (in jaws) in flight. Flatworms (bottom right) are mostly aquatic and feed on earthworms, snails, and water animals.

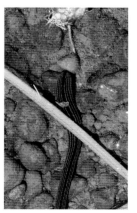

Dragonfly Dynamics

The aerodynamics of dragonfly flight is completely different than in fixed wing aircraft. New fluid dynamic studies, computer modeling, and chaos theory mathematics have cracked the puzzle of how they hover so well. The secret is in the dynamic eddies that curl off the top of the moving, rough wings. These long-lasting vortexes create half the lift associated with each wing-beat. They do this because they shed in both clockwise and counter-clockwise directions in one beat. The shear between both is called an unsteady effect, which creates velocity when the wing oscillates rapidly. An example of these eddies can be seen when a sheet of paper is left to fall, zigzagging down. Dragonflies take care to keep their flight muscles at premium working temperatures, as they need maximum power to lift off. When cold, some species can turn black to absorb more heat. When hot, dragonflies turn their tails toward the sun to minimize sun trapping.

This dragonfly scoops up prey by making a basket of its legs. It is a perch-based hunter. Other dragonflies are roamers that coast the airways looking for food. In Kakadu, the dominant species of flying dragonflies, like butterflies, is season-specific. Opposite page: rainbow lorikeet camouflage.

early morning, it goes to eat in the morning and afternoon, resting at midday. It plays by hanging upside down on wires and rolling over onto its back. The flock has a rolling action on the ground with birds at the back flying to the front constantly to get at new food. Little corella eats grass seed, berries, roots, shoots, and larvae. It forms lifetime pairs and retains ownership of its nest site that is usually in a eucalypt hole and sometimes in a termite mound.

Territory Wildlife Park

60km/37mi south of Darwin you can see the world-class Territory Wildlife Park. This is designed with large open enclosures in the latest conservation zoo style to show habitats and provide a wonderful way of seeing the wildlife close-up. Large wilderness areas, aviaries, a nocturnal house, an aquarium, and an animal care center are sprawled across the park. Tour wagons connect everything, and there is a 6km/3.6mi walking trail.

Where's Waldo? The rainbow lorikeet's colors provide excellent camouflage.

Arnhem Land

Permits are required for Arnhem Land hiking. Willis Walkabouts and a select handful of outfits have permits and offer bushwalking expeditions. The Walkabout Lodge and Hideaway Lodge offer accommodation in Nhulunbuy, which is the bauxite town at the tip of Gove Peninsula 750km/465mi northeast of Katherine. Permits to drive there across the Central Arnhem Road can be obtained from the Northern Land Council at Nhulunbuy (08-8987-2602), but book many months in advance. A visitor's permit is also required for beach and river visits from the Dhimurru Land Management Aboriginal Corporation office, (08-8987-3992).

Katherine/Nitmiluk National Park

Thirteen honey-and-red sandstone gorges can be seen by canoeing and walking the Katherine River in Nitmiluk National Park 100km/62mi south of Kakadu. All the gorges can be seen if you camp overnight at Smith's Rock at the fourth gorge. If you do this, you'll avoid the tour groups that go to the first two gorges on day cruises. You can spot Aboriginal rock art on the gorge walls as you paddle. During the dry season, beach the canoe at the fifth gorge and walk the rest from there. The river becomes a torrent of white-water in the wet season, so check for access. Call (08-8972-1886) for canoe rental and visitor information.

4WD in Kakadu

Most roads in Kakadu are paved, so a 4WD vehicle is not required.

Accessible by 4WD only: Jim Jim Falls/Twin Falls Track; West Alligator Head Track; Guratba and Gimbat; Maguk; Alligator Billabong Track; Yurmikmik and Gunlom during the wet season. Drive slowly after rainfall, as dirt road surfaces can become very spongy and give the illusion of the driver being in control. Watch for drop-offs caused by water rivulets cutting across the track and its edges. To drive across deep fords, the tradition in the rest of Australia is that one person wades in front of the vehicle to direct the driver away from hidden holes eroded by floodwaters. Do not try this in Kakadu, as there is the danger of being grabbed by a crocodile. The pungent smell of seaweed and salty oceans that may suddenly surround you in the middle of the land-locked wetlands is a clear signal that you are near a large saltie crocodile. Wild pigs should also be avoided as their tusks are dangerous.

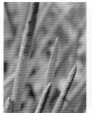  

An Edith Falls hike is 80km/50mi if you want immersion. Otherwise there are many delightful shorter walking tracks taking from a few hours to a few days around the gorge and surrounding bushland. Take the bus from Katherine, a city and major bus stop on the Stuart Highway, if you do not have transportation. Call 08-8972-1886 for hiking maps and visitor information. If birdwatching is your thing, you may see Gouldian finches and hooded parrots outside the town of Katherine.

Mary River

A night on a Mary River houseboat passes dawn and dusk, heralded by the blue-winged kookaburra. Or a Rock Hole Boat Ramp Cruise on the Mary River will add to your Kakadu adventure. Turn north off Arnhem Highway about two hours from Darwin toward Kakadu onto the unpaved Point Stuart Road. Wildman River Wilderness Lodge and Point Stuart Wilderness Lodge provide basic accommo-dation, with Point Stuart offering its own cruise and walking trail where you may see the Aboriginal people's delicacy, the non-venomous, slow-moving file snake. The Mary River has major conser-vation problems due to ocean intrusion after dike breakdown from buffalo damage, and an enormous project is in place to restore this important wetland. Another access point to the Mary River is at touristy Mary River Park 3km/1.8mi west of Bark Hut Inn. Bird-watching tours are available from Crocodile Cruise (08-8978-8877).

Spike rush (Eleocharis dulcis, flower spikes, flowers, and stems above) has transparent floatation chambers that glow in the sunlight. This rush covers vast areas of floodplain in which crocodiles and birds hide. Among the green are camouflaged beauties like this caterpillar (above).

Litchfield National Park

Croc-free swimming holes abound in this beautiful waterfall-filled park on escarpment two hours south of Darwin. Florence Falls, Tolmer Falls (no swimming here, to protect the orange horseshoe bat), Wangi Falls (year-round), and Sandy Creek Falls (4WD only) can be reached most easily from the road starting at Batchelor. You can take a round trip by exiting along the unpaved road leading out to Berry Springs. If you have a good 4WD, visit the sandstone formations of the Lost City, a turnoff south from Litchfield Park Road 6.4km/4mi after the Florence Falls exit.

Frill-necked lizard on tree trunk (above). Gubara Pools (below)

Cool Tropics Tips

Temperatures in the Top End range on average from 21–37° C/70–98.6° F with warmer months within this range falling during the dry season when skies are clear.. Humidity from October through March is high; otherwise, it's low.

• Wear a brimmed hat. Plan for activities in the early morning and late afternoon to miss the midday sun.

• If you get overheated, cool down immediately by moving into the shade, spraying clothes with water, and drinking bottled water.

• Wear nylon clothes designed for the tropics. These should be loose fitting to let air circulate freely. Long sleeves and long pants are ideal to avoid insects and reduce direct sun.

• Take 1 liter of water for every hour walked and drink often. You'll sweat most of the water off.

• Keep alcohol-based hand cleansers with you: they cool as effectively as they clean.

To reach the park take the Stuart Highway south from Darwin for 112km/69mi, turn west on Batchelor Road to Batchelor; this continues as Litchfield Park Road. There is an information office as you enter the park (08-8999-4555). Remarkable magnetic termite mounds can be seen on the north side of Litchfield Park Road within the park. So-called magnetic mounds are oriented so that the midday sun hits the nest's knife-edge, minimizing the sun's fiercest heat after warming it up pleasantly at dawn.

Gibb River Road

This 675km/420mi 4WD outback route goes to Derby through the Kimberleys and King Leopold Ranges in Western Australia. A large diversity of bird species may be spotted, including Gouldian finches, pictorella mannikins, red goshawks, and black grasswrens. From Katherine, take Route 1, the Great Northern or Victoria Highway, to Kununurra. Go west for 25km/15mi and turn off to the Wyndham sign. Gibb River Road starts at a west turn about 3km/1.8mi further on. Check out the flying foxes at Tunnel Creek and the 2,000-year-old hollow boab tree, into which prisoners were once thrown. Kimberley Tourist Office, Kununurra (08-9168-1177), gives information about off-route supply stores.

Speargrass flowering

8
Western Australia

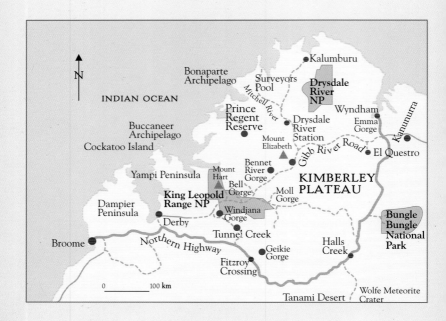

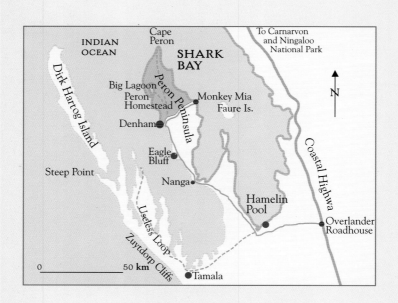

Western Australia

The 2.6 million square kilometers (a million square miles) of Western Australia can be particularly desolate, windy, and unpopulated. But it hides pearls, diamonds, and the center of diversity for many uniquely Australian flowers. In fact, its flower species are exported at 30 million Australian dollars a year, many for new xerophytic gardens that minimize use of water. A high percentage of garden and public plantings in California and Israel are of Australian plants. The southwestern corner is popping with 7,000 species of wildflowers with colored spikes and waxy whorls.

As you stand on the coastal cliffs and are buffeted by the incessant winds, you can get a feel for the brilliantly hued Indian Ocean and all its mystery. Halfway up the coast is Shark Bay, where the oldest living descendents from the Earth's first life forms still grow in strange reefs by the beach. Farther north, the stunningly diverse Ningaloo Reef and its migrating whale sharks can be explored. And the new wilderness frontier for all Australia lies in the remote gorges of Pilbara and the Hamersley Mountains, the tiger-eye-striped Bungle Bungle and the rugged Kimberley mountains in the north. To grasp something of the true grit once required of people by this different land, read the noted biography *A Fortunate Life*, by an Australian pioneer who greeted hardships with heroic effort.

Don't Miss

❖ Purnululu/BungleBungle National Park
❖ Ningaloo Reef & Coral Coast
❖ Walpole-Nornalup
❖ Monkey Mia and nearby Stromatolites at Hamelin Pool
❖ Desert wildflowers

When to go

❖ Whale shark season in March and April around Ningaloo Reef
❖ Marine turtle hatching in April
❖ Grevilleas, banksias, dryandras, everlastings, and kangaroo paws flower from August to November

Eco-watch

Salinization caused by irrigation and removal of deep-rooted native trees is causing "white death" over major sections of the wheatbelt in southwestern Australia. Salt stored deep in the earth is being brought into the root zone. Major re-vegetation and drainage programs are trying to reverse the trend. 36% of rivers in the area are now too salty to drink in this significant ecological crisis.

Gum Central

Illyarrie gum (*Eucaluptus erythrocorys*, above) is endemic to southwestern Australia and its large pompoms show the three elements shared by all Myrtaceae: lid, flower cup, and in-your-face stamens. Myrtaceae is a world-wide family that includes eucalypts, guavas, *Leptospermum* tea trees, *Syzygium* cloves, the pimento or allspice genus, myrtles, *Callistemon* bottlebrushes, and *Melaleuca* paperbarks. The similar flowers of the last two genuses are closely related.

Three branches of Myrtaceae evolved in or near Australia: eucalypts, *Calistemon* bottlebrushes and paperbarks. These are also found in New Caledonia and New Guinea.

Wildflowers

The southwest is the center of diversity for the Australian Proteaceae family and Eucalypt genus, and this is a major draw for tourists in Perth. Red and green kangaroo paw and other bizarre wildflowers are celebrated with incredible displays in and around the city of Perth, including at the Kings Park Wildflower Festival and at John Forrest National Park.

Perth is the hub of several extensive wildflower drives that are best during springtime between August and October, though if you are there at other times, you are still likely to see some species in bloom. Wildflower Way is studded with everlasting species and is over 230km/150mi long, running north inland between Dalwallinu and Mullewa. Mullewa is 97km/60mi from Geraldton. The Geraldton wax flower from this area is a major export wildflower. From Perth, the southern end of Wildflower Way is reached by taking the Northern Highway to Dalwallinu (160km/99mi). The everlastings, however, are not as totally Australian in evolutionary terms as the more varied displays of Proteaceae to be found near the southwestern coast. It is here that flower density peaks. A brochure on wildflower trails is offered by the Western Australian Tourist Centre, at the corner of Wellington Place and Forrest Place in Perth (1-300-361-351). The native flora of Western Australia is protected and should not be taken.

Fitzgerald River National Park

The amazing variety of 1,748 flower species found in the Mallee woodland and heathland of this park comprise 20 percent of the state's plant species total, crammed into this 0.2 percent of western Australia's land area. 75 are endemics, mostly located in its low-lying Barren Mountains. This intensity of unique flora has earned this park a place as a UNESCO World Biosphere Reserve. The remote park is located on the beautiful south coast between Bremer Bay and Hopetoun. Reach it by road from Perth or by plane via closer Albany and then by road. In winter, look for calving southern right whales from Point Ann.

Although this park is extremely rugged with a low level of accessibility and tour options, it is a true wilderness area with notable delights. You can camp at Quoin Head or stay outside the park. Check out park information (08-9835-5043). The whorled leaf spires of the famous royal hakea (*Hakea victoria*) rise above the heathland with intense colors that cannot

Spectacular flowers can be a car-stopping experience. The tightly whorled, stalkless silvery leaves of the mottlecah (Eucalyptus macrocarpa) look more like those of a succulent than a eucalypt. It has the largest flowers of any eucalypt, and these give it away. The similarly dramatic rose mallee (Eucalyptus rhodantha, above) has smaller leaves and may be a variant, not a separate species.

Fitzgerald Flowers

The most noticeable flowers are concentrated in the western and Barrens area of Fitzgerald River National Park, and include the locally endemic red claw-shaped flowers of the Barrens clawflower (*Calothamnus validus*) and red flower spikes of frothy Barrens regelia (*Regelia velutina*), which has geometrically-placed opposing leaves that trace a square shape. You are likely to see many endemic green and red-bracted flowers of the quaalup bells (*Pimelia physodes*) during peak flowering season (Jul–Sep). Stunning Proteaceae include showy banksia (*Banskia speciosa*), with its deeply serrated leaves; lantern bush (*Hakea victoriae*); and the huge flowers of the woolly banksia (*Banksia baueri*). The golden-flowered bell-fruited mallee (*Eucalyptus preissiana*) is common here and in the Stirling Range, and like other mallees, has many spreading limbs rising from lignotuber roots. The four-winged mallee (*Eucalyptus tetraptera*) has square-shaped winged fruits (Sep–Dec). It is found in the Stirling Range and on southern sandplains and in the park through to Israelite Bay. There are many orchid species to be discovered in the park, including the stunning sun orchid Queen of Sheba (*Thelymitra variegata*) with red, gold, and purple six-petaled flowers.

Fitzgerald Animals

The heathland itself may not be particularly pretty, but this is a critical reserve of international importance. Of the 22 native mammal species found here, several were previously thought to be entirely extinct—or at least within western Australia. Among those rediscovered are the dibbler, a small carnivorous and nectivorous marsupial with white eye rings, and the heath rat. The dibbler is being carefully conserved by the Marsupial Research Centre at Macquarie University, in association with the Perth Zoo. The red-tailed wambenger, western mouse, woylie, and Tammar wallaby are also found in this area. The 210 bird species you may see or listen to include the malleefowl, a common bird befriended by the Malleefowl Preservation Group. Sought-after species include Western whipbird, blue-breasted fairy wren, spotted pardalote, and purple-gaped and white-eared honeyeaters. The only place you will find the endangered ground parrot is in this park and the one at Cape Arid. You are unlikely to see it unless you flush it out, as the parrot creeps around the ground foraging and only flies or calls just before sunrise and sunset. There are 42 reptiles, including an endemic skink around Ravensthorpe Range.

Pincushion hakea (Hakea laurina) *flowers April-July and its pom-poms turn darker red from cream as they mature. This can be found in sandy areas between Narrogin, Albany, and Israelite Bay.*

be reproduced in the many found in cultivated gardens: you have to come here. This is because the new flower-spike leaves borrow nutrients from old ones, turning them crimson, gold, and magenta over a period of years. But they do this optimally only when the soils are as poor as they are in this area. Potting soils make the colors bland. Royal hakea is endemic to the Fitzgerald River and Stirling Range areas.

This park is large enough to be one of the few places where there has been retention of the essential mosaic system of different vegetation types and fire regimes on which so many fast-disappearing Australian native mammals depend, so there are many rare marsupials. The mix of wet and dry habitats also explains why there are more recorded frogs, mammals, and birds than any other Western Australia reserve, according to Keith Bradby, author of *A Park in Perspective,* which details its geology and natural history.

The quartzite barrens are peaking coastal hills on the southern side of the park that were once islands in a moat of shallow warm seas filled with sponges. When the oceans retreated, they left spongelite cliffs made of the silica sponge skeletons filled in by sediments. You can see these soft rocks along the Hamersley and Fitzgerald River valleys. The main area of the park is flat, with four rivers cutting through it, bordered to the north by the granite of the incredibly ancient Yilgarn Block from the core of western Australia's continental crust.

A map of the 4WD trails and campgrounds in the Fitzgerald River Park and roads from Bremer Bay–Hopetoun is available from the Royal Automobile Club of Western Australia in Albany or in Perth at 228 Adelaide Terrace. CALM Jacup office offers a detailed Fitzgerald River park guide featuring camping sites and bushwalking information (08-9835-5043). The park pass is available from CALM or when you reach the park information office. Bremer Bay Hotel (08-9837-4133) is a place to stay nearby if you do not want to camp in the rugged park, which does not offer drinking water at campsites. Farm-stays and bed-and-breakfasts are also dotted around the park and along the pretty coastline.

Kangaroo Paw

The state flower, red and green kangaroo paw (*Anigozanthos manglesii*, lower image, flowering Aug–Nov) can be found wild from Shark Bay to Manjimup.

The kangaroo paw is a monocotyledon with spear-shaped leaves, found mainly in Australia and Africa. 85 species and 7 genera are found in Australia. Several species of the long-lasting arid-resistant varieties of the *Anigozanthus* genus (below) are cultivated by nurseries for gardens and florists worldwide.

Protea Boomers

The success of Australian Proteaceae and closely related African Protea was due to to their bird and mammal pollinators plus their special root systems that chisel off scarce phosphorous. In very arid areas of Australia, insects now replace birds as pollinators, but the Proteaceae's original unfoldment excluded a dependence on insects. Most flowers in other countries suddenly proliferated in association with insects. Proteaceae relatives are found in Asia, Africa, Central America, and China, with over half of the species evolving from Australia's southwest. Australian Proteaceae include banksias, hakeas, dryandras, grevilleas, isopogons (or cone flowers), persoonia (or geebungs), and petrophiles (pixie mops).

Albany

The old whaling port of Albany can be used as a hub to explore several interesting reserves and distinctive flower districts. Within easy driving distance of Albany's own flower region, you can find outstanding wildflowers in the Jarrah Forest, Karri Forest, Stirling Range, Wheatbelt roadsides, Southern Sandplains along the coast, and the Fitzgerald River National Park. There are fascinating birding areas as well. At Two People's Bay Nature Reserve just east of Albany, the rare noisy scrub-bird, western bristlebird and western whipbird may sometimes be found. To the west of Albany along the beautiful South Coast Highway 121km/75mi you will find Walpole-Nornalup National Park, which has a contemporary Treetop Walk and Tingle Shelter for visitors to immerse themselves in the Santa Claus-girthed 70m/228.9ft red tingle trees (*Eucalyptus*

Tall and stately sandhill spider flowers (Grevillea stenobotrya) *are found rising above other shrubs on red sand dunes throughout inland Australia.*

Possum banksia (Banksia baueri), also known as woolly banksia, is found in the Fitzgerald National Park all along the southern coast of western Australia from Pallinup River to the Oldfield River. The huge feathery cones remain long after the nectar dries up, though these and the rusty new flowers may be hidden in the foliage.

Nectar spikers

Banksias are Proteaceae that are minutely adjusted for cooperative evolution with their pollinators. They evolved from the start with the birds of the honeyeater family. Honeyeaters sip the 25% sugar nectar, but need additional nitrogen. Many honeyeaters get this by hunting insects. Other honeyeaters visit selected banksia species that add amino-acids to nectar, which few other flower species do. The honey possum (*Tarsipes rostratus*) is found only in southwestern Australia, associated with banksias, bottlebrushes, hakeas, and dryandras. It is not a possum but a minute relict from an otherwise extinct family of marsupial pollinators. Banksia pollen has twice the level of protein than other plants (up to 42%). This is key for the honey possum because it only eats nectar and pollen, the only non-flying animal to do so. It digests the pollen completely and pollinates by carrying pollen on its fur. Honey possums have special mouths adapted to keep up their unusually high metabolic rate. Their long tongue is stiffened with keratin to reach into the flowers, and tipped with brush-like projections to capture pollen as well as nectar. Ridges on the mouth palate scrape the pollen off with each slurp. Their stomachs have been adapted as storage vessels to fill with nectar.

jacksonii). There in the Karri forest of *Eucalyptus diversicolor*, native *Wisteria hardenbergia* hangs among the branches, rare *Dryandra* and *Darwinia* bloom, and over 50 orchid species can be found. Good Karri forests can be found here and also at the Porongurup National Park north of Albany, where you may see red-eared finches in the understory, plus quokkas and emus.

North of Porongurup you can drive to the stunning Stirling Range National Park which is about a third of the way to Perth on the Albany–Bordon road. This offers 1,200 plant species including 60 endemics and is known for its wildflower intensity. Allow at least an extra half day to take the tourist drive which goes through the middle of the jagged hills on Stirling Range Drive, where you may see many beautiful wildflowers including the multicolored isopogon and blue dampiera flowers. The fast Great Southern Highway or Albany Highway will return you to Perth through the rolling wheatbelt.

Turning the Sky Blue

Single-celled cyanobacteria of the kind found in stromatolites (below) evolved a new kind of photosynthesis that was 18 times more efficient at trapping sunlight. They did this by splicing two genes together that coded for photosynthesis. This resulted in chlorophyll that worked harder at charging a high-energy electron, taken from water's hydrogen, with light energy. The gene splicing capability is used now in biotechnology. Cyano-bacteria changed the face of the earth. For the first time, these organisms trapped enough energy to split water and produce oxygen. They became abundant 2.3 billion years ago. Stromatolites grow 5cm/2in each hundred years, 10 times slower than coral. As the level of oxygen in the atmosphere increased from a trace to its current 21% about 1.8 billion years ago, floating gold particles flocculated from the oceans into solid gold nuggets (an effect of dissolved oxygen), and metallic iron oxidized into red ore sediments now seen all over Australia. Gold can still be found in mines, by following the "carbon leader," a vein of black organic material. This was oxygenating cyanobacteria that contributed to bringing the gold out of suspension.

Dryandra Forest Reserve

The Wandoo woodland found in Dryandra reserve is a remnant that represents the habitat before it was enveloped by the surrounding wheatbelt. The charming, medium-sized numbat (*Myrmecobius fasciatus*) is protected on this reserve, and is worth looking for during the day. This is one of the few places where you are likely come across it in full view. The marsupial numbat eats termites. Other rare mammals here include the fungus eating woylie and the Tammar wallaby. The woylie is important for distributing fungus spores, which it does not digest. Fungus species help other plants withstand dessication by ducting water to plants from distant rock crevices. Mycorrhizal fungi deliver essential trace elements into plant roots directly, in exchange for sugars. Therefore the woylie is an unlikely but essential link to keeping most plants in wilderness areas thriving under poor nutrient conditions, as found in much of Australia. To the west of this reserve, between Collie and Perth in the Jarrah Forest, a poison baiting program called Operation Foxglove started in 1994. The poison used is fluoroacetate, a local-plant toxin to which endemic animals have

Domed stromatolites in Hamelin Pool (above), microbial mats (opposite page top left and right), and oxygen production (bottom left and right).

grown immune, but not feral predators. The fluroacetate toxin successfully lowered the level of introduced red foxes to such an extent that woylies, which foxes had wiped out locally, were able to be reintroduced.

The rainbow bee-eater, painted button-quail and elegant parrot, are notable birds found at Dryandra. This small parrot is a grass-seed-eating parrot. It is found in many aviaries where there are several color variations bred. Nocturnal birds include the weird-looking incredibly camouflaged tawny frogmouth. You can spot these at night from their eye-shine. Stay in nearby Narrogin, which is located 301km/187mi south of Perth along the Southern and Brookton Highways.

Shark Bay

The Shark Bay region is a vast 2.3 million ha/5.5 million acres but the ecotourism side is on a small scale. The coast on which Shark Bay lies was so desolate-looking to the first Europeans who sailed by them that they wrote them off. Only our understanding has changed. The site has been put on the ecotourist map for several reasons. The most important is the living stromatolite community in Hamelin Pool, one of the handful of places in the world

Varieties of Life

Fifty species of cyanobacteria are found in Shark Bay. The very large mushroom-like domes are formed from 4-mµ-long organisms that glue sediment to calcium carbonate using sticky mucus. Others form microbial mats of flat ooze. Some microbial mats actually change their own environment by exuding foaming agents to reduce the size and impact of waves. Shark Bay structures date back 3,000 years. The oldest fossils discovered in the world, in the carbon leader of the Pilbara gold fields near "North Pole" in northwest Australia a few hundred miles from Shark Bay, are of bacterium-like filaments 3.5 billion years old. Stromatolites were extremely successful and dominated oceanic life from then until 360 million years ago. Stromatolites grow in pace with the day/night cycle. During the night, the cyanobacteria are dormant and a thin layer of ocean sediment forms on top. As it gets light, the cyanobacteria extend their filaments toward the light through the sediment particles, photosynthesizing and metabolizing dissolved nutrients. Calcium from seawater prevents cell division, and so is toxic to these cells. Cyanobacteria have evolved a way of combining calcium with dissolved carbon dioxide to produce a chalky waste and their reef, effectively removing the poison.

Project Eden

Project Eden is a major conservation effort located in the large Peron Peninsula (right) where native animals are starting to thrive once again. Project Eden has succeeded in its first aim to restore threatened native Australian animals from fox and feral cat predation. Since 1996, 1,455 cats have been trapped, and foxes have been eliminated by the use of sodium fluoroacetate 1080 bait. This is a poison found in many plants native to Western Australia, including the *Gastrolobium* "poison peas." Woylies and other native animals are resistant to this age-old biodegradable poison, European feral animals including foxes and cats are not. Now malleefowl and woylies are being successfully re-established. Woylies, or brush-tailed bettons, are fungus-eating rat kangaroos that carry grasses for their nest in their curled tail tip. The next phase of the project will re-introduce many more native species. Some of these are the Shark Bay mouse (*Psudomys fieldi*); stick-nest rat (*Leporillus conditor*); Western barred-bandicoot (*Parameles bougainville*), currently extinct on the mainland; and mala, or rufous-hare wallaby (*Lagorchestes hirsutus*). This wallaby used to provide significant food for Aboriginal peoples.

where you can experience the cyanobacteria reefs that once dominated the earth's early life forms and turned the sky blue and the rocks red. These strange stromatolites made the area a World Heritage Site. One other reason is the bottle-nosed dolphins at Monkey Mia: these wild animals practically cuddle up to tourists, just inside the beach waveline.

Shark Bay is located about halfway up the western coast of Australia at its most western point, a day's drive north from Perth. For accommodation, Denham has a couple of good hotels and is the main fishing village of Shark Bay, 833km/516mi from Perth and 123km/76mi west of the Overlander roadhouse turnoff (not recommended for overnight stays) on the Northwest Coastal Highway. Denham was once a pearl settlement, but now the catches are regulated and include snapper, grouper, whiting, mullet, prawns, scallops and crayfish. Fish farming is

gaining status using tanks in the bay and you can visit a couple.

Shark Bay is at the intersection of the white sands blown up from the ocean floor and the red sands of the interior, blending into wonderful shades of apricot, silver, and terracotta. Combined with the intense aquas and blues of the Indian Ocean, these colors are the best I saw anywhere in Australia. This blend of colors is representative of other critical intersections. Shark Bay stands as a transition zone between the southwest and Eremaean (N) botanical provinces and has been found to be where three climatic regions overlap. Although it may not be immediately apparent, this means you'll see more flora. The rugged wattle scrub bursts into color with flowers after seasonal rains in late winter and spring. With careful searches in the low-lying brush-land of Shark Bay and unique tree heath of Freycinet Estuary, flower discovery is rewarded.

The semi-parasitic sandalwood (*Santalum spicatum*) tree is coppiced (cut and recut) for aromatic oils and wood export around Shark Bay. Packets of wood shavings are sold in local stores. Unique regeneration capabilities are found only in Shark Bay sandalwood trees: other varieties die when cut down. The only accessible tree to look at, though, is small and is

Birradas

The Big and Little Lagoons outside Denham on the road north to the Francois Peron National Park are bay birradas. These are natural evaporative claypans that provide important fish nurseries as they still link to the ocean. Horseshoe crabs, brine shrimp, and wading birds can be seen here. There are also two types of land-locked birradas found around Shark Bay. One is dried to crusty table salt (sodium chloride, above) which is bright white, smooth as ice and sparkles like snow. The western side of the Peron Peninsula overlooks distant commer-cial salt evaporation pans managed by Shark Bay Salt in Useless Loop. This salt is so pure it is used in manu-facturing. The other birrada is quite different and is made of gypsum (calcium sulphate) on which miniature bonsai stand. This type of birrada is a natural form of plaster of Paris and looks like the icing of a wedding cake: a slightly pliable off-white layer that rests on top of a dark "cake" of anaerobic ooze that can swallow up a whole truck were the driver to miss the track. Gypsum can be used to correct some soils affected by human-induced salinization, a major problem in the southwest of Australia.

Geraldton Wax

"Geraldton wax (right) thrives in sandy soils" said Jo O'Connell of the plant mail-order company Australian Native Plants, Ventura, California, "and it has the most cultivated varieties of any western Australian flower. These have been bred mostly by Californian and Israeli nurseries." This drought-resistant wildflower that tolerates soils well is the largest export flower from the Geraldton township. A more ephemeral group of flowers are the everlastings. These have long-lasting blooms with bright paper-like petals. Their blooms burst out after heavy rains and can be seen around Shark Bay and along Wildflower Way drive between Perth and Geraldton, though in winter and spring their timing is unpredictable.

on its last legs at Nanga homestead. Other stands of the tree have just been cut and it will take years before the next coppiced woods grow large enough to be seen by visitors.

The marine area is also a species-rich transitional region that combines temperate and tropical marine environments. Species include 323 fish species, 218 bivalves, and 80 coral species. One-eighth of the entire population of dugongs is found in the area around Wooramel Bank, the world's largest seagrass meadow, comprised of twelve species of seagrass. In season, you may see whale sharks, humpback whales, and large schools of playing manta rays both from boat trips. The great thing is you can also see them from dry land at Eagle Bluff between Nanga and Denham, Steep Point, and Cape Peron. Steep Point is located on a separate peninsula, which can be reached by turning west on a 4WD track after Hamelin Bay toward Useless Loop, then turning west again to Steep Point.

Stromatolites are the same today as they were 3,500 million years ago. Stromatolites are found in Hamelin Pool, signposted on Denham Road after the Overlander Roadhouse turnoff on the way to Nanga. The cyanobacteria ancestors of these reefs built up all of today's level of atmospheric oxygen and they also originated the green color in all plants. Lynn

Margulis's now-accepted controversial theory is that this happened when a green photosynthetic cyanobacteria relative was enveloped as food by a very mobile single-celled organism. But instead of eating it, the mobile microbe retained the green cyanobacteria intact. The cyanobacteria continued to synthesize and release sugars, which were wonderful food to the new host. And the green microbe preferred its new mobile home because it gave it a variety of environments in which to thrive. This symbiotic union produced the first swimming green algae, from which all plants evolved. The green packages of chloroplasts in today's plant cells still contain their own separate genetic material inherited from this cyanobacterial ancestor. Although reef-building cyanobacteria like those seen at Shark Bay are very rare, non-reef cyanobacteria are common and can be identified wherever there is a blue-green tinge in lichens, surface molds, and water blooms.

Hamelin Pool is an ocean cul-de-sac that is twice as saline as the ocean and this salt level is thought to pickle any crustacean predators that would otherwise eat all the stromatolites. This bay also has a higher than normal concentration of calcium ions due to the proximity of millions of calcium-based shells of cardiid cockle (*Fragum erugatum*) bivalves. You can sear your eyes by looking at the massed white spiral forms next door at Shell Beach. The calcium carbonate is slowly removed from the seawater and built up by the stromatolites into chalky reef structures filled with living ooze. Shell Beach is located after Nanga just north of the feral-proof fence that marks the start of the Project Eden conservation project, at the narrow Taillefer Isthmus.

Monkey Mia is the place to start for the bottlenose dolphins that have been fed daily for three generations and come close to wading visitors. Major wild dolphin research is undertaken away from the tourist end of the

*The sweet aroma of many common boronia flowers and leaves hints at the fact that they belong to the same family as citrus fruits. A pink boronia (*Boronia crenulata, top*) is found around the Stirling Range in Mallee heath. It has aromatic leaves. Boronia flowers are either bell-shaped or star-like. In 1699, William Dampier loved Shark Bay's intense violet blue flowers, including the several* Dampiera *species (bottom). Similar-shaped but yellow-flowered* Goodenia *belong to the same family.*

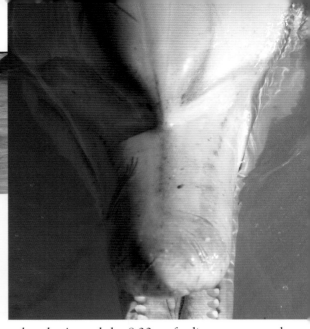

Superalliances in Shark Bay

In 1999, bottlenose dolphins in Shark Bay were the first to show us that they formed "superalliances" of individuals that cooperate to achieve group benefits. Some of these alliances, though, are organized more like gangs. Females normally live in close-knit groups of female relatives, with dissimilar call-signals. Males, with more similar call signals, generally live more independently and form temporary alliances that last a day or two. Dr. Richard Connor found, however, that when several male alliances join together, they can form super-alliances of up to 14 animals that can attack another alliance or corral a female and take her from her home group for up to four weeks. If she does not follow them as they make cavorting displays to lure her away, she gets bitten and slapped into joining them, and then is kept prisoner, encircled by the gang. Dr. Connor believes that it is this type of consensus-based social interaction that is behind the evolution of dolphins toward self-awareness and uncanny intelligence.

beach. Attend the 8:30AM feeding to see a pod of female dolphins checking the situation out before the mothers park their young in the bay. The mothers then come into the knee-deep shallows to roll over like dogs begging for food and play within inches of visitors. Some people are offered the chance to feed the dolphins. It is disappointing that there is a no-touch dolphin policy because the dolphins seem to be doing everything they can to persuade you to touch them. But the policy saves the dolphins from disease and from human dependency, and protects you from nasty dolphin bites (look at those teeth). Still, you can feel them pulling emotionally to interact more. Even with all the limitations and circus-like performance, it is still a thrill to be there.

To hear these dolphins communicating with one another, you can take a boat into the bay that is equipped with hydrophones. Shark Bay Marine Park can be explored on these cruises, which depart from Denham and Monkey Mia.

Some boat dives also reach the wooden Gudrun Wreck off the tip of Cape Peron, rated by the Western Australian Maritime Museum as one of the state's best wreck dives. Experienced divers will see estuary cod, cleaner wrasse and green moon wrasse, scissortail sergeant, lined butterflyfish, angelfish, and surgeonfish varieties. Venomous sea creatures to watch out for include the blue-ringed octopus, stonefish, seasnakes, and bristleworms.

Take a boat to the Bernier Islands, one of the three major refuges around Shark Bay for the conservation of five endangered animals. These—the Shark Bay mouse, banded hare-wallaby, rufous hare-wallaby, western barred bandicoot, and the burrowing bettong—were threatened after European introduction of competing species and destruction of native habitats. Four of these now occur nowhere else besides Shark Bay, yet used to be widespread in Australia. Dirk Hartog Island is the place to go for green and loggerhead turtle hatching at Turtle Bay, the most important site for Loggerheads in Western Australia. This island was sighted in 1660 by Dirk Hartog, the captain of the Eendracht, a Dutch trading ship. Shark Bay was named in 1699 by William Dampier who discovered its pearls when he spent a week exploring the area from the English ship *Roebuck*.

On Edel Land, you may see tracks of the sandhill frog, which buries itself in the sand head first and needs no surface water. It has no tadpoles and lays eggs in the sand. Sandhill frogs come out at night to eat ants. 12 threatened reptiles found around Shark Bay include the Baudin Island skink and woma python. The thorny devil lizard is found in red sand dune country on Peron Peninsula roads and the Nanga Coastal Highway south of Carnavon.

Endemic Avians

Emu are cooperative seed dispersers that are one of the few non-flying animal species you are likely to see during the daytime around Shark Bay. Look around the pond (below) at the old sheep station of Peron Homestead. This artesian well used to provide water for 17,000 sheep, which have now been removed for Project Eden. The well's flow rate has declined 40% since being drilled. There are 230 bird species to be found around Shark Bay, including the threatened brownish thick-billed grasswren, previously found throughout western Australia, and still seen running along the ground with erect tail around Monkey Mia. The Monkey Mia walking trail leads to a bird hide at an artificial dam where zebra finch can be spotted. The Southern emu-wren is an endemic Dirk Hartog variety in the process of splitting off into a new species. More widespread are the black cockatoos (above).

Dolphin Language

Dolphins, chimpanzees, and humans are the only animals to have sex for fun and to build social bonds. The social interactions, large brains, and language of dolphins are so sophisticated that many people believe they have very high intelligence. Their language is being studied for signs of knowing speech. Scientific proof is elusive, however. Dolphins are great mimics, imitating the sounds and movements of other animals and divers. Dolphins appear to communicate as part of their socialization. Sound travels 5 times faster in water than in air, and has no directional bearing. Dolphin brains are about half the size of that of humans, and are structured completely differently. They have no frontal lobe, as in humans, and none of the primate brain's granule cells, but have evolved self-awareness even so. This self-awareness achieved headline news recently when Diana Reiss and Lori Marino, in two separate projects, found that dolphins passed the "mirror test." Dolphins responded to locating ink spots placed on their own bodies, using a mirror. This indicated to the researchers that the dolphins were self-aware of themselves in the mirror. It was previously thought that the only self-aware animals were humans over 18–24 months, and higher apes.

Ningaloo Reef

Ningaloo Reef is famous for the swimming with bus-sized whale sharks, diving from its Navy Pier, and for exploring its extensive 260-km/161-mi fringing coral reef that lies so close to shore that you can easily swim to it. Ningaloo Marine Park rivals the Great Barrier Reef in world-class diving, although covering a smaller 4,000 square km. SCUBA diving is best around April to November, to avoid high winds, cyclones, and high temperatures. During winter from August to October whale watching outings are offered from Exmouth and Coral Bay, and divers at the Fish Pit may see humpback whales.

Whale sharks *Rhincodon typus* are the largest sharks and also the largest fish in the world. They congregate around Ningaloo from mid-March to mid-May, although snorkeling trips from Exmouth using spotter planes start mid-April and extend through early or mid-July. These fish swim at shallow depths, providing wonderful opportunities to snorkel. No-touch diving is observed, and divers are limited to small groups.

180 species of corals are found here, including branching forms found in shallow coral gardens. A week after full moon during March or April, the excitement of coral spawning can be observed at Coral Bay or around Exmouth, an annual event coloring the ocean pink with sperm and eggs.

Fantastic dive sites are numerous. Start with shore dives from the excellent Coral Bay foreshore or at Turquoise Bay halfway between Exmouth and Coral Bay which has shore diving, great brain and massive coral, and outlying coral bommies which can be reached from dive boats or shore. Tiger Wall, Wobbegong Wall, Nick's Lumps, and the Blue Hole offer limestone gullies with fantastic coral around this Westside area, which reaches 18 meters from dive boats. Pilgramunna Ledges has a lot of coral fish life 10 meters from the shore. Lighthouse Bay contains perhaps the largest fish schools, nudibranchs, cleaner shrimp and octopus to be seen. In this bay, Blizzard Ridge is a primary underwater photo destination. The crystal clear waters and more colorful reefs of the Murion Islands at the tip of the North West Cape can be reached during weekly dives for snorkelers and SCUBA.

Above all, do not miss the fish surrounding the Navy Pier, which you should arrange to dive through Coral Coast Dive Shop in Exmouth 08-99-49-1004 phone 08-9949-1044 fax or ccd@nwc.net.au. At this site, divers are surrounded by butterflyfish, angelfish, trevally, barracuda, sweetlips, spangled emperors, and snapper. You may be nudged by the huge resident potato cod and estuarine grouper. Brilliantly colored nudibranchs undulate through the waters, and the pier is decorated by delicate sponges, some fire coral (don't touch!), and seasquirts. Maximum depth is 15 meters.

Dive Companions

If you want to swim among the yellow polka-dotted whale sharks, the largest fish in the sea, one place to find them reliably is around Ningaloo. Whale sharks swim in equatiorial waters and are being hunted for meat and fins in many other countries. As laws are changed to prohibit this, the fishing trade is being replaced in some areas with dive income from whale shark snorkeling expeditions. By supporting these activities, you are protecting these harmless giants worldwide. Whale sharks are not whales but sharks. They are as large as a Greyhound bus (six to ten times longer than you are), weigh about thirteen tons as adults, and have a 1.4m/4ft mouth. Viewed from above, this large mouth gives their body a blunt front-end similar to that of a jet engine. Whale sharks feed off plankton. They occasionally use their 300 rows of file teeth to gulp schooling fish (and pocket wallets), but their primary feeding strategy is to swim through water agape so they can sieve microscopic plankton using their gill rakes. They siphon 6,000L/1,500gal an hour. Sometimes they hunt krill aggressively, but are not a danger to humans. Whale sharks around Ningaloo are males that come for the plankton bloom immediately after coral spawning in March or April.

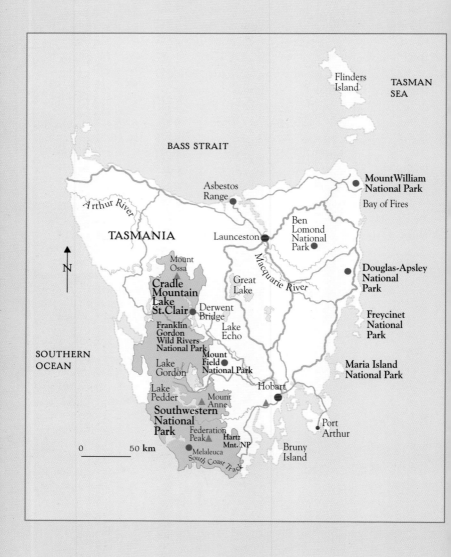

Flinders
Island

TASMAN
SEA

BASS STRAIT

Arthur River

MountWilliam
National Park

Bay of Fires

Asbestos
Range

TASMANIA

Ben
Lomond
National
Park

Launceston

Macquarie River

Douglas-Apsley
National
Park

Mount
Ossa

Great
Lake

Cradle
Mountain
Lake
St.Clair

Derwent
Bridge

Freycinet
National
Park

Franklin
Gordon
Wild Rivers
National Park

Lake
Echo

Maria Island
National Park

SOUTHERN
OCEAN

Lake
Gordon

Mount
Field
National Park

Lake
Pedder

Hobart

Mount
Anne

Port
Arthur

Southwestern
National
Park

Federation
Peak

Hartz
Mnt. NP

Bruny
Island

N

0   50 km

Melaleuca
South Coast Track

9
Tasmania

Tasmania

Tasmania is the bushwalking paradise with many extended walks, alpine climbs, bike rides, kyaking beaches, and wilderness retreats for city-bound souls. The remote expedition that awaits the adventurous is fantastic, whether or not you have prior experience. The Tasmanian Wilderness World Heritage Area is the main destination, covering about a quarter of the island. With Fiordland in New Zealand and Los Glaciares in Argentina, these rugged mountainous terrains are the only remaining temperate wilderness regions in the Southern Hemisphere. To explore the peaks and beaches, you need to don your hiking boots or swimmers. But if you want to get completely away from it all without walking more than an hour to get there, go to the Bay of Fires Lodge (03-6331-

2006) by the beach in Mount William National Park. This is a highly acclaimed small new ecolodge surrounded by pademelon and Tasmanian devil territory, designed by an award-winning architect for the best interaction with nature.

The heathland that folds in side-by-side with Tasmania's forests and alpine herb fields represents an essential community that probably started alternative lines of species, which flourished as arid-land take-overs when the Gondwanan rainforests receded. This is why the heathlands of Tasmania are more diverse than its woodlands. It is in these remote, wet heathlands of Australia where, paradoxically, its arid species originated. Drenching water is no help to a plant when temperatures are too cold for microorganisms to grow fast enough to release nutrients, or when drying winds scour mountain tops. These conditions create nutrient deserts similar to those found in arid areas, despite the apparent abundance of water. It is under these conditions that early varieties of the world's Heath family plants unfolded. You can see what some of these original forms looked like in the Gondwanan spikes of eerie-looking pandani (*Richea pandanifolia*) trees, an endemic Tasmanian signature scattered across mountainsides, the tallest member of the Heath family in the world. Tasmania has several of these endemic *Richea* species and you'll see their white colored flower spires and palm-like leaves swathing the mountain sides.

Seasons to visit

December through April are best for hiking, with excellent sunny, warm days. But snowy Antarctic weather or the wet "roaring forties" can blast you at any time. Even experienced Tasmanian wilderness travelers have been caught unprepared and have not survived hypothermia in midsummer after an all-shorts sun-bake. Be prepared.

Eco-Watch

The trees of Tasmania dwarf others in age: a Huon pine on Mount Read may be 10,500 years old. Tasmania is 20% World Heritage site, and 10% more is in national park conservation. This protects 34% of Tasmania's temperate rainforests, but clear-cutting is still the forestry method used to level the rest. And some forests on the National Wilderness Register are being rolled back into commercial logging sites.

The Tasmanian Wilderness Society is fighting a difficult battle to challenge logging in key areas. The Australian Bush Heritage Fund (GPO Box 101, Hobart, 7001, Tasmania), is buying back land to manage critical areas for conservation. The fund started in Tasmania with the purchase of Liffey Valley by Bob Brown, who turned over his American award, the Goldman Environmental Prize, to start the fund. International and Australian support for this work is enabling the Fund to purchase ecologically priceless habitats in other parts of Australia. Author Mary White reports this, and also notes with sadness that 90% of Tasmanian timber is woodchipped and only 5% is sawn. Even ancient Huon pines aged 3,000 years old are not protected. This, despite Australia's commitment that it would not use rainforest timber.

Bird Restoration

Tasmanian birds are few and far between, yet the endemic green rosella, migratory orange-bellied parrot, and elusive ground parrot draw bird-watchers to Tasmania. The Melaleuca airstrip is the start of the South Coast Track and end of the Davey Track and is near a hide overlooking a corner of what until recently was the only orange-bellied parrot breeding site in the world. This colorful green and orange bird migrates from salt marshes in southern Australia. The saltwater habitat is diminishing, along with these birds. A significant captive breeding program has been put in place. Each year, a plane-load of captive-bred young birds are brought back from the Australian mainland to restore another coastal site in Tasmania where wild birds had previously died out. The released birds have paired up and started to successfully migrate back and forth from the Australian mainland, to the delight of program coordinators.

The ground parrot is a nocturnal bird that has withdrawn from much of Australia to Tasmania, Fraser Island, and small areas in southern Australia after European development. It is extremely difficult to find, although you may flush it out from buttongrass tussocks.

Before You Go

Carried by hikers, a new fungal disease *Phytophthora* sp. is killing many ancient native pines, especially pencil pines in Pine Lake area. Clean your boots each day and especially before commencing any bush walks after being outside the area. Phosphonate aerial spraying is being tried, and the main affected area quarantined, but traces have been found in many areas including Melaleuca.

Walking for Endurance

The deep isolation of a long-distance walking expedition across Tasmania's crags, called "bushwalking" in typically Australian understatement, adds a special dimension to the need for preparedness and strategy before and during the hike. Learn from those who have gone before.

The Discovery Channel's *Eco-Challenge*, the precursor to *Survivor*, was an Australian endurance race spanning over 300 miles and six days. According to Tom Mueller, a travel writer, those who won were not the military teams, because they tried to burn through pain, and they burned out instead. The ones that finished at all were teams of self-described "ordinary" people who loved a joke, were interested in learning from one another, and

resolved issues openly as a team. Nice people got there first. And "first" was something that evolved, with some teams jubilant at crossing the finishing line last because they had had such a meaningful synthesis of group initiative.

The same applies to any multi-day hike. A good group of companions can make the difference between a washout and a cele-bration. Yet keeping up with the team is an interactive process. If muscles start to burn, give them immediate attention to avoid blisters at all costs. Adjust your load regularly and walk to spread your weight across as many muscle groups as possible. Roll the whole foot on and off as you go up a hill, rather than springing off your toes. Accurate footwork is essential on many of these paths, and injuries are more common when the mind is tired. So watch out on the way down a long hill, and follow your intuition about when to take rest breaks. Otherwise it will be "oooops . . . "

Tasmanian cities are flowering with outdoor stores and expedition companies. Check equipment and clothing lists, hiking

Banksia marginata (below) is the only banksia found inland in Tasmania, primarily on heathland. Three eucalypts vie for status as the tallest tree in the world, reaching 90m/294.3ft in Tasmania: Eucalyptus regnans *(right) prefers wetter southeastern-facing areas,* E. obliqua *is more fire resistant and found on drier ridges, and* E. delegatensis *is found from 350–1,150m/1,144–3,760ft high.*

Heath Flowers

One of the most varied of Tasmanian habitats, these diverse sedgelands boast 165 species of wildflower. One of the staple foods of ground parrots and orange-bellied parrots is buttongrass (*Gymnoschoenus sphaer-ocephalus*), prevalent in heathland on plains and slopes up to 1,000m/3,270. This is associated with tea-tree (*Leptospermum nitidum*, above), which scent the air with their characteristic aroma. Tea-tree shrubs can grow for over 100 years and are interpsersed with paperbarks (*Melaleuca sp.*). *Melaleuca squamea* is a common shrub that has pink paint-brush flowers at the tips of its branches. Parrot foods include seeds and berries of silicon-edged cutting grass (*Ghania grandis*); *Boronia citrioda*, recognized by its lemon-scented leaves; and *Cyathodes juniperina.* These gradually build up peat fibers that do not decay due to cold and wet conditions, which suppress bacterial decomposition. The peat here is up to 3,500 years old. European peat bogs date to around 5,500 years.

Colonies

Beachfleas and beach-hoppers are some of the unusually diverse endemic amphipods and crustaceans found in Tasmanian habitats from beach sands to mountaintop moss forests. Freshwater crayfish or yabbies actually cultivate entire colonies of endemic invertebrates like these in their tunnels, animals that they later eat. Near Lake Pedder these endemics include the syncarid crustaceans *Allanaspides helonomus* and *A. hickmani*.

guidelines, and registration fees with your expedition leaders. Take thermal underwear, good raingear, and heavy-duty waterproof boots, plus nylon shorts, sunscreen, and a hat. Invest in the best hiking socks you can afford. Take no cotton clothes, as this fiber absorbs heat when wet and can cause hypothermia. The only cotton you will need is a lens cloth for your camera. Wool and polyester can be damp or wet while retaining warmth. The UV levels in Tasmania are particularly high due to the ozone hole in Antarctica, which closes up again (reducing the danger) during the summer months, when you are likely to be there.

Read "Welcome to the Wilderness: Bushwalking Trip Planner for Tasmania's World Heritage Area" on www.parks.tas.gov.au and from the Tasmanian Parks and Wildlife Service, 134 Macquarie Street, Hobart 7000 (03-6233-3382). This office supplies excellent maps.

South Coast Track

In many ways, the South Coast Track is a metaphor for what life is really about. How you

Deadman's Bay with cormorant drying its wings. To reduce boyancy Cormorants have no oil on their feathers, so they can swim deep to catch fish using their wings for propulsion.

complete it is what counts. There is something especially good about going on a trip that demands that life's little necessities be left behind in order to hope to complete it. Good looks won't get you there, but a good attitude will. Perhaps the fact that you truly have to leave everyday cares behind and are immersed in vast skyline-to-skyline wilderness is one reason why this is rated among the world's best wilderness walks. The track spans boggy coastal heaths, buttongrass moorland, wilderness beaches, alpine herbfields, elfin rainforests, and eucalypt forests, with stunning views along the way. A couple of rivers need to be crossed, one by fording, the other by boat. Your expedition covers about 85km/53mi in about nine days and the ocean is warm enough in summer for good bathing. The region is within Southwest National Park in the Tasmanian Wilderness World Heritage Area and includes historic

Universal Solvent

All of water's physical properties make it well-prepared to foster life. It:
• rapidly diffuses dissolved gases: oxygen takes 1/100th of a second to pass through a cell, so the first organisms did not need complex circulatory systems;
• has the lowest viscocity of all liquids except ether, which means that blood and sap do not shear or damage the delicate molecules carried;
• absorbs more heat than most liquids when the environment temperature increases by one degree, so we don't literally boil over when we go hiking;
• conducts 4 times more heat than similar fluids, which means that our bodily hot spots are spread quickly and comfortably;
• has the highest evaporative cooling effect among common liquids: a damp patch of lawn cools the equivalent of several air conditioners;
• is among the liquids that display the "non-Newtonian" property of reduced resistance as pressure increases if mixed with particles such as red blood cells, aiding circulation;
• dissolves nearly all known compounds to detectable levels.

Aboriginal Sites

Bushwalkers may come across Aboriginal middens (below left) of shells and other artefacts, or ochre handprints on cave shelter rock walls (below right). Tasmania was occupied by Aboriginal groups for about 36,000 years, with mainland land bridges coming and going three times during this period. The few Tasmanian Aboriginal peoples left today continue some of their traditions, such as muttonbirding and cultural activities. They have no separate Aboriginal settlements within Tasmania, having been cleared by European settlers. Louisa Bay near the South Coast Track is a major Aboriginal site. Louisa Bay Aborigines settled here 3,000 years ago and may have occupied the area previously during stone-age activities 11,000 years ago. Very early habitation in Tasmania was in caves, but in more recent times, the Aboriginal people of Louisa Bay built more comfortable dome huts. The most recent settlement was mostly a seasonal affair for hunting southern elephant seals, Australian fur seals, and seabirds until 200 years ago, using bark-bundle canoes. These Aboriginal groups ate *Cyathodes juniperina* and other berries and practiced burning to yield green pick for the wombats and wallabies.

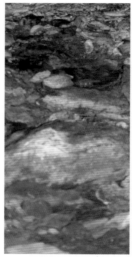 

Cave sentinels stand guard over smoke-blackened Aboriginal rock shelters (below left) in the form of the endemic Tasmanian cave spider (Hickmania troglodytes, top.) This is no ordinary spider. Its sheet web spans the entire arch of this cave like an extra dose of Halloween. "Toe to toe" it measures 170mm/7.6in. Discovered 1883, its six relatives are found in China, Chile, Argentina, and the US. All of them are primitive hermits—it was the rocks that moved them.

Cushion Plant

Cushion plants create their own microclimates several degrees warmer than their wind-blasted alpine surroundings. Their tight fibers catch wind-blown nitrogen-rich debris. One cushion may be several unrelated coexisting plant species. Donatia novae-zelendiae is the commonest cushion plant (left). It is also found in New Zealand, though most Tasmanian cushion plants are endemic. Alpine sundew Drosera arcturi grows on top of the pillows. Cushion plant moth species have highly restricted alpine ranges and dig into the middle of the cushion, where they lay eggs attached to a silk thread leading to the way out.

Aboriginal sites. It takes longer to complete than the Overland Track, and, as a result, fewer people take it on. However, the South Coast Track does "fit" into a two-week international trip, including catch-up days in Sydney and Hobart, plus flying time. One of this track's advantages is that, other than your own group, there is hardly a soul that you pass on the way, unlike the more popular Overland Track. This pristine quality is such a rare experience that it is sought after. Those hikers that you do meet share a bond that draws you together. The experiences of the trip will remain with you years after your return.

The sometimes ankle-wide track is beautifully engineered with steps or boardwalks in places and is based on an Aboriginal trail. There are various options, but the best approach is to fly into Melaleuca airstrip, then take nine days to walk east to Cockle Creek with a rest day and some side trips to Aboriginal middens and exquisite bays. Go with a guided group: never travel alone as there are real dangers along the way, particularly in the gurgling peat. Recently, one lone male hiker apparently disappeared in the peat bogs, with just glasses and a log entry to tell he was there. A woman hiking alone disappeared in midsummer. One recommended program is offered by Tasmanian Expeditions; their guides exceed expectations in terms of camping

Alpine

The primitive-looking pandani (*Richea pandanifolia*) tree (right, with leatherwood blossoms at the top of the Ironbound Range) is a celebrated Tasmanian endemic unrelated to the pandanus or palm species which it resembles. Pandani pushes myrtle and King Billy pine out of the way on wet southern-facing quartzite high-altitude slopes. Pandani is associated with pineapple grass (*Astelia alpina*), a young plant in evolutionary terms, dating to 50 million years ago. Pandani is a member of the Heath family and is a Gondwanan relict. Nine species of endemic richea shrubs are found in Tasmanian sub-alpine and alpine herb fields. Scoparia (*Richea scoparia*) shrubs blanket mountain flats with dense red, pink, gold, and white flower spikes. *Richea dracophylla* (above, after flowering) has white flowers decorated with brown bracts and is found in mountain shrubberies and rainforests.

cooking, knowledge of wildlife and wildflowers, group pacing experience, and sheer strength.

"You'll find your legs on the Ironbound Range," several South Coast Track graduates told me in the weeks before I embarked (you meet them everywhere, it seems.) But only those who complete it know what that means. This is a do-able hike for fit walkers with some outdoor experience and the common-sense to train with a backpack before departure. This is made even more enjoyable if you have an experienced buddy who offers to split tent-carrying days and share camping tips that make all the difference. If you go with a good guide, he or she will "tune up" the group even if the group is not well-matched. In my experience, two other groups were not well guided, and pushed beyond the capabilities of some walkers. These groups fell apart and encountered injuries instead of enjoying everything, an outcome that could have been avoided with a more cooperative approach.

Melaleuca to Cox Bight/Point Eric

Take a light plane from Hobart to Melaleuca, maximum four per plane. After landing at

Melaleuca airstrip, take time to visit the orange-bellied parrot hide where its conservation news is detailed and wild birds may be occasionally spotted. Their total population is only between two and three thousand. From there, the track is over wide-open heathland filled with buttongrass, paperbark, and tea-tree with boardwalks over boggy areas brimming with predatory plants. You'll see some bare areas created by recent fires that have burned thousands of years of peat back to the rock. At the bay, look across to the white beacon of Cox Bluff, which signals rocks from 600 million years ago.

Cox Bight to Louisa Bay

The path from Cox Bight winds up over Red Point Hills with a good view of the coastal bays. Reaching Louisa Bay involves a side trip that leaves the main track to reach one of the most important Aboriginal sites on the route. The alternative is to stay on the track and camp inland at Louisa Creek. To reach Louisa Bay, the conservation-oriented approach is to walk by fanning out over the sedgeland south as, initially, there is no track. Ironically, although the knee-high scrub may appear monotonous, heathlands are the most diverse of Tasmanian habitats. Yabby turrets are signs of burrows in their thousands beneath your feet that shelter entire food chains of crustaceans. The buttongrass also shelters hollow runs made by predatory marsupials including the mouse-sized swamp antechinus (*Antechinus minimus*), a carnivore that chomps on arthropods, and dusky antechinus (*Antechinus swainsonii*), which eats herbivores its own size including mice. These are so ravenous in their attacks that their own young are in danger. Probably to protect the oncoming young, they have evolved a timed safety device. Male antechninuses die at about a year old shortly after violent mating. Their breeding activity is so intense that there is an unusual breakdown

Alpine Zoos

Tasmanian alpine communities are of great zoogeographic interest. Look around boulders for the metallic skink (*Leiolopisma*, top) here for 12,000 years, from Asia, and the moth of the diurnal primitive subfamily Archiearinae. The endemic archaic Gondwanan dragonfly (*Archipetalia auriculata*) breeds in alpine streams. The Tasmanian race of *Echidna* (below) is much furrier than those on the mainland, with shorter spines. It slurps termites and slugs through its straw-like beak.

Moss Forests and Animals

The verdant forests of moss plants usually have a broader world distribution than their animals, reflecting a moss-covered earth of prehistory. Hymenophyllum sp. (top) is a worldwide genus of delicate epiphytic filmy ferns with membranous fronds. In Tasmania they are found in association with Eucaluputs regnans and Nothofagus cunninghamii where they grow from shady trunks like waterfalls. Thallose liverworts carpet damp forest floors and put slivers of cloned tissue in splash cups (second from top), ready to launch them to nearby sites during heavy rainfall. Their umberella-like fruiting bodies (third from top) distribute spores after sexual reproduction. Acaena novae-zealandiae (fourth from top) looks moss-like, but is a perennial wet moorland flowering creeper found at many elevations. Umbrella moss (Hypopterygium sp., fifth from top) looks like a miniature umbrella-topped tree and is common in damp areas in Tasmania and world-wide. Forest ferns range from the soft treefern (Dicksonia antarctica) found in gaps in the eucalypt and myrtle forests to Polystichum proliferum (bottom) in sandy coastal forests. Dicksonia flourished 135–190 million years ago, and ferns originated about 395 million years ago.

Lichens are dramatic and diverse survivors, some reconstituting after 62 weeks without moisture. They disappear when pollution levels climb so they are becoming less familiar. Lichens and cyanobacteria are the only organisms to break down rocks into minerals that other plants can metabolize. As a result, they are earth's original colonizers. All lichens are in fact a sandwich of algae (or sometimes cyanobacteria) and fungi working in tandem. Tasmanian lichens range from the pale fruticose Sphaerophorus tener (opposite page) in deep rainforest mosses on tree trunks of the Ironbound Range, to the bright orange Bay of Fires lichens. These are found at the edge of Mount William National Park on the east coast of Tasmania. This park is known for its wilderness hikes and stunning bay-side.

High altitude damp logs and moss contain some of the most bizarre animals. Velvet worms, mountain collembola, and moss bugs have remained relatively unchanged for hundreds of millions of years and pre-date the most primitive insect. They have helped us trace the location of the shifting continents of Gondwana. If you are fortunate, you may spot one of these delicate creatures between moss fronds or under Nothofagus trees.

Velvet worms (Onychophorans) are beautiful predators found in damp rotting logs in the fern gullies of upper cloud forests. They may be purple, with a gorgeous furry texture and patterned highlights. They can be a couple of inches long, have no wings, use hydraulic pressure to move, and retreat to damp burrows after hunting on moist days. They are found in two groups, originally separated by a Gondwanan desert 200 million years ago. The southern group of species is found in New Guinea, New Zealand, temperate Australia, Tasmania, Madagascar, South Africa, and Chile. The northern group is found in India, the Himalayas, West Equatorial Africa, tropical America, the West Indies, and Malaya. Velvet worms are neither insects nor worms, though physiological evidence shows worms are closely related. RNA analysis is contradictory and indicates that spiders, crustacea, and insects are more closely related to them than worms. They may even be the "missing link" between the two groups. Velvet worms spit glue threads at prey and predators. They wind in their prey by eating these threads, then partly digest their meal externally, as spiders do, before chomping the rest up. Their sexes are separate. Their breathing pores and velvety skin are not resistant to any kind of drying out, unlike insects, whose pores can close. Tropical species are viviparous and nourish their young with a true placenta, while temperate species lay eggs.

Rare mountain collembola (Ceratrimeria dendyi and C. tasmaniae) can be found in the mosses under Antarctic beech on the damp heights of Mount Wellington and elsewhere. These purple and yellow wingless creatures are up to a half-inch long, undulate with soft, caterpillar-like bodies and have a similar Gondwanan distribution to the velvet worms. The collembola that we are usually familiar with are the springtails that jump around our feet on algal strands at the beach, or that stain snow violet with their masses in remote heathlands. The two species in Tasmania don't appear to have springing tails, though—they waddle along instead.

Several moss bugs (Peloridiidae) are found in Tasmania, with the related moss bugs Hemiodoecus leai and Hemiodecellus fidelis found in Patagonia, New Zealand, Tierra del Fuego, Lord Howe Island, New Caledonia, and Australia (McPherson Range of Queensland/Mount Wanungura, New England National Park, and Victoria). All but one moss bug species is wingless and they crawl around slowly on stumpy legs. They live in damp moss and under logs, as they have for the last 200 million years.

Moss Birds

The endemic West Tasmanian scrubtit uses the mosses and ferns to build its domed nest atop soft tree ferns. It breeds from September to January. It shares spiders and beetles with 2 other birds by using separate feeding patterns. The scrubtit preens tree trunks, the endemic Tasmanian thornbill picks along outer branches, and the white-browed scrubwren searches the ground. Some nests are also distinctive while using moss as a base. The Tasmanian thornbill builds a cup nest hanging from twigs, using plant fiber ropes. The more common, but nevertheless beautiful, pink robin sews its moss nest together into a delicate cup using spider webs. It then camouflages this using a sprinkling of lichens.

of the male immune system and males die quickly, removing them from being a threat to new members of the species.

Louisa Island in the bay can be reached if the tides are right, passing an Aboriginal midden on the north side of Louisa Bay. Louisa Bay was a critical site for Aboriginal activities. Short-tailed shearwaters breed on the island in burrows November through April, after migrating all the way from Siberia and Alaska.

Louisa Bay to Louisa River

Buttongrass is traversed in several undulations until reaching the deep forest patch of the Louisa River campground. You may spot a furry echidna snuffling around for termites and slugs among the clumps. When threatened, they tend to dig a hole with their immensely strong backward-facing claws. They are so strong that they can claw their way through a refrigerator door. The eastern side of the camp is reached by boulder-hopping using a fixed rope. The site is a fascinating riverside setting within the heart of dense temperate rainforest encircled by mature specimens of some of the tallest trees in the world, *Eucalyptus regnans*.

Louisa River across Ironbound Range to Deadmans Bay

The path over Ironbound Range goes pretty-much straight up at first through blanket moor to alpine habitats at about 900m/1,000ft. It then follows a very long and steep series of downward steps for several hours, winding through rocky and clay-based rainforest. Myrtle beech (*Nothofagus cunninghamii*), sassafras (*Atherosperma moschatum*), and pandani (*Richea pandanifolia*) are so stunted they light up with an eerie green glow of Antarctic light perfumed by leatherwood at high altitudes. As you go lower the air warms up and the scent of mushrooms grows. As you get nearer the ocean, the aroma of tea tree (*Melaleuca* sp.) starts to

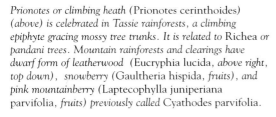

Prionotes or climbing heath (Prionotes cerinthoides) (above) is celebrated in Tassie rainforests, a climbing epiphyte gracing mossy tree trunks. It is related to Richea or pandani trees. Mountain rainforests and clearings have dwarf form of leatherwood (Eucryphia lucida, above right, top down), snowberry (Gaultheria hispida, fruits), and pink mountainberry (Laptecophylla juniperiana parvifolia, fruits) previously called Cyathodes parvifolia.

pervade the air. The views on the way up and the luminous elfin rainforest on the way down can be the highlights of the entire trip, but this section should be planned for carefully as the day is an exceptionally long, arduous challenge. The end may be sticky, as the path goes across a peat bog that may plunge you at least knee-deep when wet. Good gaiters are essential in these conditions. To minimize the significant danger of erosion damage, hikers should walk on the trail, not around it, however peaty. The peat took several thousand years to build up, but can be destroyed in two.

Deadmans Bay to Osmiridium Beach

Deadmans Bay is surrounded by a curtain of endemic leatherwood and rainforest trees that

Southern Pines

Huon pine (*Agarostrobos franklinii*) lives to 3,000 years in riverine lowland habitats. It is the main logging pine in Tasmania and reaches a huge girth of 2.5m/8ft although it does not grow particularly tall. King Billy pine (*Athrotaxis selaginoides*) lives at high altitudes. Both pines are associated with myrtle beech (*Nothofagus cunninghamii*, below), a flowering tree. King Billy lives to be 1,000 years old and bears cones. Each of these trees are Gondwanan, originating over 90 million years old.

Endemic celery top pine
Phyllocladus
aspeniifolius.

Rainforest

Tasmania's fantastic temperate rainforests gradually replace eucalypts if fire does not interruupt, taking about 400 years in theory. A new study in this region shows that these rainforests can regenerate even after fire. Myrtle Beech (*Nothofagus cunning-bamii*) is the dominant rainforest tree, with deciduous beech (*N. gunni*) also found here. Their Southern Beech genus probably originated in South America or Africa. Endemic leatherwood (*Eucryphia lucida*) grows with sassafras and myrtle, and is a small bushy tree with relatives in Chile and mainland Australia. Its beautiful white blossoms and their heavy honey scent give it away. Leatherwood honey is a Tasmanian specialty and has overtones of aromatic oils.

Sassafras Atherosperma moschatum.

reach down to sea level. The track passes through very boggy rainforest that can slow walking to a crawl, with hikers pulled down by heavy backpacks re-loaded from a food drop site nearby. It is a good idea to take a rest day at this point and split this part into two. Prion Beach is an extensive sandy beach along a peninsula that crosses the mouth of New River Lagoon. It is the historic site where the two main Aboriginal clans of the area met for cultural exchange and for trade. This community activity is what made the South Coast Track in the first place. A set of boats is moored ready to take backpackers across the lagoon: follow the clear directions or you'll maroon those following you.

Osmiridium Beach to Surprise Bay and then Granite Beach

You can camp at New River Lagoon or Osmiridium Beach, then climb through mixed forest to Surprise Bay. Behind Surprise Bay beach at the east end there are limestone bluffs that bubble with fossil trilobites from 490 million years ago. There was no land-based life at that time. Sister fossils located in Victoria Land, Antarctica so closely matched that they connected these lands together. These two areas were once in the same place, but their continents have moved apart. The fossils are like words on pages of a book that was closed and is now open. Camp here or move on to Granite Beach. Views of Precipitous Bluff in the background are stunning. This mountain was formed of molten dolerite that pushed through older rocks about 160 million years ago, when birds started to fly. The dolerite formed a life-raft for many species as conditions changed and Australia drifted off.

Granite Beach to South Cape Rivulet

Climb over the difficult South Cape Range of sandstone and dolerite to 430m/11,495ft, with good views and a long way down through

undulating forests and boggy areas that may require care to get through without falling in. Take a leaf out of Buddhist philosophy: the way to get through the neck-deep quagmires is to look neither to the right, nor to the left, but to take the middle path. This way, you will locate the submerged thin central branch that the path builders have laid down to hold your weight. Miss it and you can go in deep. Believe in miracles and you can walk straight through. Once you complete that stage, the South Cape Rivulet needs to be waded to reach the sea-level campsite set under lofty eucalypts. At night, listen for warring Tasmanian devils circling the camp. You'll likely spot their footprints in the sand next day.

South Cape Rivulet to Cockle Creek

The final half-day may be surprisingly demanding as foot-work still needs thought, even though this is entirely on the flat. This is due to the rough conditions of the path until it becomes boardwalk. To start with, the coastal rocks of South Coast Bay are fascinating, being sedimentary deposits laid down when mammals originated on earth 200 million years ago. You can get a close look by visiting Lion Rock at low tide. After walking over the black siltstone deposits of ancient vegetation at Coal Bluff nearby, the track turns inland. Blowhole Valley can be delightfully filled with heathland wildflowers in early summer. A bus pickup should be arranged in advance with Tasmanian Wilderness Travel (03-6334-4442) for the 2 1/2 hour road to Hobart.

Port Davey Track

The Port Davey Track in the Tasmanian Wilderness World Heritage Area takes 4–5 days over 70km/43mi. This passes over low-level buttongrass plains by Lake Pedder, a contro-versial artificial lake flooded for a hydroelectric project. It wiped out an important habitat of

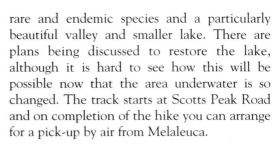

Streams

Copper-colored streams (above) are pigmented with tannic acid salts that seep from peat bogs. You are likely to see rock-climbing galaxias (*Galaxias brevipinnis*, below, under spiderweb) which is the forefather of all Australia's galaxias fish. It is found in many lakes, including Lake Will and Lake Windermere, and streams of Tasmania. Unlike most Australian freshwater fish species that emerged and evolved from saltwater oceans after Gondwana split up, the galaxias never left the continent. This torpedo-shaped galaxias grows to 20cm/18in and can climb over rocks into high mountain lakes and streams using its front fins as flippers. Other wetland rarities include the Tasmanian tree frog (*Litoria burrowsi*).

rare and endemic species and a particularly beautiful valley and smaller lake. There are plans being discussed to restore the lake, although it is hard to see how this will be possible now that the area underwater is so changed. The track starts at Scotts Peak Road and on completion of the hike you can arrange for a pick-up by air from Melaleuca.

The Overland Track

The Overland Track linking Cradle Mountain with Lake St. Clair is in the north of the Tasmanian Wilderness World Heritage Area. This destination is the most popular choice for Tasmanian ecotravellers who want to walk for several days in wonderful country. The Overland Track encompasses 80k/50mi, taking eight days with side trips. Temperate rainforests, waterfalls, heathlands, alpine herbfields, and mirror-calm alpine lake-sides are en route. Huts are available in addition to camp sites. If you want to experience the area without camping, you can reach Cradle Mountain summit in one hiking day if the weather is good, staying at Waldheim Cabins. From Waldheim at the start of the Overland Track, there are several additional short walks that take you into the rainforest and moorland, and around Dove Lake to give you an idea of the surroundings without needing a tent. Day walks around Lake St. Clair and the surrounding mountainous area at the other end of the track can be reached by staying at Derwent Bridge, 167km/103mi from Hobart. Maps and information are available from the Cradle Mountain Visitor Centre (03-6492-1133) and at city bookstores.

Waldheim to Waterfall Valley via Crater Lake

Waldheim is a replica of the historic chalet in Cradle Valley that was started as an ecolodge by the Weindorfers in 1912 (altitude, 1,000m/ 3,270ft). It is surrounded by temperate rainforest dominated by Tasmanian myrtles (*Nothofagus cunninghamii*) and King Billy pines. Look for red Tasmanian waratah around Cradle Valley in December, visited by honeyeaters. A few pandani dot the understory and creekside. Initially, there are three tracks to choose from but they merge into the Overland Track below Cradle Mountain. Walking by the glacially formed Crater Lake is one option, when the track passes Marions Lookout. In the fall, deciduous beech or "fagus" (*Nothofagus gunnii*) turn copper around the lake, the only native deciduous tree to do so in southern Australia, drawing many people for a visit. It is a much more restricted species of *Nothofagus* and this is one of the few places in which it can be found. The beautiful dolerite columns of Barn Bluff can be seen: take the side track to Barn Bluff by turning west half way along Cradle Cirque (after passing the Lake Rodway Track). The cirque is a semicircular stone formation carved by turning glaciers.

Cradle Mountain summit can be reached by taking the turnoff 100m/327ft southeast of Kitchen Hut: first turn left to Face Track and Hanson's Peak then an immediate right to the dolerite-peaked Cradle Mountain. It takes about two hours to complete the 3.5km/2.1mi climb to increase your elevation 300m and then return back to Kitchen Hut. The elevation at the top is 1,545m/5,099ft. You will encounter alpine vegetation sheared by wind on the way, plus a large boulder field as you wind upwards. Look for mats of creeping pine (*Microcachrys tetragona*), and pom-poms of pink mountain berry (*Laptechophylla juniperiana parvifolia*), previously called *Cyathodes parvifolia*. On top you can identify the vista points by checking the plaque. On this mountainside and others, the leaves of lemon-scented boronia (*Boronia citriodora*) perfume the air, its four-petaled pink flowers being very distinctive. But much more restricted is the frothingly white-flowered lily-like milligania (*Milligania densiflora*), only found

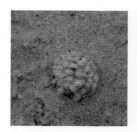

Scats (top to bottom): seagull seed casts; endemic black currawong casts of pink mountainberry seeds; eastern or spotted-tailed quoll scat is somewhat pointed with fur, feathers, insect, and bone fragments; Tasmanian devil scat is more oblong with hair and bone fragments; wombat (not shown) puts large cube-shaped territory markers on top of rocks and in the center of tracks.

Wet Sclerophyll Berries

Native plum (*Cenarrhenes nitida*, top) is an endemic Proteaceae tree that weaves itself into the understory of wet sclerophyll.

Turqoise berry (*Drymophilea cyanocarpa*, second from top) and tussocky blue berry (*Dianella tasmanica*, third from top) are lilies found in wet hillsides of Tasmania, Victoria, and New South Wales. Cheeseberry (*Cyathodes gluaca*, above) is a common endemic Tasmanian shrub with puffy berries found on wet hillsides to 1,100m/3,597ft.

on the slopes of Cradle Mountain, around D'Alton Falls and around Waterfall Valley Hut. It comes from a unique group of flowers found only in Tasmania.

The track from Marions Lookout to Waterfall Valley can be very exposed in bad weather, so take extra care. You will pass through tall snow gums (*Eucalyptus coccifera*) at Fury Crossing. Herbfields dot the snow patches along Cradle Cirque as you drop down into the woodlands of Waterfall Valley. Bleached trees and branches indicate past fire damage. Bennetts wallabies, nocturnal eastern quolls, and wombats frequent the woodland around the huts.

Waterfall Valley to Lake Windermere

You climb gently to the woods and moorland around Lake Windermere. Denser rainforests on southen-facing slopes are dominated by Tasmanian myrtle, pencil pines, and snow gums, and on northern-facing slopes these patches change to extensive buttongrass moors. You will see many turrets sticking up around the buttongrass, burrows of the endemic land yabbie. Windermere Hut's fauna include nocturnal Tasmanian pademelons and endemic black currawongs in search of berries, carrion, and insects.

Windermere to Frog Flats and Pelion Plains

The Pine Forest Moor has a number of open tarns, and the Forth Gorge Lookout view is stunning. More fluted dolerite columns can be seen on Mount Oakleigh to the east. At Pelion Creek and on to Frog Flats you are surrounded by rainforest sprinkled with leatherwoods, then you will climb slowly up through woodland until Pelion Plains. In the streams and lakes you may spot rock-climbing galaxias (*Galaxias brevipinnus*), a fish that can climb mountainous streams, and a shrimp-like creature (*Anaspides*

tasmaniae), which reaches about 18mm/¾in. This endemic mountain shrimp lacks the usual tail-flick mechanism developed by less primitive crustaceans to escape predators. It remains a living relict that has not evolved further than it was when it originated around 250 million year ago.

Pelion Plains to Kia Ora

Pelion Plains open up with tussocks of snowgrass (*Poa gunnii*) which are food for wallabies, corbie grubs, and six species of brown butterfly caterpillars. Look for flowers of the daisy bush (*Olearia* sp.), bauera (*Bauera ruboides*), Christmas bells (*Blandifordia punicea*), and mountain rocket (*Bellendena montana*). The track then climbs to Pelion Gap at 1,126m/3,682ft through rainforest, a climb of 300m/981ft in elevation. A side track leads west to the fluted dolerite columns of Mount Ossa, 1,617m/5,287ft, Tasmania's highest mountain. This takes about 3 to 4 hours return. As you pass these mountains, look for several species of bright green cushion plants that join many individual plants together to protect plants and insects in the warmer climes beneath their mantle. You may also spot the colorful flower spikes of the Gondwanan scoparia (*Richea scoparia*) and the red flattened

Boggy Glades

In summer, peat bogs ripple with purple and white. Bladderwort or fairies' aprons (*Utricularia dichotoma*, above left) has a large lower purple petal "apron." Its roots have a small below-ground cup, or bladder, in which small water fleas and insect larvae are trapped and digested to extract nitrogen and phosphorous. Triggerplant (*Stylidium graminifolium*, above right) whacks pollen onto probing insects using a jointed trigger of stamens, style, and stigma that slowly reset after release. Forked sundew (*Drosera binata*) has linear leaves with glandular hairs to trap insects, and large sweet-scented white-petaled flowers (above left). Several Gondwanan eyebright species on drier heaths include the endemic *Euphrasia collina diemenica,* with its delicate pink, yellow, and white petals, and common *Euphrasis striata,* with striped petals.

Precipitous Bluffs

Magma was directly thrown up from deep in the earth and intruded the sedimentary rocks near the surface as a result of the pressure from Gondwana fracturing to bits 170 million years ago, and this has created much of Tasmania's dramatic skyline. The magma cooled and crystallized into fluted dolerite columns. These were revealed after the softer sedimentary rocks eroded over time, producing some of Tasmania's more dramatic skyline. This process has slowly unearthed Precipitous Bluff (above) near the South Coast Track, Cradle Mountain, Mount Ossa, and Barn Bluff by the Overland Track, the Hartz Mountains, Mount Eliza, Mount Field, Mount Wellington, Mount Picton, and many more Tasmanian monuments. Other Tasmanian mountain formations are made of dolomite which is a form of limestone, plus mudstone, quartzite, and glacial deposits.

fruits of mountain rocket (*Belendena montana*) that look like drooping hyacinths. The track descends to woodlands and the Kia Ora hut, which is surrounded by cider gums (*Eucalyptus gunnii*), the most frost tolerant eucalypt. Yellow-throated honeyeaters sip the nectar of its blossoms and chocolate wattle bats nestle under loose bark.

Kia Ora to Windy Ridge

The 100-year-old white skeletons of burned King Billy pines poke through the vegetation around the Du Cane Hut, which sits between Cathedral Mountain and Falling Mountain. The green Macleays swallowtail butterfly caterpillars lives off the leaves of the root-beer-scented sassafras trees dominating the rainforest that unfolds from Du Cane. King Billy pines and myrtle trees are common. Several waterfalls are worth the short side trips: Boulder Falls, D'Alton Falls, Ferguson Falls, and Hartnett Falls lead into the Mersey River. Each of these takes about a half hour to visit. The Du Cane Gap sports pineapple grass, an endemic lily that lives up to its name.

Windy Ridge to Narcissus Bay and Lake St. Clair

Windy Ridge hut is at the foot of a cirque or glacial bowl made 20,000 years ago. Nectar-filled flowers of *Banksia marginata*, needle hakea (*Hakea lissosperma*), gum-topped stringybark (*Eucalyptus delegatensis*), and *E. pauciflora* forest surround the track as you walk toward Narcissus Bay at Lake St. Clair. Large yellow wattlebirds, endemic strong-billed honeyeaters, black-headed honeyeaters, and migratory swift parrots visit these blossoms in summer, the parrots on their way to and from breeding sites in southeastern Tasmania. Hidden among these eucalypts may be one of the most primitive cicada genuses known, *Tettigarcta tomentosa*, found only in Tasmania. The other species of this genus is found in Australia and both are living

Carnivore Collection

Carnivorous marsupials of the Quoll family are doing well in Tasmania. On the mainland, these species are in rapid decline. One theory is that canine distemper brought by European pets added to the pressure of dingoes, feral cats, and feral red foxes. But the prevailing view is that the dingo, never found in Tasmania, left a gap in which Tassie's marsupials could thrive. Cat-sized spotted-tail quolls (*Dasyurus maculatus*), eastern quolls (*Dasyurus viverrinus*), Tasmanian devils (*Sarcophilus harrisii*) (left), mouse-sized dusky antechinus (*Antechinus swainsonii*), swamp antechinus (*Antechinus mimus*), and white-footed dunnart (*Sminthopsis leucopus*) are nocturnal carnivores that you may see, especially at dusk around cabins and tent sites. The dunnart can eat its body weight in a night. The thylacine (*Thylacine cynocephalus*) was a large carnivore last recorded in 1936. A Tasmanian bounty accounted for 2,184 killed and it rapidly died out. Several sightings were reported in the 1980s in Tasmania and the mainland (to which some had been transferred), but these sightings have not been confirmed. The Sydney Museum is engaging in a credible effort to clone and bring to life a thylacine from DNA in preserved museum specimens.

relicts of what cicadas used to be like before they chirped, when these cicadas prevailed. These are the largest insects to communicate old-style, using low-level vibrations that transmit through the host plant rather than air to potential mates. They have no tympanic apparatus found in the more evolved cicadas, and make no audible sound. It is possible that this early form of signaling evolved into the audible noise produced by modern cicadas.

Narcissus to Cynthia Bay around Lake St. Clair

You can walk close to the shore around the glacially hollowed-out Lake St. Clair on the Overland Track, or take the detour to the views of Byron Gap leading to muddy Cuvier Valley Track. Both options meet at Cynthia Bay, the end of the trail. Lake St. Clair has been ground out by glaciers from four ice ages and is the deepest lake in Australia at 167m/546ft. It was dammed in 1937, raising the water level 3m. Rainforest trees surround the lake and some of the 80 species of birds recorded here may be spotted. There are many day hikes around Cynthia Bay for those wanting to avoid the entire Overland Track. Or you can take the ferry from Narcissus Hut to and from Cynthia Bay. If you have a party of four or more, call using the radio at Narcissus Hut at the northern end of Lake St. Clair.

Resources

HOW TO BE AN ECOTOURIST

An ecosafari is a great way to be immersed in the "no worries" Australian culture and wilderness while getting a close look at wildlife. Safari options include single and multi-day excursions with camping or accommodated stays. Many of the resources listed below are very small businesses. Ecolodges offer sustainable practices that many vacation resorts do not. Here are ways to improve your choices:

1 Avoid mass-tourism sites that overload the area with unsustainable practices and disturb animals as they look for food.
2 Select operators who contribute financially to conservation and cultural projects and employ local people.
3 Select accommodations that minimize their environmental impact and promote sustainable approaches.
4 Do not interfere with animals or marine life by touching or chasing them.
5 Follow local conservation laws and observe sanitary guidelines for disposal of waste.
6 Take only photos and leave only footprints. Walk on the center of paths to limit erosion, even if boggy. In arid areas, even footprints destroy sensitive fungal crusts essential to the region's ecological wellbeing, so be sensitive to each habitat.

Ecotourism Accreditation

Take ecotourism accreditation with a grain of salt. The Ecotourism Association of Australia (www.ecotourism.org.au) accredits member organizations based on their own statements. There are some gaps and a wide range of quality represented. For example, there are several organizations listed in the following resource section, particularly in Tasmania, that should be accredited for the excellent nature-based, sustainable services that they offer, but are not due to the newness of the accreditation program. Some more-recently accredited organizations may be in the process of working out the kinks that more experienced operators have down pat.

※ Advanced Ecotourism Accreditation
❋ Ecotourism Accreditation
🔊 Recommended
🔲 Member of Dive Queensland
❖ Nature Tourism Accreditation

General Resources

Andrew Isles Natural History Books recommended for new and out-of-print Australian titles; internet and mail service
Rear of 115 Greville Street/PO Box 2305, PRAHRAN 3181, Australia
03 9510 5750 t   03 9529 1256 f
www.Andrewisles.com

Bird Australia
415 Riversdale Road, Hawthorn East, VIC 3123
03 9882 2622

Earthwatch Institute Headquarters excellent Australian conservation programs for volunteers, teacher education awards
3 Clock Tower Place, Suite 100, Box 75, Maynard, MA 01754-0075, USA
978-461-0081 or 800-776-0188 within the US
www.earthwatch.org
info@earthwatch.org

Earthwatch Australia
126 Bank Street, S Melbourne, VIC 3205, Australia
03-9682-6828 t 03-9686-3652 f

Phone numbers

800 numbers are for within Australia only and cannot be called internationally, unless otherwise specified. Add a 1 prior to the 800 number to connect. To call the regular numbers from outside Australia, drop the first zero and add the international code and country code. From the US these are 011-61.

First Aid

Phone ooo for emergencies within Australia to connect to police, fire, and ambulance services.

Snakebites

Australian snakes and sea snakes are among the most toxic in the world. You are unlikely, though, to come across them. Look before you step or place your hands. Generally, snakes will remove themselves when they see you, but some species are aggressive and can move toward a threatening intruder, so back slowly away. Sea snakes rarely bite, and when they do, the snake often chooses not to inject venom. Treat as if it is a venomous bite, just to be safe.

The venom of Australian snakes is different to that of North American snakes and the treatment is not the same.

1 Apply a stretchy wide pressure bandage over the bite area and limb. Do not use a narrow torniquet and do not incise the wound.
2 Immobilize the limb with a splint.
3 Reassure the victim and transport to hospital immediately using a radio or cell phone to keep in contact with the hospital.
4 If necessary, use manual or mouth-to-mouth resuscitation and keep airways clear. Elevate legs if the victim threatens to lose consciousness. Only use electric shock treatment if advised by a doctor to do so.
5 It is not necessary to identify the snake in order to select the right antivenom.
6 You or the hospital may consult the Australian Venom Research Unit.

Other Venomous Animals

Get immediate medical attention for venomous sea stings and apply artificial respiration if necessary. Bluebottle jellyfish, blue-ringed octopus, cone shells, sting rays, stinging coral species, and lionfish are a few of the many venomous sea creatures to avoid, as their stings can be lethal or exceptionally painful. Wear hiking boots when exploring coral pools and do not touch coral when diving. Do not swim from northeastern beaches during box and blue jellyfish spawning season. The outer reef itself is less jelly-prone because jellyfish do not spawn there, but instead mass in mangroves and estuaries. Vinegar is no longer recommended for jellyfish stings as one type is made worse with this treatment. Hot water can help denature the jellyfish venom.

In Tasmania, jumper ants are venomous. Avoid their anthills as their sting can cause severe reactions that have been known to be lethal.

Stinging Plants

In the Wet Tropics, avoid touching the two species of stinging tree as the reaction is severe, though the rash is not considered life-threatening. Three types of toxin are involved so these are difficult to treat and the irritation can persist for weeks.

Swimmer's Ear

This itchy condition is caused by a fungal infection that brews well in the tropics and can ruin a holiday. This may be alleviated by mixing equal parts rubbing alcohol, vinegar, and water. Swab the ear with this, then dry carefully. This adjusts the ecological balance of the ear and helps prevent the fungus from growing. The fungus loves an alkaline (basic), humid environment that the acid and the drying alcohol neutralize.

Heat Stroke

Plan ahead to avoid heat stroke and the less dangerous, but still challenging, heat exhaustion. Wear a hat, sun lotion, and loose clothes, and drink lots of water. In the tropics, avoid activity around noon when the sun is much, much stronger than in temperate zones because its rays are near-vertical and so concentrated into a smaller area. Allow 1 liter of water per hour walked and take frequent breaks to cool down.

Heat stroke can be lethal. The individual stops sweating and their temperature increases. They feel hot and dry and become confused to the point where they may lose consciousness. Get immediate medical attention, while soaking the victim's clothes with cold water, giving them cool, not cold, water to drink if conscious, and fanning them.

1. SYDNEY & CENTRAL PACIFIC COAST

National park information, maps, & permits

NSW National Parks & Wildlife Service
102 George Street
The Rocks
Sydney, NSW 2000
02-9253-4600
Dorrigo National Park 02-6657-2309
www.npws.nsw.gov.au

NSW National Parks & Wildlife Service
Blue Mountains Heritage Centre
Govetts Leap Road
PO Box 43, Blackheath NSW 2785
02-4787-8877

Lamington National Park
(under Queensland National Parks & Wildlife Service)
07-5544-0634

Ecosafaris & cruises

Aussie Bushabout Holidays ❋
Blue Mountains bushwalking holiday, bushabout weekend, Wollemi day trip, wilderness retreat
PO Box 606, Lithgow, NSW 2790
02 6352 1133 p 02 6352 1133 f
ausbush@lisp.com.au
www.ausbush.com.au

Blue Mountains 4WD Ecotour ✄
PO Box 1433, Lane Cove, NSW 1595
02 9418 7222 t 02 9418 6163 f
adventure@bushlimo.com.au
www.bushlimo.com.au

Ecolodges

Carrawirry Cabins ✄
PO Box 84, Dungong, NSW 2420
02 4992 1859 t 02 4992 3255 f
carrawirry@turboweb.net.au
www.barringtontops.org.au

Four Horizons Eco Lodges ✄
Georges Rd, Watagan National Park
Hunter Valley, NSW 2325
02 4998 6257 t 02 4998 6237 f
info@fourhorizons.com.au
www.fourhorizons.com.au

Hookes Creek Forest Resort ✄
384 Jems Creek Road
via Gloucester, NSW 2422
02 6558 5544 t 02 6558 5552 f
info@hookescreek.com.au
www.hookescreek.com.au

Kanimbla View Environmental Retreat ✄
PO Box 252, Blackheath, NSW 2785
02 4787 8985 t 02 4787 6665 f
kanimbla@lisp.com.au
www.kanimbla.com

Midginbil Hill Country Resort ✄
252 Midginbil Road, Midginbil via Uki
via Murwillumbah, NSW 2484
02 6679 7158 p 02 6679 7120 f
midhill@midginbilhill.com.au
www.midginbilhill.com

Yeranda at Barrington Tops ❖
Kalimna & Pindari cottages
Main Creek, Dungong, NSW 2420
02 4992 1208 t 02 4992 1208 f
ros@yeranda.com.au
www.yeranda.com.au

Gardens, sanctuaries, & aquaria

Australia Zoo
native animals & jumping crocodiles;
Steve Irwin's family zoo is a low-key, well-kept sanctuary for native and feral Australian animals. Catch a wave from Steve Irwin as he drives off to his next film assignment
Glasshouse Mountains Tourist Route
Beerwah, QLD 07 5494 1134
www.crocodilehunter.com

Brisbane Botanic Gardens
20,000 native and exotic plants,
Aboriginal plant trail
Mount Coot-tha Road, Brisbane
07 3403 8888

Forest Glen Sanctuary
drive-through sanctuary, hand-feed deer, cuddle koalas
Tanawha Tourist Drive, near Mooloolaba,
Forest Glen, QLD 4556
07 5445 1274

Underwater World
swim with sharks, subsonic adventure ride, barrier reef fish, sea otter splash
1 hour N of Brisbane on Parkyn Parade
Mooloolaba, QLD
07 5444 2255 international infoline
07 5444 8088 general inquiries

Ecosafaris

Off Beat 4WD Tours ✄
PO Box 1660, Noosa Heads, QLD 4567
07 5473 5135 t 07 5473 5135 f
mikeandsue@offbeattours.com.au
www.offbeattours.com.au

Southern Cross 4WD Tours
window to the wilderness day tour to Lamington and Tamborine National Park;
Gloworm tour
PO Box 359, Jimboomba, QLD 4280
07 5547 7120 t 07 5546 0018 f
info@sc4wd.com.au
www.sc4wd.com.au

Ecolodges

Binna Burra Mountain Lodge ✕
(Lamington NP)
Binna Burra Road
Beechmont, QLD 4211
07 5533 3622 t 07 5533 3658 f
takeahike@binnaburralodge.com.au
www.binnaburralodge.com.au

O'Reilly's Rainforest Guesthouse ✕
(Lamington NP)
Lamington National Park Road
Canungra QLD 4275
07 5544 0644 t 07 5544 0638 f
peter@oreillys.com.au
www.oreillys.com.au

2. LORD HOWE ISLAND

National park information, maps, & permits

Lord Howe Island Visitors Center
02-6563-2114

Lord Howe Island Marine Park
02-6563-2359
www.lordhoweisland.info

Accommodations

Milky Way Holiday Apartments
within easy reach of restaurants
Old Settlement Beach
Lord Howe Island NSW 2898
02-26563-2012 t 02-6563-2164 f

Capella Lodge & White Gallinule Restaurant
Booking: PO Box 296
Cronulla NSW 2230
02-9544-2273 t 02-9544-2387 f
www.lordhoweisland.info/stay/capella.html

Arajilla Retreat
(previously Trader Nick's Resort)
small luxury retreat and restaurant
Old Settlement Beach
Lord Howe Island NSW 2898
02-6563-2022 t 02-6563-2022 f
www.lordhowe.com.au

3. FRASER ISLAND

National park information, maps, & permits

Queensland Parks & Wildlife Service
PMB 10 MS2173
Rainbow Beach, QLD 4581
Fraser Island 07-4127-9191
Fraser Island permits 07-3227-8185

Ecosafaris & cruises

Fraser Island Adventure Tours ✕
4WD tour
PO Box 1009, Mooloolaba, QLD 4557
07 5444 6957 t 07 5478 0622 f
www.fraserislandadventuretours.com.au

Just Paddlin' Canoe Tours ✻
half-day & full-day ecotours
73 Endeavour Drive, Cooloola Cove
via Tin Can Bay, QLD 4580
07 5486 4417

The Fraser Island Company ✕
ranger-guided day & day tours
PO Box 5224, Torquay, QLD 4655
07 4125 3933 t 07 4125 4199 f
toptours@bigpond.com
www.fraserislandtours.com.au

Noosa 4WD Eco Tours ✻
Beachcomber Tour: half-day or full-day
PO Box 1189 Noosaville DC, QLD 4566
07 5449 1400 t 07 5471 0688 f
lyn@noosa4wdtours.com.au
www.noosa4wdtours.com.au

Tasman Venture II
whalewatching
363 Great Sandy Straits Marina
Hervey Bay, QLD 4655
07-4124-3222

4WD rentals

Shorty's 4WD Hire
Fraser Island 07-4127-9122
Fraser Beach 4x4 Hire
Fraser Island 07-4127-9145
Kingfisher Bay 4WD Hire
Fraser Island 07-4120-3366
4WD Hire Island Explorers
07-4124-3770
Rover Rentals 07-4124-3655

Ecolodges

Kingfisher Bay Resort ✍ ✕
world-class ecolodge with ranger-guided
walks and wilderness adventure tours,
dolphin watch, camping tours
(located on W Fraser Island)
GPO PO Box 913, Brisbane, QLD 4001
07 3032 2822 t 07 3229 7435 f
gary_smith@kingfisherbay.com
www.kingfisherbay.com

Camping

Cathedral Beach Camping Park
(privately run) 07 4127 9177

Queensland Department of Environment and Heritage Camp Sites: Dundubara
(east of Lake Bowarrady), Waddy Point
(eastern beach), Wathumba (west coast,
be prepared for "mossies" and sand flies);
all sites include toilets and hot showers.
Lake Boomanjin and Lake McKenzie sites
are overused and not recommended;
Central Station offers toilets, hot showers
and drinking water facilities.

Services

Queensland Ambulance Service:
07-5441-1333

Automobile mechanical services:
Orchid Beach 07-4127-9188,
Eurong 07-4127-9188.
Eurong towing: 07-4127-9188.
Yidney Rocks towing: 07-4127-9167

4. QUEENSLAND WET TROPICS

National park information, maps, & permits

Queensland National Parks
& Wildlife Service
Naturally Queensland Information
Centre
160 Anne Street
Brisbane QLD 4000
Postal address: PO Box 155
Albert Street, Brisbane QLD 4002
07-3227-8186
Cairns office
2–4 McLeod Street
Cairns, QLD
07-4046-6602
Wooroonooran 07-4078-6304
www.env.qld.gov.au

Ecosafaris

Adventure Company ✼
Bartle Frere wilderness walks, outback rock
art/great northern safari, Mulgrave River
wilderness canoeing
PO Box 5740, Cairns, QLD 4870
07 4051 4777 t 07 4051 4888 f
adventures@adventures.com.au
www.adventures.com.au

Adventure Connection
6-day Cape York safari, Daintree safari,
Kuranda safari, 3-day Undara, dive
training; trained botanists and zoologists as
guides
Lot 1, Captain Cook Hwy, Clifton Beach,
Cairns, QLD 4874
07 4059 1599 t
07 4059 1614 f
info@palmcove.com
members.ozemail.com.au/~adconn

Araucaria Ecotours ✼
3-day wildlife ecotour
Running Creek Road, MS 768
Via Rathdowney, QLD 4287
07 5544 1283
ecotoura@eis.net.a
www2.eis.net.au/~ecotoura

Aries Tours ✼
night safari tour, southern sky tour,
rainforest tour
16 Barnett Place, Ernest, QLD 4214
07 5594 9933 t 07 5594 9922 f
clare@ariestours.com

Australian Natural History Safaris ✎
Daintree, Mitchell River, & Mount Lewis
rainforest & outback safaris; personal
safaris for up to 4 people
Thylogale Nature Refuge
Port Douglas, QLD
07 4094 1600
armbrust@anhs.com.au
www.anhs.com.au

Australia Wildlife Tours ✎✎
tableland wildlife mountain safari; night in
the rainforest; jungle adventure picks up
from Port Douglas, Cairns, and Kuranda
and visits national park and private
sanctuary to see endangered wildlife and
other animals.
Currawong Fauna Sanctuary
PO Box 43
Kuranda QLD 4872
07 4093 7287

Bat House
wild bat rescue station and education
center, visitors can volunteer (near
Coconut Beach Resort)
Cape Tribulation Tropical Research
Station, PMB 5
Cape Tribulation, QLD 4873
07 4098 0063

Billabong Sanctuary ✳
Bruce Highway, Townsville, QLD 4816
07 4778 8344 t 07 4780 4569 f
rangers@billabongsanctuary.com.au
www.billabongsanctuary.com.au

Billy Tea Bush Safaris ✳
Daintree to Cape Tribulation day tour,
9-day drive/fly Cape York safari, 14-day
Cape York camping safari
PO Box 77N, Cairns, N QLD 4870
07 4032 0077 t 07 4032 0055 f
info@billytea.com.au
www.billytea.com.au

Currawong Fauna Sanctuary
see Australian Wildlife Tours

Chris Dahlberg
birdwatching river tours on the Daintree
River, 4-day birder tour
07 4098 7997
Chrisd@internetnorth.com.au
www.members.ozemail.com.au/~fnq/daintree

Cooper Creek Wilderness Tours ✼
day walk, night walk
PO Box 590, Mossman, QLD 4873
07 4098 9126 t 07 4098 9097 f
walks@ccwild.com
www.ccwild.com

Cruise Maroochy Eco Tours ✼
Dunethin rocks cruise, nocturnal nature
cruise
PO Box 210, Maroochydore, QLD 4558
07 5476 5745 Bookings 1800 333 242 t
07 5476 9234 f
tours@cruisemaroochyeco.com
www.cruisemaroochyeco.com

Daintree Rainforest Environmental Centre ✄
PMB 28, via Mossman, QLD 4873
07 4098 9171 t 07 4098 9171 f
drec@internetnorth.com.au

Daintree River Cruise Centre ✄
07 4098 6115 t 07 4098 6208 f
jesserae@tradesrv.com.au

Diamantina Outback Tours ✄
PO Box 335, Winton, QLD 4735
07 4657 1514 pt 07 4657 1722 f

Fine Feather Tours
full-day, half-day, and wet season explorers
PO Box 853, Mossman, QLD 4873
07 4094 1199 t 07 4094 1199 f
info@finefeathertours.com.au
www.ozemail.com.au/~fifetour

Foaming Fury ❋
full-day Russell River rafting
PO Box 460, Cairns, QLD 4870
07 4031 3460 t 07 4031 7460 f

Kirrama Wildlife Tours
Klaus Uhlenhut's renowned birdwatching tours to the Iron Range, Cape York Peninsula, tropical North Queensland, Kakadu NP, Katherine NP, and Papua New Guinea;
English and German spoken
PO Box 1400 Innisfail, QLD 4860
07 4065 5181 t 07 4065 5179 f
email: kirrama@znet.net.au
www.gspeak.com.au/kirrama

Jungle Tours & Trekking
Outback, Cape Tribulation, Atherton Tableland, Great Barrier Reef
PO Box 179, Westcourt, Cairns, QLD 4870; 07 4032 5600 t 07 4032 5611 f
reservations@jungletours.com.au
www.jungletours.com.au

Raft'n'Rainforest Company
48 Abbott Street, Cairns, QLD 4870
07 4051 7777 t 07 4051 4777 f

Reef & Rainforest Connections ❋
Cape Tribulation 4WD day tour, Mareeba wetlands and skyrail 4WD safari, Cape Tribulation and Bloomfield Falls 4WD safari, Daintree River and Mossman Gorge day tour
PO Box 717, Port Douglas, QLD 4871
07 4099 5777 t 07 4099 5510 w
daytours@reefandrainforest.com.au
www.reefandrainforest.com.au

Rose Gums Wilderness Retreat ❋
PO Box 776, Malanda, QLD 4885
07 4096 8360 t 07 4096 8230 f
info@rosegums.com.au
www.rosegums.com.au

Savannah Guides ✍
wilderness challenge, Diamantia outback tours, Undara experience, Adel's Grove,
Cobbald Gorge tours, Croydon historic precinct, Norman River cruises, outback Aussie tours, Hells Gate, far out adventures, gecko canoeing, Odyssey Safaris, Bedrock Village tours, venture north, traveltrain, Davidson's Arnhem Land safaris. Winner of many national and international ecotourism awards
57 McLeod Street, PO Box 8043
Cairns, QLD 4870
07 4058 0952 t 07 4058 1109 f
info@savannah-guides.com.au
www.savannah-guides.com.au

Suncoast Far North 4WD Safaris ✄
day tour to Daintree–Cape Tribulation–Bloomfield Track
327 Spence St, Cairns, QLD 4870
07 4035 2275 t 07 4035 2276 f
info@suncoast-safaris.com.au
www.suncoast-safaris.com.au

Tjapukai Aboriginal Cultural Park
Creation Dance Theatre
Queensland tourism awardwinners, international dance tours;
adjacent to the Skyrail Rainforest Cableway, Kamkerunga Road, PO Box 816
Smithfield, Cairns, QLD 4878
07 4042 9999 t 07 4042 9990 f
tjapukai@tjapukai.com.au
www.tjapukai.com.au

Wait-a-While Rainforest Tours ✍ ✄
Daintree wilderness experience, mountain wildlife experience
Pick-ups from Cairns and Port Douglas
Tropical Beachside
59 Wonga Beach Road
Wonga Beach, QLD 4873
07 4098 7500 t 07 4098 7600 f
wildlife@waitawhile.com.au
www.waitawhile.com

Wet Tropics Safaris
safari to Daintree and on to Bloomfield Falls via Cape Tribulation
owner-operated, up to 6 people
PO Box 209, Stratford, QLD 4870
07 4034 2233 t 07 4034 2266 f

Wilderness Challenge Pty Ltd ✄
Daintree, Cape Tribulation, and Mossman Gorge safaris
PO Box 254, Cairns, QLD 4870
07 4055 6504 t 07 4057 7226 f
info@wilderness-challenge.com.au
www.wilderness-challenge.com.au

Wildscapes Safaris ✄
nocturnal tour, the secret world of the platypus; Queensland Tourism Awardwinner, platypus research; closed-circuit TV records wilderness experiences; accessible to the disabled.
PO Box 510, Smithfield, QLD 4878
07 4057 6272 t 07 4057 8093 f
info@wildscapes-safaris.com.au
www.wildscapes-safaris.com.au

Wooroonooran Safaris ✹
Wooroonooran Tour, Lake Barrine eco-
walk, Mt Bartle Frere trekking tour, the
Goldfield Trail trekking tour
PO Box 2670, Cairns, QLD 4870
07 4058 1505
oliver@wooroonooran-safaris.com.au
www.wooroonan-safaris.com.au

Queensland Ecolodges

Bloomfield Rainforest Lodge
Bloomfield River cruise, roaring Meg Falls
safari, Cooktown safari, Hope Islands
cruise, Aboriginal cave painting tour to
Laura; luxury ecolodge accessed by plane
then boat launch within the Cape
Tribulation National Forest, 2 hours N of
Cairns
Bookings: Trailfinders, 194 Kensington
High Street, London, W8 7RG, England
Bookings (London): 020 7938 3939
www.bloomfieldlodge.co.uk

Book Farm ✹
Maleny Rainforest writing workshops,
advanced illustration workshops
330 Reesville Road
Maleny, QLD 4552
07 5494 3000 t 07 5494 3284 f
jillmorris@greaterglider.com
www.greaterglider.com

Broken River Mountain Retreat ✹
guided spotlight walk, canoe tours, guided
rainforest walk & guided birdwatch
Eungella, QLD 4757
07 4958 4528 t 07 4958 4564 f
brmr@easynet.net.au
www.brokenrivermr.com.au

Carnarvon Gorge Wilderness Lodge ✹
guided activities & nature lodge
Carnarvon Gorge
via Rolleston, QLD 4702
07 4984 4503 t 07 4984 4500 f
info@carnarvon-gorge.com
www.carnarvon-gorge.com

Cassowary House
guesthouse and birdwatching haven
Black Mountain Road
Kuranda, QLD 4872
07 4093 7318 t 07 4093 7318 f
sicklebill@austarnet.com.au
www.cassowary-house.com.au

Coconut Beach Rainforest Resort ✹
Daintree Rainforest National Park
expedition, rainforest villas
PO Box 334H, Edge Hill, QLD 4870
07 4053 1100 t 07 4053 1200 f
marketing@coconutbeach.com.au
www.coconutbeach.com.au

Couran Cove Resort ✹
Couran Cove environmental walk
PO Box 224, Runaway Bay, QLD 4216
07 5529 6399 t 07 5529 6858 f
couran@fan.net.au
www.couran.com

**Daintree Cape Tribulation Heritage
Lodge** ✹
PMB 14, Mossman, QLD 4873
07 4098 9138 t 07 4098 9004 f
heritage@c130.aone.net.au
www.home.aone.net.au/heritagelodge/

Daintree Ecolodge & Spa ✹
5-star spa; Queensland Awards for Best
Resort and for Conservation; (4km from
Daintree Village)
20 Daintree Road, Daintree, QLD 4873
07 4098 6100 t 07 4098 6200 f
info@daintree-ecolodge.com.au
www.daintree-ecolodge.com.au

Daintree Wilderness Lodge ✹
awarded the Cassowary Award for Best
Practice in Ecotourism
83 Cape Tribulation Rd, Alexandra Bay
PO Box 352, Mossman, QLD 4873
07 4098 9105 t 07 4098 9021 f
reservations@daintreewildernesslodge.com.au
www.daintreewildernesslodge.com.au

Ferntree Rainforest Resort
4WD safaris, guided walks, reef and river
tours, Ferntree Restaurant; located
140km/87mi from Cairns at Cape
Tribulation
Queensland Tourism Award Winner
Cape Group, PO Box 334 H
Edge Hill, QLD 4870
07 4053 1100 t 07 4053 1200 f

**Fur 'n' Feathers Rainforest Tree
Houses** ✹ ✹
Atherton Tableland
MS 1877, Malanda, QLD 4885
07 4096 5364 t 07 4096 5380 f
stay@rainforesttreehouses.com.au
www.rainforesttreehouses.com.au

Hanging Rock Chalets ✹
PO Box 383, Currumbin, QLD 4223
07 55330327 t 07 55330327 f
hangingrock@bigpond.com
www.hangingrockchalets.com.au

Lotus Bird Lodge ✹
PO Box 187, Clifton Beach, QLD 4879
07 4059 0773 t 07 4059 0703 f
lotusbird@iig.com.au
cairns.aust.com/lotusbird

Possum Valley Rainforest Cottages ✹
Evelyn Central
Via Ravenshoe, QLD 4872
07 4097 8177 t 07 4097 8177 f
possumvalley@iig.com.au
www.bnbnq.com.au

Red Mill House ✹
b&b, specialized Daintree River tours,
Chris Dahlberg's birding safaris; original
plantation-style home in wildlife-rich
grounds with hosts Diana and Geoff Fowkes
Daintree Village, QLD 4873
07 4098 6138
redmill@internet north.com.au

Sanctuary Retreat ✕
72 Holt Rd, Bingil Bay, QLD 4852
07 4088 6064, 1800 777 012 t
07 4088 6071 f
seek@sanctuaryatmission.com
www.sanctuaryatmission.com

Silky Oaks Lodge ✕ ✍
luxury ecolodge, Mossman Gorge walk,
night spotlight walk, Australian wilderness
experience, spa
PO Box 396, Mossman, QLD 4873
07 4098 1666 t 07 4098 1983 f
silky.oaks@poresorts.com

Undara Lodge ✕
sunset tour, half-day lava tube tour
PO Box 6268, Cairns, QLD 4870
07 4031 7933 t
07 4031 7939 f
info@undara.com.au
www.undara.com.au

5. GREAT BARRIER REEF

National park information, maps, & permits
Great Barrier Reef Marine Park Authority
2–68 Flinders Street
PO Box 1379
Townsville, QLD 4810
07-4750-0700 t 07-4772-6093 f
www.gbrmpa.gov.au

Diving & kayaking
Absolute Scuba 'n' Snorkeling ✖
6/1 Dan Street, Capalaba, QLD 4157
07 3245 1005 t 07 3245 2953 f
abscuba@powerup.com.au

The Adventure Company ✕
tropical islands kayaking
PO Box 5740, Cairns, QLD 4870
07 4051 4777 t 07 4051 4888 f
adventures@adventures.com.au
www.adventures.com.au

Aristocat Reef Cruises ✖
Shop 18, Marina Mirage
Port Douglas, QLD 4871
07 4099 4727 t 07 4099 4565 f
reef@aristocat.com.au

Aussie Sea Kayak Company ✕
Fraser Island, Sunshine Coast,
Whitsunday Islands & Lindeman Group
Sea Kayak Tours
Shop 9, The Wharf
Mooloolaba, QLD 4557
075477 5335 t 07 5477 5662 f
www.ausseakayak.com.au

Baraka Australia ✕
5-day Crystal Waters-based adventure tour
36 Crystal Waters, MS 16
Maleny, QLD 4552

07 5494 4555 t 07 5494 4770 f
info@baraka.com.au
www.baraka.com.au

Cairns Dive Centre ✖
overnight on-reef dives
PO Box 2401, Cairns, QLD 4870
07 4051 0294 t 07 4051 7531 f
info@cairnsdive.com.au

Cairns Reef Dive ✖
overnight on-reef dives
PO Box 1554, Cairns, QLD 4870
enquiries@cairnsreefdive.com.au

Captain Cook Cruises ✖
extended live-aboard dives
PO Box 4927, Cairns, QLD 4870
07 4031 4433 t 07 4031 6983 f
cruise@captraincook.com.au

Dive Dive Dive ✖
PO Box 5309
Manly, QLD 4179
07 3890 4443 t 07 3890 2788 f
vantage@powerup.comau

Fantasea Cruises ✳
recommended for the low-key sailing
focus: day cruise to reefworld, seasonal
whale watching, reef sleep overnight
accommodation, half-day cruise to
Whitehaven Beach
PO Box 616, Airlie Beach, QLD 4802
07 4946 5811 t 07 4946 5520 f
info@fantasea.com.au
www.fantasea.com.au

Low Isles Sailaway ✳
sailing day tour to Low Isles
Port Douglas Tourist Information Centre,
Port Douglas, QLD 4871
07 4099 5599 t 07 4099 5070 f
sailaway@reefandrainforest.com.au
www.reefandrainforest.com.au

Magnetic Island Sea Kayaks ✦
PO Box 130, Magnetic Island, QLD 4819
07 4778 5424 t 0747785457 f
misk.digby@bigpond.com
www.seakayak.com.au

Mantaray Charters ✳
day trips in the Whitsundays
PO Box 839, Airlie Beach, QLD 4802
07 4946 4579 t 07 4946 4988 f
mantaray@whitsunday.net.au
www.whitsunday.net.au/mantaray

MarineAir Seaplanes ✳
PO Box 349, Cooktown, QLD 4871
07 4069 5915 t 07 4069 5915 f
marineas@tpg.com.au
www.marineair.com.au

Mike Ball Dive Expeditions ✖
extended live-aboard dives
143 Lake Street, Cairns, QLD 4810
07 4031 5484 t 07 4031 5470 f
resv@mikeball.com

Ocean Rafting ✲ Whitsundays Boat Tours
PO Box 106, Cannonvale, QLD 4802
07 4946 6848 t 07 4946 4122 f
oceanrafting@airlie.net.au
www.oceanrafting.com

Oceanspirit Cruises ▩
PO Box 2140, Cairns, QLD 4870
07 4031 2920 t 07 4031 4344 f
reservations@oceanspirit.com.au

PADI ▩
2 62/68 Digger Street, Cairns, QLD 4870
07 4051 3184 t 07 4041 0684
padi-adm@padi.com.au

Prosail Dive ▩
PO Box 24, Airlie Beach, QLD 4802
07 4948 8612 t 07 4946 4788 f
safari@mackay.net.au

Quicksilver Connection ✀ ▩
reef biosearch, wavedancer dive
Marina Mirage, PO Box 171
Port Douglas, QLD 4871
07 4087 2100 t 07 4099 5525 f
enquiries@quicksilver-cruises.com
www.quicksilvers-cruises.com

Reef Dive Whitsundays ▩
16 Commerce Close
Cannonvale, QLD 4802
07 4946 5473 t 07 4946 5007 f
info@reefdive.com.au

Reef Magic Cruises ▩
PO Box 905, Cairns, QLD 4870
07 4031 1588 t 07 4031 3318 f
magic@reefmagic.com.au

Reef Sea Charters ✲
diving & snorkelling tours
PO Box 5515, Cairns, QLD 4810
07 4041 3055 t 07 4039 0487 f
info@reef-sea-charters.com.au
www.reef-sea-charters.com.au

Surfers Paradise Divers ▩
Stradbroke Island Coast
PO Box 475, Surfers Paradise, QLD 4217
07 5591 7117
spd-oz@yahoo.com

Taka II Dive Adventures ▩
extended live-aboard dives
PO Box 6592, Cairns, QLD 4870
07 4051 8722 t 07 4031 2739 f
takadive@takacom.au

Tallarook Sail & Dive Charters ▩
Shop 1, Beach Plaza, the Esplanade
Airlie Beach, QLD 4802
07 4946 4777 t 07 4946 4633 f
tallark@Whitsunday.net.au

Tusa Dive Charters ▩
PO Box 1276, Cairns, QLD 4870
07 4031 2490 t 07 4031 0672 f
info@tusadive.com

Undersea Explorer ✀
adventure diving & research expeditions
PO Box 615, Port Douglas, QLD 4879
07 4099 5911 t 07 4099 5914 f
undersea@ozemail.com.au
www.undersea.com.au

Wavelength Reef Charters ✀
snorkeling tour, dolphin watch cruise,
half-day whale watch cruise
Wavelength Tour Shop
Shop 2, 38-42 Wharf St
Port Douglas, QLD 4871
07 4099 5031 t 07 4099 5031 f
info@wavelength-reef.com.au
www.wavelength-reef.com.au

Coral Cay & Island Resorts
mainland ecolodges in Great Barrier Reef
coastal areas offer transfers to reef dive
boats for day and extended trips. *See*
Queensland Wet Tropics for listings.

Bedarra Island Resort
hyperluxurious beach getaway,
connections to Dunk Island dives
PO Box 268, Mission Beach, QLD 4852
07 4068 8233 t 07 4068 8215 f
800 225 9849 from within the US
bedarra_island@bigpond.com

Brampton Island Resort
Whitsundays; coral reef close by; access by
boat from Shute Harbor
Via Mackay, QLD 4740
07 4951 4499 t 07 4951 4097 f
800 225 9849 from within the US
resorts.reservations@poresorts.com
www.bramptonisland-australia.com

Daydream Island Resort
Whitsundays; transfer from Shute Harbor
by boat or helicopter to this all-island
resort
Novotel Daydream Island
PMB 22, Mackay, QLD 4740
07 4948 8488, 800 075 040 t
07 4948 8499 f
www.daydreamisland.com.au

Dunk Island Resort
QuickCat day trips to the outer reef from
Dunk Island
PO Box 212, Mission Beach, QLD 4852
07 4068 8199 t 07 4068 8528 f
800 225 9849 from within the US

Fitzroy Island Resort
a party resort
52–54 Fearnley Street, PO Box 1109,
Cairns, QLD 4870
07 4051 9588 t 07 4052 1335 f
info@fitzroyislandresort.com.au
www.fitzroyislandresort.com.au

Green Island Resort ✀
Coral Cay; a brief jet-catamaran ride
27km east of Cairns
PO Box 898, Cairns, QLD 4870
07 4031 3300 t 07 4052 1511 f
res@greenislandresort.com.au
www.greenislandresort.com.au

Haggerstone Island Guest Houses
Outer Barrier Reef, Upper Cape York
Peninsula; the ultimate in wilderness living
and diving; 6–8 guests in 3 palm-thatched
guest-houses; access via charter plane from
Cairns and 20-minute boat trip
Haggerstone Island, Far North QLD
07 3876 4644 t 07 3876 4645 f
www.great-barrier-reef.com/haggerstone
or PO Box 153H Edge Hill, QLD 4870
01 4511 1883 t 01 4521 1883 f
www.haggerstoneislands.com

Hamilton Island Resort
Whitsundays; 20 minutes by boat from
Shute Harbor or 2.2 hours by plane direct
from Sydney
Hamilton Island, QLD 4803
07 4946 9999, 800 075 110 t
07 4946 8888 f
www.hamiltonisland.com.au

Hayman Island Resort
Whitsundays; 2.5 hours flight from Sydney,
by boat from Shute Harbor, or by flying to
Hamilton Island, then short boat trip
Hayman, QLD 4901
07 4940 1234 t 07 4940 1567 f
Reservations: 02 9268 1888 t
02 9268 1899 f
reserve@hayman.com.au
www.hayman.com.au

Heron Island
Coral Cay
PO Box 616, Gladstone, QLD 4680
07 4972 9055, 07 4972 5166 t
07 4972 0244 f
800 225 9849 from within the US
resorts.reservations@poresorts.com
www.poresorts.com.au

**Hinchinbrook Island Wilderness
Lodge & Resort**
Point Richards; Australia's largest island
national park; fly to Cairns or Cardwell
and transfer to Reef Watch
PO Box 3, Cardwell, QLD 4849
07 4066 8585 t 07 4066 8742 f
info@hinchinbrookresort.com.au
www.hinchinbrookresort.com.au

Lady Elliot Island Resort
Coral Cay; excellent visibility;
southernmost island on the reef; 70-km
flight from Bundaberg or Hervey Bay using
Whitaker Air; budget to luxury prices
PO Box 206 Torquay
Lady Elliot Island, QLD 4655
07 4125 5344, 1800 072 200 t
07 4125 5778 f
www.ladyelliot-island.com

Lizard Island Resort
plain luxury marlin fishing lodge
PMB 40, Cairns, QLD 4970
07 4060 3999 t
from within the US: 800 225 9849
07 4060 3991 f
resorts.reservations@poresorts.com
www.poresorts.com.au/lizard

Long Island Resort
Whitsundays; beach resort close to
Shute Harbor
Club Crocodile Long Island Resort
Shute Harbour, QLD 4901
07 4125 2343 t 07 4125 5514 f
www.clubcroc.com.au

Magnetic Island Resort
national park, koala reserve, beach
activities
Mandalay Avenue, Nelly Bay
Magnetic Island, QLD
07 3876 4644 t 07 3876 4645 f
www.magneticisland.info

Orpheus Island Resort
beach resort; half-hour from Townsville or
one hour south of Cairns by seaplane; dive
center for outer reef excursions
PMB 15, Townsville, QLD 4810
07 4777 7377, 800 077 167 t
07 477 7533 f
www.orpheus.com.au

Camping on the reef
Queensland Parks & Wildlife Service
provides information on the many reef
island campsites
2–4 McLeod Street
PO Box 2066, Cairns, QLD 4870
07 4046 6602 t 07 4072 3080 f

6. RED CENTER

National park information, maps & permits
**Parks & Wildlife Commission of the
Northern Territory**
Alice Springs office
PO Box 1046
Alice Springs, NT 0871
08-8951-8211

Ecosafaris & guides
Ayers Rock Tour & Information Center
can arrange guided activities
08 8957 7324

Desert Tracks
1–8 day tours organized by the
Pitjantjatjara people
contact Ayers Rock Resort for more
information

Trek Larapinta ❋
guided walks on the Larapinta Trail
22 Chewings St, Alice Springs, NT 0870
08 8953 2913 t 08 8953 2933 f
charlie@treklarapinta.com.au
www.treklarapinta.com.au

Uluru-Kata Tjuta Cultural Centre
art, aboriginal cultural tours, bushwalks,
bush tucker, base trail
08 8956 3138

Red Center ecolodges

Ayers Rock, Kings Canyon, and Alice Springs Resorts are run by one company and offer several levels of excellent accommodation, from camping to semi-luxury, all designed for minimum environmental impact. Each price level is given a separate hotel name but in fact these are all part of an extended architectural community. There are no other alternatives to choose from at Uluru or Kings Canyon. Alice Springs, though, has a wide variety of choices.

Ayers Rock Resort
Yulara Drive, Yulara, NT 0872
08 8956 2100 t 08 8956 2156 f
www.ayersrockresort.com.au

Frontier Kings Canyon Resort
Ernest Giles Road, Watarrka National Park
Kings Canyon, NT 0872
08 8956 7442
www.ayersrockresort.com.au

Glen Helen Resort
neither luxury resort nor ecolodge, by the beautiful Larapinta Trail and Mereenie Loop; camp site plus basic accommo-dation, good food, and occasional music
Namatjira Drive, PO Box 2629
West MacDonnell Ranges, Alice Springs, NT 0871
08 8956 7489 / 800 896 110 t
08 8956 7495 f
res@glenhelen.com.au

7. TOP END & KAKADU

National park information, maps, & permits

Parks & Wildlife Commission of the Northern Territory
Darwin office
PO Box 496
Palmerston, NT 0831
08-8999-4555
Katherine office
PO Box 344
Katherine, NT 0851
08-8973-8888

Ecosafaris & bushwalking

Billycan Safaris
5-day 4WD Arnhem Land (Mount Borradaile), 2-day Kakadu, 4-day Katherine, Kakadu, and Litchfield camping safaris; German and English spoken
res@billycan.com.au
www.billycan.com.au

David Bishop with Victor Emanuel Nature Tours
Australia highlights bird specialty tour
1 800 328 VENT from the US
info@ventbird.com
www.ventbird.com

Davidson's Arnhem Land Safaris
original Mount Borradaile campsite, 60 miles N of Jabiru; member, Savannah guides; arranges permits to the Arnhem Land base camp and safaris departing from Darwin
PO Box 41905 Casuarina, NT 0811
08 8927 5240 t 08 8945 0919 f
infor@arnhemland-safaris.com
www.savannah-guides.com.au

Discovery Ecotours
4WD and minibus Kakadu, Arnhem Land (Oenpelli and Mount Borradaile), Litchfield, Coburg Peninsula camping safaris,1-day and 2-day Uluru and Olgas tours (no big buses, university-trained biologist guides), Ayers Rock observatory night sky recommended, 12-day Centralian Desert safari;
Ecotourism Award winner
08 8956 2536
bookings@ecotours.com.au
www. discoveryecotours.com.au

Far Out Adventures ✀
Katherine explorer, Northern Australian Aboriginal experience, Northern exposure, urban recovery, Australia naturally ecosafaris; Ecotourism Award winner & member, Savannah Guides
5 Rutt Court, Katherine, NT 0851
08 8972 2552, 02 6557 6076 t
02 6557 6076 f
mike@farout.com.au
www.farout.com.au

Go Bush Safaris
conservation-informed walking, hotel and camping safaris; discovering Tasmania; Kimberley adventure, Fraser Island and whale watching, Mungo Mutuwintji, Kakadu in the wet, Lord Howe Island, tropical rainforest and reef, Shark Bay and WA wildflowers, Blue Mountains bush Christmas
PO Box 71, Gladeville, NSW 1675
02 9817 4660 t 02 9816 1642 f
enquiries@gobush.com.au
www. gobush tours.com.au

Denise Goodfellow (Lawungkurr Maralngurra)
individual ecosafaris; expert wildlife guide and author/illustrator of recommended *Birds of Australia's Top End*
15 Somerville Gardens, Parap, NT 0920
08 8981 8492
goodfellow@bigpond.com

Australian Ornithological Services
(formerly Inland Bird Tours)
Kakadu/Kunanurra/Darwin, Great Victoria desert bird safaris
PO Box 385 South Yarra, VIC, 3141
03 9820 4223
enquiries@philipmaher.com
www.philipmaher.com

Kirrama Wildlife & Klaus Uhlenhu Safaris: *see* Queensland Wet Tropics listing

Odyssey Safaris ✁
3-day Kakadu adventure, 5-day Kakadu
discovery, 10-day Kimberley, 3-day
Nipamjen wilderness escape; member,
Savannah Guides
PO Box 3012, Darwin, NT 0801
08 8948 0091, 1800 891 190 t
08 8948 0646 f
rick@odysaf.com.au
www.odysaf.com.au

Peregrine Bird Tours
2 Drysdale Place
Mooroolbark, VIC 3138
03 9726 3343 t 03 9727 1545 f
birding@peregrinebirdtours.com
www.peregrinebirdtours.com

Savannah Guides: *see* Queensland Wet
Tropics listing
info@savannah-guides.com.au
www.savannah-guides.com.au

**Umorrduk Aboriginal Safaris &
Australian Wilderness Expeditions**
day safaris from Imilgil, a tent camp in
Arnhem Land
08 8941 3882

Willis's Walkabouts ✁
Kakadu and Arnhem Land bushwalking
expeditions
08 8985 2134
www.bushwalkingholidays.com.au

Wilderness Challenge ✁
Cape York "Frontier" 4WD safari, the
Kimberley complete, Cape York
"Adventurer" 4WD safari, Gulf Savannah
wanderer 4WD safari, Kakadu and Gulf
Drover, Gulf and Kakadu Overlander
PO Box 254, Cairns, QLD 4870
07 4055 6504 t 07 4057 7226 f
info@wilderness-challenge.com.au

Kakadu ecolodges & accommodations

All Seasons Kakadu Resort
hotel cabins and campground near park
entrance
Arnhem Highway, 42km/26mi west of
Bowali Visitor Center
1 800 818 845 in Australia
08 8979 0166 t 08 8979 0417 f

Gagudju Crocodile Hotel in Jabiru
package tour hotel and campground in
mining town
1 800 835 7742 in the US and Canada,
0345 40 4040 in the UK, 0800 801 111 in
NZ, 1 800 808 123 in Australia or 08 8979
2800 t 08 8979 2707 f

Gagudju Lodge Cooinda
centrally located by Yellow Waters; good
ecohotel, backpacker trailers, and
campground
800 835 7742 from the US and Canada;

1 800 500 401 from Australia;
0 800 801 111 from New Zealand;
0345 40 4040 from UK;
08 8979 0145 t 08 8979 0148 f

Tent-only campgrounds with toilets and
hot showers are located at Gunlom,
Mardugal Billabong, Muirella Park, and
Merl. These may be closed during the wet
season. Take mosquito repellent and pitch
tents away from the water's edge and the
crocodiles. Free, quieter "bush camps" are
situated throughout the park in marked
sites. These have basic toilet facilities.
Bowali Visitor Center has a map with
locations.

Arnhem Land ecolodges
Seven Spirit Bay
Arnhem Land luxury ecolodge, Aboriginal
traditions, and safaris
08 8979 0277 t 08 8979 0248 f

8. WESTERN AUSTRALIA

National park information, maps, & permits
**Conservation & Land Management
(CALM)**
Hackett Drive
Crawley, WA 6009
08-9442-0300
Kimberley: 08-9168-4200
Plbara: 08-9143-1488
Denham: 08-9948-1208
Albany: 08-9841-7133
www.calm.wa.gov.au

Ecosafaris & cruises
Abrolhos Islands
122 islands, 90 seabird species
60km west of Geraldton
Batavia Coast, Geraldton, WA
08 9921 6800 t 08 9921 3617 f
abrolhosbookings@wn.com.au
www.abrolhosislands.com.au/eco-
abrolhos.htm

Aristocat 2
dolphin and dugong cruises, Shark Bay
Marine Reserve
Dept of Conservation license to access
restricted dolphin and dugong zones
08 9948 1446
www.monkeymiadolphin.com

Boranup Eco Walks ✺
wild walk, forest walk, night walk
RMB 335 Sebbes Road
Forest Grove, WA 6286
08 9757 7576 t/f

Christmas Island Wet & Dry Adventures
08 9164 8028 t/f
diving@christmas.net.au

Coates Wildlife Tours ❀
naturalist-lead safaris to the Kimberley,
Karijini and Rudall River National Parks
and the Kennedy Ranges and Mt
Augustus, and Kimberley Coast cruise
Unit 1B, 28 Baile Road
Canning Vale, WA
08 9455 6611 t / 800 676 016 t
08 9455 6621 f
coates@iinet.net.au
www.coates.iinet.net.au

Design A Tour
4WD Cape Range, Hamersley Range,
Millstream National Parks, and Ningaloo
Marine Park
PO Box 122, Denham, WA 6537
08 9948 1880 t 08 9842 2809 f
www.dat.com.au

Discover West
single and multi-day ecotours in WA;
some are coach/bus tours, others are small
4WD safaris; 13-day Broome Darwin safari
via Mitchell Falls; 8-day Broome Darwin
safari; 22-day WA adventure safari, Bungle
Bungles discovery fly-in and more
77 King Street, PO Box 7355
Perth, WA 6850
08 9486 4122 t
08 9486 4133 f
In Australia, 1 800 999 243
Free fax from US, 1 866 553 3343
www.discoverwest.com.au

Darngku Heritage Cruises
Bunuba-guided fishing and heritage tours
to Darngku, Geikie Gorge National Park,
West Kimberley
Mowie Enterprises, PO Box 94
Fitzroy Crossing, WA 08 9191 5552 t
08 9191 5553 f fitzroytb@bigpond.com
www.darngku.com.au

Exmouth Diving Centre
whale shark dives, Point Murat Navy Pier,
PADI 5-star IDC; provides dive cruises
and accommodation links
Payne Street, Exmouth, WA 6707
08 9949 1201 / 800 655 156 t
08 9949 1680 f
bookings@exmouthdiving.com.au
www.exmouthdiving.com.au

Indian Ocean Diving Academy
Christmas Island
08 9164 8090 t/f
office@ioda.cx
www.ioda.cx

Kimberley Birdwatching Wildlife & Natural History Tours ❀
Gibb River road, Pelagic trip, black
grasswren tour, northwest coast nature
cruise, Kimberley wildlife coastal luxury
cruise, best of birding wildlife boat cruise,
best of Kimberley naturetrek, Mount Hart
and Lower Isdell River tour
PO Box 220, Broome, WA 6725
08 9192 1246 t 08 9192 1246 f
kimbird@tpg.com.au
www4.tpg.com.au/users/kimbird

Kimberley Dreams
4WD Darwin, Katherine, Kununurra,
Bungle Bungle, Gibb River Road, Broome
safaris, homestay itineraries based in
Darwin
PO Box 37070, Winnellie, NT 0821
08 8942 0971 t 08 8942 0974 f
www.kimberleys.com.au

Kimberley Wilderness Adventures
Award-winning camping or
accommodated safaris, 7-day Broome to
Darwin, 2-day Bungle Bungle Fly/4WD,
7-day Gibb River Road, Bungle Bungle
from Broome, 9-day Bungle Bungle, Gibb
River Road, and more options.
Shop 4, 31 Carnarvon Street
Broome, WA
08 9168 1144, 800 804 005 t
08 9192 5761 f
bookings@kimberleywilderness.com.au

Ningaloo Reef Diving Centre
Coral Bay manta rays, whale sharks,
snorkeling, diving; provides dive cruises
and accommodation links
Book with Exmouth Diving Centre
08 9949 1201, 800 655 156 t
08 9949 1680 f
bookings@exmouthdiving.com.au

North Star Cruises
luxury cruises around the Kimberley Coast
and islands
Shop 2, 25 Carnarvon Street, Broome
08 9192 1829 t 08 9192 1830 f

Odyssey Safaris ❁
3-day Kakadu adventure, 5-day Kakadu
discovery, 10-day Kimberley, 3-day
Nipamjen wilderness escape
GPO PO Box 3012, Darwin, NT 0801
08 8948 0091, 1800 891 190 t
08 8948 0646 f
rick@odysaf.com.au
www.odysaf.com.au

Osprey Wildlife Expeditions
Nullarbor down-under wildcaves
expedition, whales & wildcaves expedition
PO Box 738, Stirling, SA 5132
08 388 2552

Outback Coast 4WD Tours ❀
recommended for local charter tours
PO Box 91, Denham, WA 6537
08 9948 1445 t 08 9948 1005 f
djevans@wn.com.au

Over-the-Top Adventure Tours
Broome to Cape Leveque and more in
WA, 1–6 days
PO Box 5921, Broome, WA 6725
08 9192 5211 t/f
info@4wdtourswa.com
www.4wdtourswa.com

Safari Treks
13-day Kimberley adventure from Broome,
15-day canning stock route from Perth,
pinnacle 4WD day safari from Perth, 8-
day Mount Augustus wildflower safari from

Perth
Unit 1, 11 Foundry Street
Marylands, WA
08 9271 1271 t 08 9271 9901 f
crane@safaritreks.com.au
www.safaritreks.com.au

Shotover Monkey Mia Wildlife Sailing ✀
expect the unexpected, wildlife and
dolphin experience, dugong experience
Monkey Mia, WA 6537
08 9948 1481, 800 241 481 t
08 9948 1471 Free-, fax 800 241 480
service@monkeymiawildlifesailing.com.au

Stirling Range Retreat ❋
guided orchid and wildflower walk
Chester Pass Rd, Stirling Range, WA 6338
08 9827 9229 t 08 9827 9224 f
stirlingrangeretreat@bigpond.com
www.stirlingrange.com.au

Tree Top Walk
experience the Tingle Forest at canopy-
level; 430km south of Perth and 100km
west of Albany
Valley of the Giants Road
Denmark, WA
08 9840 8263 t
valley@denmarkwa.net.au

West Kimberley Tours
Windjana Gorge/Tunnel Creek day safari,
2-day Windjana Gorge safari, 4-day West
Kimberley safari
Lot 180 Bell Creek Way, Derby, WA
08 9193 1442, 800 621 426 t
08 9193 1590 f
derbytb@comswest.net.au
www.westkimberleytours.com.au

Wondergoodie Aboriginal Safaris
Wyndham and Kununurra 4WD day tours
c/o Wyndham Tourist Information Centre
Kinberley Motors, PO Box 38
Great Northern Highway, WA 6740
08 9161 1281 t 08 9161 1435 f
mail@thelastfrontier.com.au

Yardie Creek Tours ✀
Westtreks
PO Box 687, Exmouth, WA 6707
08 9949 2659 t/f
yct@nwc.net.au
www.nwc.net.au/yardiecreektours

Western Australian ecolodges & island resorts

Environmentally sustainable ecolodges are
rare in WA, as is accommodation in
general in this sparsely populated area.
The exceptions are the Indian Ocean
resorts, which offer adventure exploration
away-from-it-all. Most national park
accommodation is camp sites and
backpacker bunk huts. Southern WA has
some delightful farmstays along the coast
that are worth exploring. For Ningaloo,
check with Exmouth and Ningaloo Diving
Centres for up-to-date information on
accommodation.

Christmas Island Resort
red crab migration, java trench wall dives;
fly from Jakarta, Perth, Singapore
(seasonally), or Cocos Islands.
Waterfall Bay, Christmas Island, WA
08 9164 8888 t 08 9164 8833 f
www.christmas.net.au

Cockatoo Island Resort ⚓
Buccaneer Archipelago cruising,
whalewatching; celebrated new nature
destination, 1-hour flight from Broome,
35-min flight from Derby
08 9191 7477 t 08 9191 7484 f
www.cockatooisland.com
info@cockatooisland.com

Heritage Resort Hotel
Corner Knight Terrace & Durlacher St
PO Box 410, Denham, WA 6537
08 9948 1133 t 08 9948 1134 f

Yelverton Brook Eco Retreat & Chalets ✀
c/o PO, Carbunup River, WA 6280
08 9755 7579 t/f
retreat@yelvertonbrook.com.au
www.yelvertonbrook.com.au
info@sharkbaycottages.com.au

9. TASMANIA

National park information, maps, & permits

Tasmanian Parks and Wildlife Service
Department of Primary Industries, Water
& Environment
GPO Box 44
Hobart, TAS 7001
Information line 03-6233-6191
www.dpiwe.tas.gov.au

Expeditions & dives

Bicheno Dive Centre
Bicheno, Maria Island, and Governor
Island dives
4 Tasman Highway, Bicheno, TAS
03 6375 1138 t 03 6375 1504 f
bichenodivecentre@telstra.easymail.com.au
www.seanature.southcom.com.au/sitbic

Bruny Island Charters ❋
daily wilderness & wildlife boat charters
PO Box 25, Margate, TAS 7054
03 6293 1465 t 03 6234 3166 f
info@experiencetas.com.au
www.brunycharters.com.au

Close to Nature Tours
Mount Field expeditions
03 6288 1477 t 03 6288 1478 f

Craclair Tours
8- or 10-day overland track, Cradle
Mountain, Pine Valley, and Frenchman's
Cap hiking
Devonport, TAS 7310
03 6424 7833 t/f
craclair@tasadventures.com

Freycinet Adventures
2 Freycinet Drive, Coles Bay, TAS 7215
03 6257 0500 t 03 6257 0447 f
info@freycinetadventures.com
www.freycinetadventures.com

Freycinet Experience
4-day guided Freycinet ecohike
03 6375 1461
www.freycinet.com.au

Go Bush Safaris
discovering Tasmania
PO Box 71, Gladeville, NSW 1675
02 9817 4660 t 02 9816 1642 f
enquiries@gobush.com.au
www. gobush tours.com.au

Hamilton's Tasmania Discoveries
7-day classic trails
Taranna via Hobart, TAS 7180
03 6250 3230 t 03 6250 3406 f
hamilton@tasadventures.com

Inala Tours
Bruny Island tours and more
03 6293 1217
inala@tassie.net.au
www.inalabruny.com.au

Tasman Bush Tours
overland track, Cradle Mountain, walls of
Jerusalem, South Coast Track, Port Davey
track, Frenchman's Cap hikes
169 Steele Street, Devonport, TAS 7310
tasmanbush@tasadventures.com

Tasmanian Escape
4WD tours including 1-day non-hiking
visit to Cradle Mountain
171 Opossum Road
Launceston, TAS 7250
03 6344 1206 t/f
escape@tasadentures.com
www.southcom.com.au/~rexmacar

Tasmanian Expeditions
Cradle walk, Cradle Mountain trek,
Freycinet walk, South coast track
expedition, cycle Tasmania, Franklin
River rafting, Frenchman's Cap
110 George St, Launceston, TAS 7250
03 6334 3477, 800 030 230 t
03 6334 3463 f
info@tas-ex.com
www.tasmanianexpeditions.com.au

Tasmanian ecolodges
Bay of Fires Ecolodge
architecture merges with nature in a
remote, intimate, true ecolodge
Mount William National Park
03 6331 2006 t 03 6331 5525 f
www.bayoffires.com.au

Cradle Mountain Lodge
run by P&O Resorts
PO PO Box 153, Sheffield, TAS 7306
03 6492 1303 t 03 6492 1309 f
800 225 9849 from within the US

Derwent Bridge Chalets
Lyell Highway, near Lake St. Clair
Derwent Bridge, TAS 7140
03 6289 1000 t 03 6289 1230 f
4chalet@h130.aone.net.au
www.troutwalks.com.au

Silver Ridge Wilderness Retreat
Rysavy Road, Sheffield, TAS 7306
03 6491 1727 t 03 6491 1925 f
silver-ridge@tasadventures.com
www.silverridgeretreat.com.au

Index